I0796673

Skyhookers

Skyhookers

An Illustrated History of Hook-On Aircraft and Their Dirigible Motherships

William Wolf

First published in Great Britain in 2025 by
Air World
An imprint of Pen & Sword Books Limited
Yorkshire – Philadelphia

ISBN 978 1 03613 774 8

A CIP catalogue record for this book is
available from the British Library.

Typeset by Mac Style
Printed in the UK by CPI Group (UK) Ltd, Croydon, CR0 4YY.

The Publisher's authorised representative in the EU for product
safety is Authorised Rep Compliance Ltd., Ground Floor,
71 Lower Baggot Street, Dublin D02 P593, Ireland.
www.arccompliance.com

For a complete list of Pen & Sword titles please contact

PEN & SWORD BOOKS LIMITED
47 Church Street, Barnsley, South Yorkshire, S70 2AS, England
E-mail: enquiries@pen-and-sword.co.uk
Website: www.pen-and-sword.co.uk
or
PEN AND SWORD BOOKS
1950 Lawrence Road, Havertown, PA 19083, USA
E-mail: uspen-and-sword@casematepublishers.com
Website: www.penandswordbooks.com

Author Bill Wolf in his Fountain Hills, Arizona office surrounded on the back wall by the covers of his 30 books published during the past 27 years (with his final two on the way).

Contents

Foreword

From the First World War until late in the Second, first dirigibles and then large bombers were vulnerable to evolving small, fast, manoeuvrable interceptors. It was almost essential that during every bombing or scouting mission the long-range dirigible or large bomber was escorted and defended by short-range fighters. However, once the long-range aircraft surpassed the range of the escorting fighter, it was exposed. A solution seemed to have the larger aircraft carry the smaller defending aircraft until needed. This method produced the so-called composite aircraft, consisting of the manned carrier 'mothership' aircraft and the manned carried aircraft dubbed the 'parasite'. This fascinating, unexplored subject focuses on the little-known pioneering post-First World War British and American mother airships and their hook-on fighter parasites.

Acknowledgements

My lifelong hobby has been Second World War aerial combat and over the past 45 years I have collected more than 27,000 books and magazines, along with nearly 2,000 reels (2.5 million pages) of vintage wartime microfilm. Also included in my collection are thousands of aviation unit histories; intelligence reports; pilot, crew, flight, and training manuals; and technical, structural, and maintenance manuals for aircraft ordnance, armament, engines, and equipment. Thanks go to the many historians and archivists I visited from the 1980s until recently for patiently finding the thousands of documents and photos to copy. The author wishes that every person who contributed photos and materials during the past forty-five years could be specifically mentioned. Over the years, the origin of many of the thousands of photos and materials I have copied at government and military sources and from private individuals have become obscured, and I apologise in advance if some sources are miscredited. To the best of my knowledge and enquiry, the photos and drawings within are in the public domain. Many of the photos were copied before Photoshop and digital scanning and, because of their age and sources, especially many of those photos copied from microfilm, movie stills, and poor paper and print quality of pre-1940s and wartime publications are necessarily of poorer quality but are presented because of their singularity and importance to the narrative.

During 2004, after a health scare, I contacted the newly named National WW2 Museum in New Orleans, which sent a representative to consider my collection. They contracted the collection, and I willed it to them, updating the donation every five years when we updated our wills. However, in 2021, during the COVID crisis, I received a notification from them stating that the museum was no longer accepting books and was digitalising everything. Being 80 years old, I needed to find a good home for my collection. I then contacted all three service academies, several universities, and air museums but none were interested or didn't have the space. However, one Texas air museum would accept the collection only if I packed and shipped it! A book dealer would give me $25,000, if he could cherry pick 5,000 books. I have many books worth $100s! In spring 2022, I saw a Fox News interview with Dan Starks, former CEO of Abbott Laboratories, who has the wonderful National Museum of Armored Vehicles in Dubois, Wyoming. I contacted him and he flew in his private jet to Fountain Hills with his curator and accepted the books only, and then flew my wife and me back to his museum for an impressive tour. However, in the summer of 2022, we were vacationing in Breckenridge, Colorado, and I had a kidney stone that could only be treated 200 miles away in Colorado Springs. While there, we visited the National Museum of WW2 Aviation, where I discussed my collection. Bill Klears and a curator flew to Fountain Hills to assess my collection, and were very enthusiastic and accepted the entire collections, books, models, lithographs, and all. Since this museum was a much better fit for my Second World War aviation-oriented collection, Dan Starks graciously released it. During October 2023 museum personnel arrived in two 26ft trucks to spend three days packing everything and we now have a garage for the first time in twenty-four years!

Section One

Airship/Aircraft Composite Pioneers

The earliest mention of a composite aircraft was August Koch's proposed design in 1893 consisting of a prone-piloted type of hang glider attached to and to be released from a balloon. Koch's 'apparatus which endeavored [sic] to imitate the soaring of the birds' never progressed beyond the model stage.

During July 1906, Alberto Santos-Dumont, the wealthy Brazilian aeronaut, pioneering balloonist, and airship pilot residing in France, experimented with what was probably the first ever 'composite' aircraft arrangement. Santos-Dumont had constructed a canard-configured biplane, which he found that he was unable to get into the air from the ground. However, being a lighter-than-air (LTA) pilot, he considered attaching his heavier-than-air (HTA) biplane to a non-rigid airship. The first non-flight trials to simulate flight conditions showed the aircraft to have only limited control and was pulled dangerously toward the airship's envelope, nearly tearing it. The danger of these tests caused Santos-Dumont and his team to quickly abandon them, although some useful information was obtained.

On 16 March 1905, John J. Montgomery, a professor of physics, readied a man-carrying glider to be launched from under a balloon near San Diego, California. The glider was released at an estimated 800ft and glided back under Daniel Maloney's full control to an undamaged landing. Successive trials saw Maloney being launched from

Alberto Santos-Dumont, wealthy Brazilian aeronaut, pioneering balloonist, and airship pilot residing in France, has his non-rigid #14 Airship gasbag carry the 14-bis biplane aloft, but the experiment became too dangerous to continue. (*Matin*)

On 16 March 1905, aeronautics professor John J. Montgomery had Daniel Maloney, pilot of the glider The *Santa Clara*, be released while suspended from a balloon during a successful public demonstration. (*Santa Clara University*)

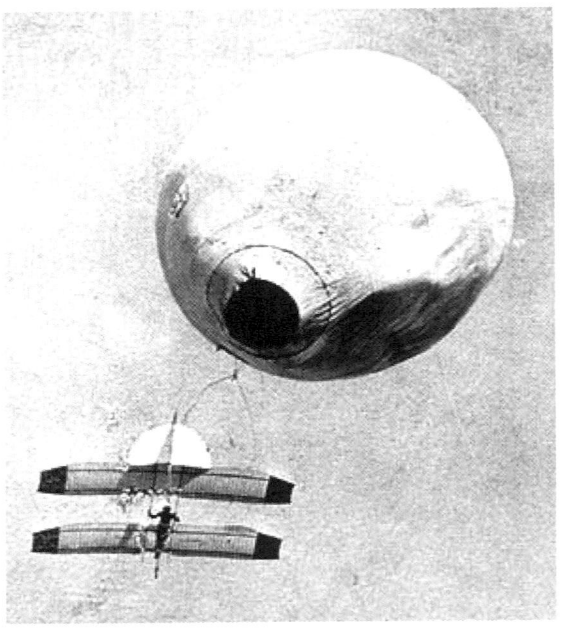

3,000ft, gaining more control over the glider on each subsequent flight. These continued into the following year, when the pair conducted exhibition flights that tragically ended in Maloney's death when his glider suffered structural failure.

As early as 1912, Count Ferdinand von Zeppelin discussed the feasibility of using aircraft in conjunction with his large Zeppelin airships in which he forecast the transport of passengers by aircraft to his airships. The idea languished into the last year of the war, when on 26 January 1918, the German Zeppelin L35 released an Albatros D.III fighter slung beneath its hull. The plane fell away at 4,600ft, and after diving about 150ft, it picked up speed and flew away for a safe landing. This was the first and only German experiment of this type, as operational technical problems and the strategic purpose of the concept were questioned and the project was abandoned.

An Albatros D.III and a Siemens torpedo glider were carried and released from beneath the Zeppelin L.35 and landed successfully during January 1918 experiments. (*Albatros-Flugzeugwerke/1917*)

Section Two

British Airship Composites First World War – 1928

In June 1912, renowned aviation analyst Fred T. Jane wrote to the British *Flight Magazine* asking: 'How long before dirigibles will grow bigger and carry aeroplanes to use against aeroplanes which attack them?'

Submarine Scout (SS) Class Blimp. (*RNAS*)

Royal Aircraft Factory B.E.2c biplane. (*Author*)

Chapter One

AP-1/B.E.2c Composite

Soon after the First World War broke out, the British Admiralty realised that German U-boats threatened Allied shipping and that airships seemed to offer a viable solution to protecting it by detecting threats. A fleet of small 'blimps' was ordered and designated the SS Class (Submarine or Sea Scout), which were essentially an aircraft fuselage without wings slung below a simple envelope. A blimp is a non-rigid airship (dirigible) without an internal structural framework or a keel. These blimps were hastily designed and developed and during March 1915, evaluation tests on the first, the 140ft-long SS2, was completed and it was introduced into service by the Royal Naval Air Service. It eventually led to three types of SS-class airships. The initial SS2 type was quickly and cheaply assembled by attaching the wingless fuselage of a Royal Aircraft Factory B.E.2c aircraft under the envelope to serve as an improvised gondola. Although not a true composite to be released, the combination would serve as a blueprint for the AP-1/B.E.2c Composite. Later SS classes included purpose-built gondolas.

The approximately 3,500 B.E.2s were single-engine tractor two-seat biplanes designed and developed at the Royal Aircraft Factory but they were becoming obsolete and vulnerable (derisively called 'Fokker Fodder') as a front-line fighter and were intended to provide a stable platform required for reconnaissance as an SS gondola. The wingless B.E.2c fuselage was stripped of various fittings and equipment and furnished with two ash skids in place of its wheeled undercarriage. An air-cooled 75hp Renault engine drove a 9ft diameter, four-bladed propeller. The pilot was seated behind the observer/wireless operator. The armament consisted of bombs carried in frames suspended about the centre of the undercarriage and a Lewis gun mounted on a post adjacent to the pilot's seat. The submarine scouts were so successful on coastal patrols that the Admiralty demanded bigger and better airships and three additional classes – 'Coastal', 'C' and 'North Sea' – were developed. Each had larger engines, envelopes and crews than the previous class, with the patrol duration increased.

Royal Aircraft Factory B.E.2c Specifications and Performance

Specifications

Crew: 2
Length: 27ft 3in (8.3m)
Wingspan: 37ft (11.3m)
Height: 11ft 1.5in (3.4m)
Wing area: 371 sq ft (34.5sq m)
Empty weight: 1,370lb (621kg)

Gross weight: 2,350lb (1,066kg)
Powerplant: 1 × RAF 1a V-8 air-cooled piston engine, 90hp
Propellers: 4-bladed wooden fixed-pitch propeller

Performance
Maximum speed: 72mph (116kmph) at 6,500ft (2,000m)
Service ceiling: 10,000ft (3,000m)
Wing loading: 6.3lb/sq ft (31kg/sq m)

Armament
Guns: Normally 1 × .303in (7.7mm) Lewis gun for observer, sometimes several
Bombs: 224lb (102kg) of bombs (usually flown as an unarmed single-seater)

At the beginning of 1915, London initiated air raid precautions and blackouts to respond to the initial Zeppelin raids. At the time, the British had few existing aircraft that had the power, speed, climb rate, or weapons to counter them. Many times, after they had laboured to reach the Zeppelin's 12,000ft operating altitude, the raider had left the area. But if they had remained in the area and the British interceptor was able to close on one, the Zeppelin commander needed only to unload ballast and climb a few more thousand feet out of danger.

Commander de Courcy W. P. Ireland of the Royal Naval Air Service (RNAS) believed that he had a solution to counter the Zeppelin's altitude advantage and requested Wing Commander Neville Usborne, renowned British pioneer aviator and commanding officer of

The AP-1 carrying the B.E.2c ascending to about 4,000ft when disaster struck. (*RNAS*)

the Kingsnorth Airship Station, to implement his idea. Ireland had envisioned his innovative anti-Zeppelin experiment by designing and developing an airship/aircraft system capable of long endurance, called the AP-1, or Airship Phase 1. Since the SS blimp already used the fuselage of a B.E.2c as its power source and control car; Ireland proposed replacing this fuselage with a complete B.E.2c (s/n 989) with engine, wings and tail assembly.

The AP1 concept was to have the SS lift the B.E.2c, which was slung under the envelope, to the Zeppelins' operating altitude and provide a loitering time while attached to the blimp far longer than the B.E.2c's usual patrolling endurance. Once a Zeppelin was encountered, the fighter pilot would activate a quick-release mechanism, and the B.E.2c would fall from the gas bag, start its engine, and then fly to intercept and attack the Zeppelin.

A full-scale test of the B.E.2c release with no crew was successful but during August 1915 this composite aircraft was tested by Flight Commander W. C. Hicks. However, deficiencies were found in its controlling gear and no attempt was made to release. The problems were remedied but it was six months later, on 21 February 1916, that the next flight to test the release with a crew was made. The SS carrying the B.E. ascended from Kingsnorth to about 4,000ft when a sudden loss of pressure in the envelope caused an unexpected loss of stability. This caused the forward suspension wires to partly release prematurely, dropping the fighter's nose and causing it to go into a sideslip. The aircraft continued to be held by its rear suspension wires and for a moment it hung inverted, but the suspension wires became overstressed and broke away. Ireland was thrown out of his cockpit and fell without a parachute into the River Medway and drowned. Usborne sat helplessly in the observer's seat, which had no controls, while the plane spun and crashed fatally into Strood Station Goods Railroad Yard. Subsequently, the Admiralty banned all further experiments and AP-2, although completed, never flew.

Between October and December 1916, six German Army airships would be destroyed by improved ground-based Home Defence B.E.2c interceptors and the raids ended as a result. The German Navy airship raiders of 1917 flew at higher altitudes to avoid interception, and the performance of the B.E.2 was inadequate for it to intercept both the airships flying at 15,000ft and the high-flying Gotha bombers that appeared during 1917, effectively ending its livelihood as an effective Home Defence fighter.

Chapter Two

HMA No. 23r/2F.1 and Sopwith Camel

Construction on the British airship HMA No. 23r was begun by Vickers on 1 January 1916 but was delayed by material shortages and strikes. Its trial flight took place at Barrow on 19 September 1917, but it was found to have less than the rated lift. The airship was allowed to begin operations by removing equipment to save weight and by replacing the Rolls-Royce engine in the new rear car with a Maybach engine from the crashed Zeppelin L 33.

HMA No. 23r Specifications and Performance

Specifications
Length: 535ft (163m)
Diameter: 53ft (16m)
Volume: 942,000 cu ft (27,000 cu m)
Useful lift: 14,600lb (6,600kg)
Powerplant: 4 × Rolls-Royce Eagle V12, 250hp each

Performance
Maximum Speed: 52mph (84kmph)

The R23 was huge at 535ft long, 53ft in diameter, and with a volume of 942,000 cu ft, rivalling contemporary Zeppelins. (*RNAS*)

2F.1 Sopwith Camel Specifications and Performance

Specifications

Crew: 1
Length: 18ft 9in (5.7m)
Wingspan: 28ft (8.5m)
Height: 8ft 6in (2.6m)
Wing area: 231 sq ft (21.5sq m)
Wing loading: 6.3lb/sq ft (31kg/sq m)
Empty weight: 930lb (422kg)
Gross weight: 1,453lb (659kg)
Powerplant: 1 × Clerget 9B 9-cylinder air-cooled rotary piston engine, 130hp
Propellers: 2-bladed fixed-pitch wooden propeller

Performance

Maximum speed: 113mph (182kmph)
Stall speed: 48mph (77kmph)
Range: 300 miles (480km)
Service ceiling: 19,000ft (5,800m)
Rate of climb: 1,085ft/minute (5.51m/s)

Armament

Guns: 2 × 0.303in (7.70mm) Vickers machine guns

During October–November 1918, experiments were conducted with the R23 carrying a Sopwith Camel 2F.1 parasite fighter. (*Author*)

Pulham Royal Naval Air Service Airship Station, Norfolk. The left shed was constructed in 1915, while the right shed was built several years later to accommodate large rigid airships such as the R34. (*RNAS*)

During October/November 1918, experiments under the command of Maj. Ivor Little were conducted using a 2F.1 Sopwith Camel parasite fighter, serial N6814, with the intention that it could be carried by an airship and released in mid-air either to repel attackers or to take offensive action. No. 23 was equipped with Little-Crook anchoring gear for releasing aircraft in flight. Trials conducted on 2 October did not involve releasing an attached Camel as flight was intended to observe any in-flight anomalies associated with a parasitic aircraft. On 3 November 1918 the unmanned Camel, with its controls locked and carrying a dummy pilot, was released from 600ft over Pulham Air Station, south of Norwich, where it glided successfully to the ground. On 6 November, Lieutenant R. E. Keyes of the RAF's 212 Squadron at nearby Great Yarmouth piloted the Camel after it was released, having no trouble starting the engine and pulling out of the dive to fly around the airship before landing safely at Pulham. No provision had been made for retrieval of the Camel in flight, as the purpose was that it should make its own return to base. As with other unusual wartime projects, further development was abandoned after the Armistice and Britain's severe post-war economic cutbacks.

Because both the German and British airship/fighter composites made no provisions for retrieving the fighter after its release, the strategic rationale of the concept was questioned. After release and engaging enemy aircraft in combat, and ostensibly driving them off, the pilot was expected to find and land on a friendly airfield. Considering that these airship/composites would necessarily have to operate over a limited area over the North Sea and would have never to be too far from the safety of terra firma, the development of a hook-on retrieval arrangement would soon begin.

On 6 November 1918, the Sopwith Camel, piloted by Lt R. E. Keyes was loaded on to and released from R23 and landed successfully. The R23 had no provision for the retrieval of the Camel in flight. (*RNAS*)

Chapter Three

HM Aircraft Carrier R33

The R30 series was the new design for the second stage of the British airship scheme, with the R31 and R32 being completed by Shorts, while the R33 and R34 were on the drawing boards during 1916. However, in September 1916 the fortuitous crash and capture intact of the Zeppelin L-33 gave the British an insight into the latest German airship technology, which the R33's builders, Armstrong Whitworth, incorporated into its design. After almost nine months in construction, the R33 was launched after the war on 6 March 1919 and proceeded to fly over the UK and Europe on shakedown flights.

During early 1920 the R33 was demilitarised and given a civil registration. In May 1920, it flew north from Pulham to Howden Air Station, Yorkshire, to conduct an experiment involving the release of a Sopwith Camel fighter aircraft from beneath the airship. The pilotless plane was launched from the airship with its engine running, over a deserted area of the North York Moors. After a successful launching procedure, it made a powered descent, crashing without catching fire due to a new type of fuel tank being tested. Nonetheless, the project was cancelled.

On 31 May 1921, due to the poor state of the post-war economy, the British government cancelled all airship development, construction and overhaul, with military airships to be scrapped. However, the civilian R33, badly in need of overhaul, was deflated and lowered on to its cradle during August 1921 and was mothballed for the next four years. Once the economy improved, the Imperial Airship Scheme decided that the R33 would be reconditioned and on 2 April 1925 it emerged from its hangar at Cardington, Bedfordshire. However, on the night of 16–17 April, the wind increased to gale force and the R33 was torn from its mast and drifted for fourteen hours at the mercy of the winds before finally being tethered. The damage incurred required almost six months to repair.

R33 Specifications and Performance

Specifications
Crew: 26
Length: 643ft (196m)
Diameter: 79ft (24.1m)
Volume: 1,950,000 cu ft (55,000 cu m)
Useful lift: 58,240lb (26,420kg)
Powerplant: 5 × Sunbeam Maori, 275hp each

Performance
Maximum speed: 62mph (100km/h)

R33 builders Armstrong Whitworth incorporated the advanced design technology found on the crashed German L 33 Zeppelin into its design of their airship. (*RNAS*)

R33/DH.53 Humming Bird Hook-On Experiments

On 5 October 1925, the R33 left its shed following repairs to conduct pressure experiments to aid the design of the new R101 airship. Ten days later R33 began a series of trials involving the launching of an aircraft hooked on to its hull to examine the viability of providing protection for an airship from enemy fighter aircraft and to furnish ship-to-shore communications similar to the way a warship used its auxiliary boats.

The British examined the available information concerning the attachment of an aircraft to an airship, the previous British AP-1/B.E.2c and HMA No. 23r/Camel Composites and those later trials in America using small Army Air Service blimps and the Sperry Messenger. From their investigation the British found that little was known about the airflow in the vicinity of a very large airship like the R33 in flight and decided that for it to be successful it would need a hook on the aircraft for hooking onto a trapeze-type device at a considerable distance below the airship. Some type of buffer assembly would be required to prevent the aircraft, once attached, from damaging itself or the airship, particularly by reducing the aircraft's sway when being pulled toward the airship. Although the US Air Service trials were successful, the Messenger parasite aircraft was attached to just a small blimp, and the information could not be made use of, since, in addition to the enormous difference in relative size between the American airship (200ft) and the R33 (643ft), no attempt to attach a trapeze closely under such a large airship had been made.

Generally, the DH.53's trapeze hook-on gear was similar to that previously used by the US Army Messenger, except that the hook did not possess its automatic releasing feature. The R33 was equipped with a large trapeze-type structure located in the forward third of its hull. For use on the very large R33 the short rigid trapeze used on the American airships at the time seemed to be impracticable and the British conducted wind tunnel tests using a small model hung on a wire structure. From these wind tunnel tests a horizontal trapeze bar hung by two approximately vertical cables attached to strong points on the airship was developed to be capable of being pulled up by a winch. The fore and aft position of the trapeze was fixed by two wires (called guys) attached to the ends of the trapeze bar and carried forward to the bow of the airship and at a relatively small angle to attach to the bow. These guys, while taking the drag of the aircraft when attached to the trapeze, were further cross braced from the corner of the trapeze to the attachment of the other guy to the airship to prevent swaying. The trapeze was about 3ft wide and was swung 30ft below the airship's hull. It was pivoted at the upper end and could be swung up by hand winches close to the airship's hull so that the parasite pilot could disembark or enter his craft. For airship launch the parasite was modified with a gantry mounted above the forward part of the fuselage.

The parasite was the small De Havilland DH.53 Humming Bird monoplane. In 1923, De Havilland had introduced its ultralight (326lb empty weight) single-seat, low-wing DH.53 powered by a 26hp Blackburne Tomtit V-2 inverted air-cooled piston engine that gave it a maximum speed of 73mph and cruising speed of 60mph over a range of 130 miles. The DH.53's Tomtit engine experienced no mechanical problems but had some difficulties when overloaded with the extra weight of the hook-on gear and due to the testing conditions. The pilot had problems bending his head back to look up to see the hook, which was installed 3ft above the cockpit and over the aircraft's centre of gravity. He also had very little sense as to the location of the horizon, as his vision was limited to either the underside of the airship or the sky.

De Havilland DH.53 Humming Bird Specifications and Performance

Specifications
Crew: 1
Length: 19ft 8in (5.99m)
Height: 7ft 3in (2.21m)
Wingspan: 30ft 1in (9.17m)
Wing area: 125 sq ft (11.6 sq m)
Empty weight: 326lb (148kg)
Gross weight: 565lb (256kg)
Powerplant: 1 × Blackburne Tomtit V-2 inverted air-cooled piston engine, 26hp
Propellers: 2-bladed fixed-pitch propeller

The DH.53 Humming Bird was a very small single-seat, single-engine, low-wing monoplane whose trapeze hook-on gear was similar to that previously used by the US Army Messenger trials. (*RNAS*)

Performance
Maximum speed: 73mph (117kmph)
Cruise speed: 60mph (97kmph)
Range: 130 miles (210km)
Service ceiling: 15,000ft (4,600m)
Rate of climb: 225ft/minute (1.14m/s)
Wing loading: 4.52lb/sq ft (22.1kg/sq m)

During these preliminaries, DH.53's method of overtaking the airship and flying into the trapeze was found to be unsatisfactory and the correct method was to have the aircraft's flight path to be about 60 degrees above horizontal so as to contact the trapeze with a certain amount of relative forward speed and relative vertical velocity. It was suggested that a propeller guard be provided to prevent the blades from hitting the wires but this was later found to be ineffective.

After several months of study and design changes, finally the R33 with the little DH.53 nestled in front of the two wing cars was ready for their debut at Pulham Airship Station and to the numerous officials, press and photographers who had waiting for good weather for the trials to begin.

Finally, on 15 October 1925 the weather cleared, and the airship was taken out of the hangar under the command of Maj. George Scott, who had commanded the R34 airship's Atlantic crossing and return in 1919, which was the first transatlantic flight by an airship and the first east–west transatlantic flight by an aircraft of any kind. Squadron Leader Rollo de Haga Haig of the Royal Air Force was chosen as the DH.53 pilot due to his record as a fighter pilot able to fly precision close formation.

The R33 climbed to 3,000ft, where Haig climbed down from the airship into the Humming Bird cockpit on a rather flimsy aluminium ladder that was twisting in the cold wind. Later the ladder was discarded and the pilot climbed down the trapeze. To make

Haig's ladder descent easier, the two forward airship engines were stopped, eliminating their slipstream over the DH.53. This also slowed the airship below the stalling speed of the DH.53 to allow it to drop clear.

Once Haig was settled in the cockpit, the airship slowed to 23mph and he received a pre-arranged signal to pull the trapeze hook release lever, allowing the Humming Bird to drop away from under the airship. By using a valve lifter, Haig released engine compression and the propeller began turning to start the engine.

By this time he was about 200ft below the airship and far behind, and he had difficulty in finally catching up. The trapeze had been lowered about 50ft below the airship and Haig and received the signal to hook on. He flew back up toward the trapeze, attempting to match the speed of the airship (44mph at 2,100ft). However, at this point Maj. Scott, the airship commander, decided that they were getting too far away from the aerodrome and decided to slow down and cancelled the hook-on signal. From under the airship Haig was only able to see the trapeze and did not see the cancellation signal,

Maj. George Scott, who captained the first transatlantic flight by an airship, was the commander of the R33 during the DH.53 trials. (*RNAS*)

Accomplished aerobatic pilot Rollo de Haga Haig was chosen to fly the DH.53 during the hook-on trials with the R33. (*RNAS*)

so he continued his hook-on approach. However, he was flying much too fast, and the hook engaged the trapeze's bracing wires and pivoted the aircraft upward to swing around the trapeze bar, with the propeller entangling a trapeze cross-bracing wire. Both the wire and the propeller broke, stopping the engine. After the initial turmoil subsided, Haig found the Hummingbird hanging on to a bracing wire with a dead engine. Haig then coolly disengaged the suspension gear and dropped off to glide to the airfield below, to be immediately surrounded by numerous press personnel. A post-flight review determined that the pilot's approach was miscalculated, and that the trapeze should have only been lowered when the aircraft was approaching from the stern, allowing the nose gear to be easily slotted into place.

The second attempt was made from Pulham on 28 October 1925, and again the DH.53 was released from the R33 and it approached the trapeze when the airship was flying at 48mph. Haig had no difficulty in immediately engaging the bar, but the Humming Bird slipped violently to one side of the trapeze due to a failure of one of the airship pulley blocks and the aircraft fell off its precarious perch as the trapeze dropped at one end and the hook slid into the corner. However, Haig was again able to drop off to land safely.

On 4 December the third attempt was made, with changes made in the interim. It was decided to increase the DH.53's engine power by installing a Bristol Cherub engine. The entire gear was reinforced and improved with additional brace wires provided and better shock-absorbing devices installed at the end of the trapeze that removed the load of the aircraft when hooking on. The trapeze itself, which had previously been provided with a dip in the centre for the DH.53 to centralise itself, was replaced by a lighter straight one, which was less likely to affect the path of the aircraft at the moment of contact.

With the airship cruising at 2,500ft and flying at 52mph, Haig approached and checked the effect of his controls on the relative motion between the Humming Bird and the trapeze bar. He found the Cherub provided extra power and made several practice attempts at hooking on with the hook locked. Finally, he attempted and accomplished a successful hook on. Afterward, he pulled himself out of the cockpit and climbed up into the airship. Haig described the feat:

> It was found that the straight trapeze bar was not all joy. It was exceedingly difficult to get to the centre. I made numerous attempts when hooked, which generally ended by sliding, with some zest, into the opposite comer. However, it was eventually accomplished, and the machine was hauled up. This operation presented no difficulty whatever and no swaying occurred. I found I could make the hauling up operation easy or otherwise by causing the nose of the plane to point up or down, i.e., either pulling on the cables or flying up. The airship, of course, was kept at a steady speed well above the stalling speed of the machine.

This was the end of the R33/DH.53 experiment and during the spring of 1926 the government announced that the experimental programme using the R33 had come to an end and the airship was to be shedded at Pulham for care and maintenance.

On 4 December 1925 de Haga Haig achieved the first British aircraft hook on to an airship (the R33) while flying the DH.53. The R33 was equipped with a large trapeze-type structure located in the forward part of its hull, forward of the two wing cars. The trapeze was about 3ft wide but was much longer than the US Army version, hanging 30ft below the airship's hull. (*RNAS*)

At the conclusion of these Humming Bird experiments, Squadron Leader Haig's report concluded:

> From the experience gained there is no doubt that, given an airship suitably designed, aircraft can be released and hooked on and housed again with ease. We have proved that it can be done and that very little more experiment is needed to make it a very straightforward job which can be carried out by any pilot who has had experience in close formation flying. For training purposes, it would not even be necessary to use an airship. Any big aircraft could have a suitable trapeze hung from it for other aircraft to practice on with dummy hooks. In wartime, a suitably designed airship would have its own scouts which would attack any enemy machines and would be capable of putting np a most redoubtable defence. One big advantage which would accrue because of the development of aircraft for this work is that such a plane need have no undercarriage and only a small hook. The engine and propeller could be designed to be efficient at some height, say 20,000 ft, and such a machine would be far superior in performance at altitude to any ground aircraft that might attack the airship as the former would be in its natural element. In view of the possibility of a landing being forced, the lightest of skids on the fuselage would be sufficient to prevent the pilot from being hurt.
>
> It is really from a commercial point of view that I see the biggest advantage, however. Instead of an airship having to carry out comparatively short trips, say from London to Egypt, and then execute a rather difficult and expensive landing to a mast, the trip would be extended, say to Cape Town, and any goods (and possibly, later, passengers) could be exchanged by merely flying a suitable aircraft up from some aerodrome en route. The airship would not even have to stop. While not wishing to press the point unduly, this arrangement seems to be ideal.
>
> The airship authorities claim, apparently quite reasonably, that the airship is the long-distance weight carrier, and the aircraft has proved a good and very rapid comparatively short distance transport vehicle. I am speaking now of aerial distances of thousands of land miles as against hundreds of land miles. Is it not obvious that the ideal is a combination of both? From what little I have seen, as a layman, of airships on the ground and at masts etc., the real troubles arise under these conditions, and as an aircraft is from this point of view, the airship is a thousand times worse. It is, moreover, a prey to every wind which blows under these conditions but, like the aircraft, nothing worries it once it is in the air. Therefore, keep it in the air as long as possible.
>
> Some day, a long way ahead, I suppose our airship liners will normally live in the air, be refuelled, re-gassed, and reloaded in the air, and only come down for docking and repairs.
>
> *Aviation*, 28 March 1927

The last two RAF Humming Birds were used in the R33 launching experiments and by 1927 the RAF disposed of all eight, which were sold as civilian aircraft. The British realised that to be useful the light Humming Bird had to be replaced by a true military aircraft and thus the DH.53 was discarded in the following year when the hook-on work was continued.

R33/Gloster Grebe Hook-On Experiments

However, by early autumn 1926, the R33 was relaunched to participate in further experiments involving the launching of fighter aircraft and for trials at the newly erected mast at Cardington. Instead of the diminutive DH.53 Humming Bird, the R33 was equipped with two more formidable Gloster Grebes, which had a loaded weight of about 2,500lb.

With the development of the powerful 325hp Armstrong Siddeley Jaguar III engine, the British aviation industry based its new designs around that power plant. Gloster developed the prototype Grebe I, powered by the 400hp Jaguar IV, from the then experimental Gloster Grouse. The Grebe II entered service in 1923 as the RAF's first post-war fighter aircraft. It was a fast (top speed 152mph), wooden, sesquiplane (a type of biplane where one wing, usually the lower, is significantly smaller than the other) with fabric covering. Gloster produced 133 Grebes, including the four prototypes, 108 Grebe II single-seat fighters, and 21 two-seat dual-control trainers. Grebes remained in RAF service for almost five years until replaced by Armstrong Whitworth Siskins in mid-1928. The Gloster Company's successor was the Gamecock.

Gloster Grebe Specifications and Performance

Specifications

Crew: 1
Length: 20ft 3in (6.17m)
Wingspan: 29ft 4in (8.94m)
Height: 9ft 3in (2.82m)
Wing area: 254 sq ft (23.6 sq m)
Wing loading: 10.3lb/sq ft (50kg/sq m)
Empty weight: 1,720lb (780kg)
Gross weight: 2,614lb (1,186kg)
Powerplant: 1 × Armstrong Siddeley Jaguar IV 14-cylinder, air-cooled, radial piston engine, 400hp
Propellers: 2-bladed wooden fixed-pitch propeller

Performance

Maximum speed: 152mph (245kmph) at sea level
145mph (233kmph) at 10,000ft (3,000m)
Endurance: 2 hours 45 minutes
Service ceiling: 23,000ft (7,000m)

Armament

Guns: 2 × 0.303in (7.7mm) Vickers machine guns

The airship composite tests were under the overall command of Major G. H. Scott with Squadron Leader R. Booth acting as captain. Two Grebes of the Royal Aircraft Establishment were assigned for the tests, J7385 and J7400, piloted by Flying Officers Robert Linton Ragg and Mackenzie Richards. One of the Grebes was suspended amidships and the other one aft of it. Each Grebe was suspended by a central quick-release attachment to the aircraft's top centre section. There were three struts to prevent oscillation while the aircraft was hanging on the R33's trapeze, two to the wings and one to the fuselage near the tail. There was a flexible piping running from the keel to the side of the fuselage, which conveyed the mixture from the Bristol gas starter in the airship to the Grebe's Jaguar engine. The pilots had to enter their cockpits via precarious rope ladders from openings in the airship's keel.

The R33 took off from Pulham on 21 October 1926 carrying two Grebes. One was carried well aft and the other was slightly abaft the control car. When the R33 climbed to 2,000ft, the release was delayed when the Grebes had initial engine problems. Mackenzie Richards in the rear Grebe was released first and cleared the airship, Ragg, in the second aircraft, was not released until an hour and a half later due to continued engine problems. Both Grebes flew their scheduled flights around the mothership and returned to base, while the R33 landed at Cardington.

On 3 November 1926, trial landings were made by the R33 at a new mooring mast at Cardington. During these tests two Grebes were carried although they were not launched. On 17 November the airship attempted to demonstrate this experimental work before attending British Commonwealth premiers, but low clouds prevented the efforts to launch the two Grebes. Two Grebes were flown from the airship when the R33 flew from Cardington to Pulham on 23 November. The Grebes, piloted by Squadron Leader B. S. Baker and Flight Leader F. H. Shales, were released and landed safely at Pulham. On the following day the British discontinued further hook-on attempts. Soon after these tests the R33 was deflated and placed in the Pulham shed for long-term storage. It languished until metal fatigue was discovered in its framework, causing it to be dismantled during 1928. The forward part of the R33 control car is on display at the RAF Museum in Hendon.

The Cardington shed No. 1 was the largest in Britain at that time, providing space to enable the construction of two rigid airships. The second shed on the right was built later. (*RNAS*)

During 1923, the Gloster Company modified their Sparrowhawk fighter trainer into the Grebe single-seat, single-engined, fabric-covered, wood construction biplane powered by a 400hp Jaguar IV engine. (*RNAS*)

Two Grebes were suspended by a central quick-release attachment to the aircraft's top centre section under the R33's keel preparatory to being dropped from the airship in flight. The R33 took off from Pulham on 21 October 1926 with both Grebes launched and they then flew their scheduled flights around the mothership and returned to base. No hook ons were attempted during the Grebe trials. (*RNAS*)

Section Three

American Airship Composites: Sky Hookers of the 1930s

On 12 December 1917, the navy successfully released the first American aircraft, a Curtiss JN-4 Jenny biplane, from an airship, the non-rigid Goodyear/Goodrich C-1 Blimp. (*USN*)

Curtiss JN-4 Jenny, 'The airplane that taught America to fly'. (*Author*)

Chapter One

Early Concepts

One of the more unique chapters in American aviation history involved the operation of airship motherships carrying parasite aircraft during the end of the First World War and into the 1920s and 1930s. The US Navy initially designed lighter-than-air rigid airships during 1916 and after the war it became convinced that these would have an important function in future naval campaigns by extending long-distance scouting for the Fleet.

During November 1918, Navy Lt George Crompton Dirigible Officer of the Rockaway, Long Island Naval Air Station (NAS) New York, designed a hook, called a 'pelican hook', for carrying and releasing an aircraft from an airship. A Harvard University graduate, Crompton was a member of the first lighter-than-air class trained by the Goodyear Rubber Company at Akron, Ohio. He was designated Naval Aviator Number 100 on 21 September 1917, and then served at Naval Air Station Montauk, Long Island, New York, during the war. He collaborated with 1Lt A. W. Redfield, commanding officer of the 52nd Aero Squadron at Mitchell Field, on determining the specifics of the hook's operation. Compton was to fly a Navy non-rigid Goodyear/Goodrich C-1 Blimp (USN serial #4118) and Redfield an Army Curtiss JN-4 Jenny. An initial concern was if the JN-4's engine could be started in the air, but Redfield proposed the use of a compression release, and found that after cutting his engine and releasing its compression he could dive the aircraft to get its propeller windmilling, then use the choke to start the engine.

On 12 December 1918, Crompton flew the C-1 to a rendezvous with four JN-4s (three observers) over a large field adjacent to Fort Tilden, New York. The lifting apparatus of the JN-4 had been made part of the blimp's car suspension by attaching four cables to finger-patches numbers 3 and 5 on each side of the envelope. The four cables came together in a ring about 6ft below the control car. One end of a 100ft length of half-inch cable was attached to the ring and on its opposite end was the hook and releasing device that was to carry the Jenny. While Crompton was slowly ascending by carefully releasing the ballast, the ground crew allowed the blimp to rise about 50ft and Redfield's plane was manoeuvred under the control car. The pelican hook was attached to a suspension point on the JN-4's upper mid-wing and the blimp then ascended to the end of the 100ft wire. To compensate for the weight of the JN-4, Crompton discharged 2,125lb of ballast, which made the C-1 about 75lb light, causing the blimp and aircraft to rise into the air statically. At 400ft Crompton started his engines and flew the blimp in wide spirals to about 2,600ft, where Redfield tripped his release, started his engine, and flew away for the first American, certainly unrefined, effort at combining airship and aircraft.

In the October 1923 *Popular Science*, Navy R. Adm. William Moffett had written an article, 'Sky Leviathan of Tomorrow', maintaining that Navy airships carrying aircraft, like 'lifeboats on ocean-going vessels', were a concept that would be seen soon as aircraft had already been carried, launched, and retrieved by airships. He predicted that future airships, developed for naval use, would 'carry a sting that will make it one of the most formidable contenders for supremacy of the air, sea, and earth that has ever been conceived'. Moffett continued his forecast that airships would 'carry a dozen aircraft to protect it against attack and in addition will mount a battery of guns that will command the respect of any enemy marauder'. He didn't see any problem for aircraft taking off: 'The launching of them is merely a matter of pushing the planes off into space, where they can recover themselves with the ease of a bird thrown into the air.'

Rear Admiral William Moffett, although not a pilot himself, became known as the 'Air Admiral' for his leadership of the Navy's Bureau of Aeronautics from its formation in 1921. In this role, he supervised the development of tactics for naval aircraft, the introduction of the aircraft carrier, and advocated the development of airships. (*USN*)

The October 1923 *Popular Science* contained an article by Navy Rear Admiral William Moffett entitled 'Sky Leviathan of Tomorrow', which predicted in the near future aircraft being carried, launched, and retrieved by airships. (*Popular Science*)

Chapter Two

US Army Airships and the Sperry Messenger

After the First World War, Brig. Gen. William 'Billy' Mitchell, Assistant Chief of the Air Service, had eagerly anticipated the beginning of Air Service airship operations. The innovative Mitchell predicted a time when giant Army airships would implement multipurpose roles, acting as reconnaissance aircraft, troop and supply transports, aircraft for fighting enemy airships, and as an air base on to which heavier-than-air fighter aircraft could hook, refuel, then disengage for heavier-than-air combat operations. In his 1925 book *Winged Defense*, Mitchell envisioned the airship 'as an aircraft carrier, that is equipped with aircraft which could fly away from it and return to it, so that it could go anyplace over the ocean, launch the aircraft, let them do what was desired, and then have them return'. Mitchell considered this to be possible, since 'the airship … has the greatest cruising radius of any known means of transportation, seacraft included'.

During 1919 Mitchell asked Alfred Verville of the US Army Air Service Engineering Division to design a lightweight aircraft to replace motorcycles that was to act as a liaison between Army field units. In early 1920 Verville completed a design called the Messenger that was one of the smallest aircraft ever in service for the Army Air Service. These 'motorcycles of the air' were simple, single-seat conventional biplanes powered by a nose-mounted 60hp Lowrance L-4 radial engine. The Lawrence Sperry Aircraft Company of Farmingdale was contracted to build five Verville-Sperry M-1 Messengers in April 1920, with the first flown on 1 November. The aircraft was distinguished by its small size, simple construction, and inexpensive cost, which made it ideal for testing and experimentation. The National Advisory Committee for Aeronautics (NACA) used one in its pioneering aerodynamic research programmes from 1923 to 1929, while Sperry modified twelve into the radio-controlled Messenger Aerial Torpedo.

Sperry Messenger Specifications and Performance

Specifications

Crew: 1
Length: 17ft 9in (5.4m)
Wingspan: 20ft (6.1m)
Height: 6ft 9 in (2.1m)
Wing area: 160 sq ft (14.9 sq m)
Empty weight: 623lb (283kg)
Gross weight: 862lb (391kg)
Powerplant: 1 × Lowrance L-4, 60hp

Performance
Maximum speed: 97mph (156kmph)
Rate of climb: 700ft/minute (3.56m/s)

Armament
None

September 1921 Conference Discusses Operating Aircraft from Airships

At a conference of US Army Air Service officers at Bolling Field, Virginia, on 28 September 1921, the subject of operating aircraft from airships was discussed as the Army was also interested in developing the operation of aircraft from its newly purchased Italian-built, semi-rigid airship *Roma*.

Attending the conference were Lawrence Sperry, head of the Sperry Aircraft Company (and son of gyrocompass developer, Elmer Sperry), and several Air Service officers including Lt Robert Olmstead and a Mr Stone of the Navy. Sperry proposed the mounting of a hook on the upper wing of an aircraft, which would engage the bar of a 'trapeze' suspended from the airship. The Army D-3 Goodyear (envelope)/Naval Aircraft Factory (control car) training blimp was to be used to explore hook ons to its trapeze with a Sperry Messenger.

Lawrence Sperry (in cockpit), the head of the Sperry Aircraft Company, with his father Elmer Sperry, the developer of the gyro¬compass, having a discussion by his son's two-seat Messenger biplane. (*Cradle of Aviation Museum*)

Balloon Pilot Lt Robert Olmstead (L) and pilot's aide Lt John Choptaw at the Gordon-Bennett Cup, Brussels, September 1923, where both were killed in a storm that occurred shortly after take-off. (*Agence Roi*)

After the conference, Olmstead, in reporting on the feasibility of the project, stated that the 'Sperry Messenger plane was peculiarly well adapted, for carrying on the experiment principally due to the fact that the motor starts very easily and is extremely reliable in this respect, and it is possible to start it under all conditions of temperature.' In enumerating the tactical uses of 'an aircraft such as the Messenger in conjunction with the operation of airships', Olmstead stated that:

> in coastal patrol work an airship operating at 200 miles off the coast could release planes of this type to carry messages back to bases ashore; that such planes might be released for purposes of inspecting various, suspicious-looking craft visible to the occupants of the airship, to determine whether they were friendly craft or otherwise, for it would be impossible to send an airship sufficiently close to suspicious-looking craft to make sure of their character without exposing it to anti-aircraft fire and possible destruction; that, in conjunction with land operation of larger airships such planes would be very useful in arranging for landings at places where there were no personnel trained in the manipulation of airships; for the pilot of the plane could land and take charge of landing the airship, or, in case landing was not possible, he could return to the airship, explain the situation to its commander, and arrangements could be wade to land in another location; that in actual warfare it would be practicable to utilise these planes to act as scouts for the airships and give timely warning of the approach of enemy planes or airships.

1922: The Messenger Airship Tests Approaches

On 17 July 1922, Lawrence Sperry, flying one of his Messengers, conducted unofficial approach tests with an Air Service C-2 blimp piloted by Lt Max Moyer. Neither the airship nor aircraft were equipped with an aircraft-attaching apparatus, so Sperry's limited objective was to determine how his Messenger performed when flown at the relatively slow speed of the blimp, and when flown within the area of turbulence created by the blimp's gas bag. While Moyer held the blimp on a straight course at 1,200ft over the Army's Aberdeen Proving Ground, Maryland, and into the smooth air over Chesapeake Bay, Sperry practised manoeuvring his Messenger up under the blimp's control car, reducing the Messenger's speed to that of the C-2 while gradually gaining altitude. After a few minutes of practice, Sperry was able to manoeuvre the Messenger to within 8 or 10ft of the bottom of the control car and to maintain his altitude, course, and speed without varying his position in relation to the airship. The only problem he encountered occurred when he closed within 3ft of the control car. That startled Moyer and he released ballast to climb away from Sperry, whose aircraft and open cockpit was then drenched with several hundred pounds of ballast water.

By late 1922 Sperry had designed and fabricated a trapeze apparatus for attaching his Messenger to an airship, and during late November he flew some tentative tests of the device over Mitchell Field, New York. The 15ft-long trapeze was attached under a de Havilland DH.4 Liberty biplane (No. 64553) flown by Lt Clyde Finter. The trapeze was retracted against the underside of the DH.4 while on the ground but could be lowered and fixed

1Lt Clyde Finter inspects the hook on the upper wing of the Sperry Messenger, which was to engage the bar of a 'trapeze' suspended from the DH.4. (*USAAS*)

into a vertical position once the DH.4 was airborne. Sperry's Messenger (No. 64225) was equipped with a contact stick, which was mounted vertically over the upper wing's centre section. The lower end of the 3ft-long stick was set in a pivot so it would not break upon striking the trapeze, and when the pressure was removed, the stick was sprung to snap back to its vertical position. For the tests the stick was covered with lampblack to show where it had contacted the trapeze.

Poor-quality photo of 1Lt Clyde Finter's DH.4 outfitted with a rudimentary trapeze flying above Lawrence Sperry's hook-equipped Messenger practising hook-on approaches over Mitchell Field, NY, in November 1922. (*USAAS*)

On 28 November 1922, due to rough air, Sperry in his Messenger only practised close approaches, not hook ons, to the trapeze on Finter's DH.4. During the morning of 2 December Sperry spent an hour of flying touch-and-goes over Mitchell Field, during which he attempted sixteen unsuccessful passes at Finter's trapeze. Sperry met with Finter and his back-seat observer and they determined that the problem was due to parallax, an optical illusion that is the apparent change in the position of an object resulting from a change in position of the viewer. During testing two days later, Sperry was able to allow for this and made seven out of eight successful passes (not hook ons) at the trapeze, three resulting in contacts of several seconds. Afterward, Sperry's concluded: 'that it will be a very simple matter to fly into the trapeze with a certain amount of very necessary practice, and that this ought to be easier to do than for a beginner to learn on the ground'.

After these tests Sperry's other interests would lead him away from these hook-on trials. On 13 December 1923 Sperry took off amid fog in a Sperry M-1 Messenger from Britain headed for France but never reached his destination as, tragically and ironically, Sperry lost his way in the continuing fog and his plane crashed into the English Channel, where his body was found on 11 January 1924. Only 31 years old at his death, he held twenty-three patents, mostly for inventions related to air safety.

September 1923 D-3 Blimp/Messenger Hook-On Tests

During the summer of 1923 the Sperry Company developed a practicable skyhook for the Messenger for the Army, and it was subjected to a series of static tests at McCook Field,

Army D-Class Blimp. (*USAAS*)

Ohio. The hook had a very small aperture and was mounted at the end of wooden guide bar that had its contact surface sheathed in metal. The trapeze, which was to be attached to an Army D-3 Blimp, remained basically unchanged, being a simple structure fabricated from aluminium tubing, its only complex feature being its shock-absorbing system, which was simply a set of modified Fokker landing gear shock absorbers.

About nine months after Sperry's airship approach tests and demise, on 18 September 1923, at Langley Field, Virginia, the Army Air Service duplicated the Sperry-Finter

Sperry Messenger AS 68533 was equipped with a hook-on apparatus to be used for the airship hook-on trials during subsequent years. (*USAAS*)

experiments using a D-3 Class Blimp. Lt Rex Stoner piloted the Messenger (AS 68533) while West Point graduate (1914) and First World War Balloon Corps veteran Maj. John Jouett piloted and Lt Junius Smith co-piloted the airship, with Lt Frederick Evans as the observer. After climbing to 2,000ft, Stoner's first attempt to contact the blimp's trapeze swinging below its control car missed the trapeze with its contact stick by within about 4in of the trapeze bar. On his second attempt he brought the contact stick against the trapeze bar, but with a 17mph speed differential with the airship, broke the shock absorber cord holding the stick in an upright position when contact was made, allowing it to fall to a horizontal position and terminating the day's tests.

To increase the airship's speed, new and more powerful engines were installed and on 24 September a second series of hook-on tests were conducted over Aberdeen Proving Ground, Maryland. Lt Stoner again piloted the Sperry and Lt Smith the airship, with Lt Evans as observer. To improve chances of a hook-up, the stick was fastened with elastic at the lower end so that it would bend with pressure from the trapeze. At 2,000ft the Messenger's air speed was 60mph and that of the airship 57mph. Stoner's first approach on the trapeze kept the plane at the level of the bar and while contact was made it was not maintained for more than three or four seconds. On the second attempt Stoner approached the trapeze until he was within about 200ft of it at about 30ft below and began to climb. This proved to be a highly successful manoeuvre, as the stick was brought into contact with the bar and held there for about one minute. While this contact was being maintained, Stoner tried sliding the stick up and down the bar to determine the feasibility of attaching his aircraft to the trapeze and concluded that there should be no difficulty in doing so.

On 18 September 1923, Lt Rex Stoner, flying a Sperry Messenger, determined the feasibility of attaching his aircraft to the trapeze with the US Army Blimp Airship D-3 over Langley Field. (*USAAS*)

October 1924: The TC-5 Carries and Releases the Messenger

During 2–4 October 1924, during the Pulitzer Air Races held at Wilbur Wright Airfield, Dayton, Ohio, the Messenger, again AS 68533, was once more piloted by Lt Clyde Finter, and the airship mother ship was now a TC-5 crewed by Capt. Edmund Hill, directional pilot; Lt Frank McKee, altitude pilot, one engineer, and one rigger.

The Messenger was equipped with a pyramidal apparatus on the centre section of the upper wing with a horizontal guide bar extending over the propeller that served as a propeller guard as well as a guide to slide the trapeze bar into the hook mounted at the rear of the guide bar. The aperture of the hook was only about ¼in larger than the trapeze bar, thus adding to the difficulty of hooking on. The hook was designed to automatically open in case the relative difference in speed between the plane and the airship exceeded 2mph, for it was calculated that a greater shock would carry away some part of the apparatus. The trapeze bar was mounted on the airship by two rigidly secured uprights joined at the lower ends by a crossbar. Just below this, the trapeze bar, a straight bar 3ft in length, was secured by means of a shock absorber cord that was designed to permit a fore and off movement of about 4in to absorb the shock of landing. However, this flexibility was not attained in the tests. The trapeze bar extended about 9ft below the TC-5 control car that was secured to the airship's bomb racks. The trapeze with brace wires had been installed while the airship was elevated on its mooring mast. After assembly and adjustment, the forward brace wires were released so that the trapeze could be pulled up close beneath the control car. The airship then was released from the mooring mast and manoeuvred to the flying field.

For these airship aircraft carrying/release test flights, Lt Clyde Finter piloted the Sperry Messenger, and the TC-5 was piloted by Lt Frank McKee (commander and altitude pilot), assisted by Capt. Edmund Hill (directional pilot), one engineer, and one rigger. The TC-5 was 'weighed off' about 1,200lb 'statically light', which was approximately the weight of the Messenger. Carrying 150lb of fuel, the airship was trimmed to horizontal. The TC-5's engines were warmed up, and the trapeze bar lowered into position and secured to the bomb racks. The Messenger was then manoeuvred on the ground alongside the TC-5, which rose over the Sperry for attachment to the trapeze. McKee reported in an article in *Aviation Week*, 29 December 1924: 'Quite a bit of difficulty was experienced in this operation owing to the fact that it was impossible to keep the airship under control to avoid injuring the plane when the airship was forced down due to gusts and eddies. Some slight damage was done to one wing, but this did not affect its operation in any way.' Once the aircraft was hooked on, the TC-5 was 'free ballooned' to about 15 or 20ft before its engines were throttled up. The mothership and its parasite maintained an altitude of about 150ft while flying across the length of Wilbur Wright Field, after which the TC-5 went into a climbing turn and headed into the wind with the engines at full throttle until the airship reached an altitude of 1,500ft before releasing Finter. After release Finter was to immediately turn the Messenger to the right or left to avoid possible contact should the TC-5 descend. Once in the air no difficulties were experienced by either the airship or aircraft.

McKee described the test:

> We had no prearranged signal for letting go other than for me to let him know when we had reached 1,500ft. This I did and shortly after Lt Finter released the plane. I did not realise that he was gone until I looked over the side and saw him about 100ft below and to the left. It was a matter of at least a minute before I felt the static effect of the loss of the plane. This was not particularly great owing to the fact that the motors were wide open. The ship did not gain altitude or become unmanageable in any way. At no time, either while carrying the plane or after its release, was any difficulty experienced in handling the ship. Lt Finter stated that he at all times had perfect dynamic control of his ship and could slide it either to the right or left on the bar by a slight movement of the rudder and could use his elevators in elevating or depressing the nose of his plane.
>
> *Aviation Week*, Volume 17, 29 December 1924

However, these trials convinced the Army that it should be much easier to attach an aircraft to an airship in the air than duplicate the complicated ground attachment procedure. Finter supported the Army's opinion 'that attaching the plane in the air would be a great

Control car and trapeze of the non-rigid Army TC-5 airship inside the Scott Field hangar in October 1924. (*USAAS*)

The Messenger piloted by 1Lt Clyde Finter being carried by the TC-5 to the 1,500ft dropping altitude during the Pulitzer Air Races of 2–4 October 1924 at Wilbur Wright Field Dayton, Ohio, where it was successfully launched/dropped. (*USAAS*)

deal simpler, with less possibility of injury to either personnel or aircraft, and that by taking off from the ground about 500 or 600lb light it would be comparatively easy to pick the plane up except on a very bumpy day.' The Army supposed that once aerial hook ons were perfected they could hook on and then carry at least five fighter aircraft to a large, 2 million cu ft capacity rigid airship, and later develop even larger airships capable of carrying a fighter squadron of as many as eight aircraft.

December 1924 TC-3 Hook-On Tests

During late November 1924, the Engineering Division at McCook Field (now part of the Wright-Patterson complex) were detaching the TC-5's trapeze for travel and dismantling the Sperry Messenger for transportation to the Army's lighter-than-air centre at Scott Field, Illinois. Because the Messenger's range was very short and its skyhook prevented the installation of an extra gas tank, it had to submit to the ignominy of travelling by truck to the place where it was destined to record a first in aviation history. The Messenger and personnel left McCook Field on 10 December and arrived at Scott Field the same day. The trapeze was re-rigged to the TC-3 and the Messenger reassembled, and by mid-December the two were ready for the first hook-on efforts. However, weather conditions prevented any attempts being made.

12 December 1924 Hook-On Tests

It was not until 12 December 1924 that attempts to hook a Messenger on to the TC-3 in flight were made. For these tests the airship crew consisted of Lt Frank McKee (commander and altitude pilot), Capt. Edmund Hill (directional pilot), an engineer, and a rigger, while the Sperry Messenger was again piloted by Lt Clyde Finter. Supervising the trials was an Air Service Engineering Division representative. Maj. H. A. Strauss. Lt W. L. Boyd was the Air Service pilot of the photographic aircraft, and Lewis Hagemeyer, an Engineering Division employee, was to film moving pictures of the experiment.

For these tests a fixed trapeze was used, braced fore and aft by two cables in each direction, leading from trapeze to suspension clips on the airship car. The Fokker type of trapeze bar was utilised as it was better designed to absorb not only upward thrust from the Messenger, but also the forward momentum and drag of the suspended aircraft on this bar in flight. The Messenger was not hooked on to the TC-3 while on the ground but rendezvoused with the airship in the air. Finter began his first hook-on approach from the rear and below upon the narrow bar suspended 12ft below from the bobbing TC-3 control car, which was flying at 55mph in rough air. When he closed on the trapeze bar the slipstream from the airship's propellers soon affected Finter's control of his aircraft. To carry the extra load of the parasite, the airship was flown 1,000lb lighter but to compensate

For these hook-on tests the Messenger was not hooked on to the TC-3 while on the ground but rendezvoused with the airship in the air for the first American aircraft hook-on attempt to an airship trapeze. (*USAAS*)

for this increased lift the airship could not be flown on an even keel without gaining altitude. When nosed down to counter the tendency to rise, the airship proceeded to alternately rise and fall. The disturbed air tossed Finter's aircraft upward, causing its guide bar to strike the trapeze and throwing the aircraft violently downward. Finter then swung around to make a second approach, only to be once again bounced off the trapeze. During a third attempt an air current forced the Messenger upward, breaking the propeller against the trapeze and causing Finter to carry out a forced but safe landing in a pasture. There were no spare propellers for the Messenger at Scott Field, but to avoid any further delay, over the weekend one was cannibalised from the OA-1 airship. It was tested on the Messenger and, while only turning over 1,450rpm with full open throttle, Finter decided to try again on the afternoon of the 15th if the weather permitted.

The first in-air hook-on attempts on 12 December 1924 were unsuccessful and resulted in a broken propeller but on 15 December 1924 1Lt Clyde Finter made the first successful American hook on to an airship. (*USAAS*)

15 December 1924: The First Successful Hook-On Tests

For the 15 December test the TC-3 crew again consisted of Lt Frank McKee, Capt. Edmund Hill, an engineer, and a rigger. During this second series of tests, although the winter day was crisp, clear, and below freezing, the air was smoother, and the airship was flown only 250lb light, thus permitting it to fly more nearly on a level keel. Motion pictures and stills were to be taken of both the hooking on and release by four aircraft carrying Air Service and newspaper photographers, and arrangements were made to secure copies of the films taken by commercial photographers to supplement these records.

On the first hook-on attempt, while McKee tried to hold the blimp steady at 1,500ft, Finter's Messenger approached from behind and battled through the propwash and slipstream spilling from the bottom of the TC-3. He placed the hook on to the trapeze bar but instead of coming to rest on the trapeze, it kept on going through. The hook had been equipped with a pressure-impact safety feature that would automatically release the hook if the Messenger contacted the trapeze at a speed differential of more than 5mph. It had worked too well. Finter realised that when he positioned the hook to within about 2 or 3ft of the trapeze bar the blimp's propwash and turbulence surrounding the hull and control car virtually stopped his plane and that it was necessary to apply an extra surge of power to break through this turbulence to reach the bar. He also found that this power had to be applied carefully as giving it too much speed would force it through the hook. On the second pass Finter again hooked on to the trapeze, but his speed was higher than the speed of the airship and the automatic releasing safety catch in the hook mechanism again released. While circling for his third pass, Finter decided that, instead of approaching the trapeze on a level tack from behind, he would approach several feet below the trapeze and then climb up to make his hook on. Using this tactic, he would remain outside the turbulent area until the last minute. Finter judiciously increased power, so as not to give the aircraft too much speed and cause the hook to release itself. The hook on was a success, accomplished with the aircraft flying at an indicated air speed of 62mph: a ground speed of approximately 54mph and the airship at an indicated air speed of 51mph and a ground speed of approximately 45mph. Finter thus became the first man to 'land' an aircraft aboard another aircraft in flight. Dumping ballast to accommodate the weight of its new passenger, the TC-3 then turned toward Scott Field with the Messenger hanging under its control car. Once over Scott Field, Finter released his hook and landed, to the congratulations of those few present who realised the significance of his feat. As a result of their tests, the Army concluded 'that an average pilot could make a successful hook on, provided that his overtaking speed did not exceed 5 mph'.

After the tests, Brig. Gen. Billy Mitchell enthused that test 'evidenced conclusively that articles may be delivered from an airship anywhere over a locality, passengers may be disembarked or embarked, fuel may be taken on, and last of all, the airship may be used as an aircraft carrier. This fact enhances the usefulness of the great dirigible airship many times.' (*Aviation Week*, Volume 17, 29 December 1924)

Army Blimp TC-7 was equipped with a trapeze for additional and final Army hook ons with the Sperry Messenger. Since the Navy had been assigned exclusive airship responsibility, the Army terminated its airship interests. (*USAAS*)

1925: The Army Concludes Its Airship/Aircraft Lifting/Release Trials

The Army conducted some additional hook-on experiments with their 200,000 cu ft TC-7 Goodyear blimp, commanded by Lt Karl Axtater.[1] The Sperry Messenger was flown by

1. Later, on 15 June 1928, Lt Axtater gained more widespread recognition by flying in an Air Corps TC-10 blimp, descending directly over a moving Illinois Central train and handing a mailbag to the postal clerk, thus completing the first aircraft-to-train transfer.

Cadet Bayard Carpenter on 7 September 1925 over Scott Field and again on 13 September during a flying circus over Scott Field. The results of these tests are unknown. Although these trials demonstrated airship/aircraft hook on as feasible, the Army discontinued further testing. This can probably be attributed to the Navy having been assigned exclusive responsibility for rigid airship development, and any aircraft carrying by the Army's blimps would have had to have been of a very limited scope.

The Army Air Corps Last Composite Airship Proposals

Also, in 1925 the Army, having procured the 719,000 cu ft semi-rigid Goodyear-Zeppelin RS-1, discussed fitting it with a trapeze, but this proposal was never completed. During 1930 the Army briefly considered the procurement of a very large metal-clad airship that would have carried aircraft. As late as 1934 Army airship designers were proposing a huge 13 million cu ft airship that would carry Boeing B-9, twin-engine monoplane bombers; but this project also never progressed beyond the initial prototype stage, the B-9 being quickly eclipsed by the superior Martin B-10 bomber. By this time the Army finally realised it had reached a dead end and further proposals were discontinued as the Navy had perfected aircraft hook ons, storage, and launching from their huge airships.

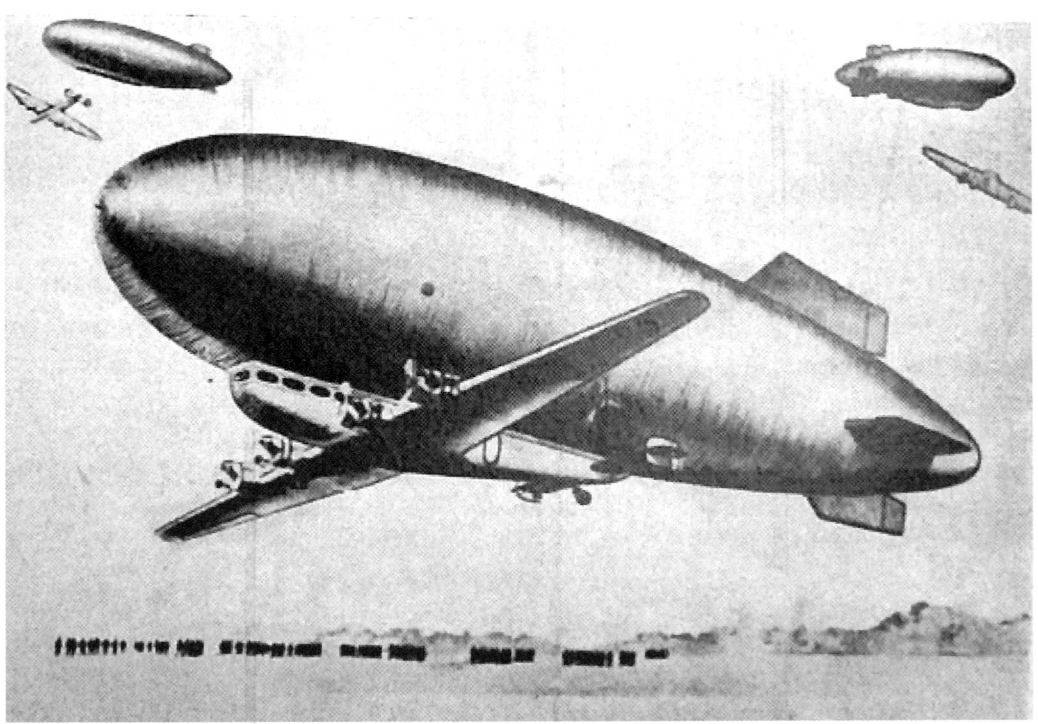

During late 1934 Army air¬ship designers proposed a huge 13,000,000 cu ft airship that would carry Boeing B-9 twin-engine monoplane bombers. (*USAAS*)

Chapter Three

The US Navy Pursues the Airship/Aircraft Composite Concept

Since the early twentieth century America had faced the dilemma of having to defend its lengthy Atlantic and Pacific coastlines against a possible European or Asian enemy fleet approaching on the open oceans. Before the days of radar and satellites the only way to detect an enemy was to physically search these vast areas; an impossibility, considering the sizes of America's Atlantic and Pacific fleets. By the beginning of the 1930s military reconnaissance aircraft had been developed but could only scout relatively short distances near the American coasts.

Another aircraft was needed for over-ocean reconnaissance and the long-range dirigible was considered the best choice for the mission. Germany developed its revolutionary Zeppelins during the First World War and afterwards continued their 'non-military'

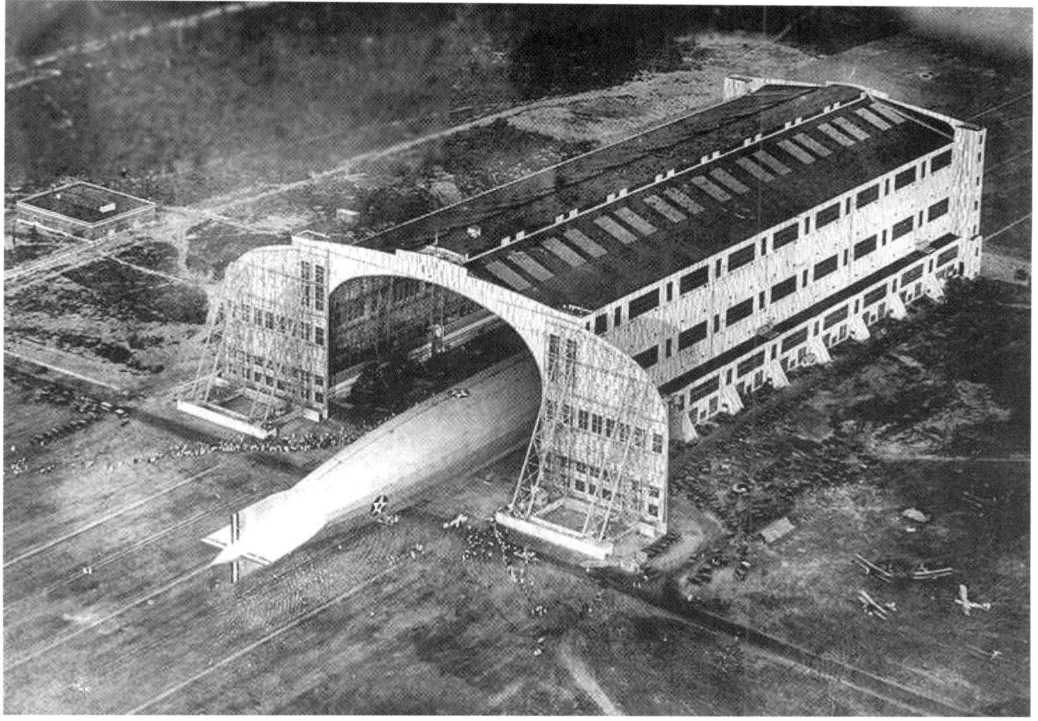

Lakehurst Naval Air Station was inaugurated by the US Navy in 1921 to serve as its LTA aircraft headquarters to store and service its huge new helium-filled airships. The huge hangar measured 966ft long, 350ft wide, and 22ft high, with a floor area of 211,434 sq ft. (*USN*)

development, followed by the British. America entered the large airship field by first building the USS *Shenandoah* (ZR-1) and receiving the USS *Los Angeles* (ZR-3) from Germany as a war reparation. These two dirigibles could cruise long distances over the oceans, but the later USS *Akron* and *Macon* were not only long-range dirigibles but were also 'flying aircraft carriers', that could carry scouting aircraft in their internal hangars and launch and recover them after they had scouted areas far from the airship.

The Navy received Congressional authorisation for two airships and the construction of a gigantic airship hangar at Lakehurst, New Jersey. During 1921 the Lakehurst Naval Air Station was inaugurated by the US Navy to serve as its LTA aircraft headquarters to store and service its huge new helium-filled airships. This new base became the experimental and developmental hub for military and commercial rigid airships as well as the control station for all Navy LTA flights. Hangar One was the first major building constructed at Lakehurst and was of conventional First World War airship hangar design. It was completed in 1921 by the Lord Construction Company, with its large trusses built and erected by the Bethlehem Steel Company. The structure was 966ft long, 350ft wide and 224ft high, with a floor area of 211,434 sq ft. At each end there were two pairs of massive, counterbalanced steel doors, with each weighing 2.7 million lb. They were moved on railroad tracks by two 20hp motors, although provisions were made to open the doors manually. Service mezzanines were located on each side of the hangar with a system of railroad tracks leading to the mooring areas outside the hangar. The hangar was used to construct the USS *Shenandoah* from 1922 to 1923. The building was large enough to house two rigid airships as well as additional non-rigid airships (blimps). The hangar also provided service and storage for other airships including the German *Graf Zeppelin* (LZ-127), USS *Macon* (ZRS-5), and USS *Akron* (ZRS-4), as well as the German LZ-129 *Hindenburg* during its well-publicised transatlantic flights. Once the *Macon* left the east coast for its new west coast home at Sunnyvale, California, the Lakehurst Air Station would never again operate a commissioned US Navy rigid airship.

Chapter Four

USS *Los Angeles* (ZR-3)

The Navy had been slated to receive two German Zeppelins as part of First World War reparations. However, before being surrendered to the Allies, both Zeppelins were sabotaged by their German crews in 1919. Following the *Shenandoah* (ZR-1) crash, in September 1925, the Navy had to re-evaluate its rigid airship programme and its military efficacy. Subsequently, the Inter-Allied Reparations Commission directed Germany to order the Zeppelin Company to construct a single new airship for the Navy to replace the two destroyed Zeppelins. Construction was to be under the direction of Hugo Eckener as the successor to Count Ferdinand von Zeppelin, who had died on 8 March 1917. Eckener had been able to keep the Zeppelin factory at Friedrichshafen viable as the Treaty of Versailles had forbidden Germans to construct airships of the size needed to operate the profitable transatlantic service. However, after much determined lobbying, he convinced the US and German governments to allow the company to construct the airship for the US as its largest Zeppelin, the LZ-126, as a passenger airship at its Friedrichshafen factory on Lake Constance.

The first Navy-built rigid airship, the *Shenandoah* (ZR-1), which was destroyed in a squall line over Ohio during September 1925, was never involved with LTA/aircraft hook-on trials and had little military practicality. It was used mainly for demonstration flights. (*USN*)

Eckener The First World War reparations LZ-126 replacement Zeppelin, the future *Los Angeles*, was built under the direction of Hugo Eckener, successor to the deceased Count Ferdinand von Zeppelin. Eckener and his crew flew the LZ-126 across the Atlantic for delivery during October 1924. (*Vervaardigingsjaar*)

After its commissioning, Lt Cdr George Steele was assigned as the commander of newly named *Los Angeles*. The lacklustre and chronically ill Steele would remain in command until May 1926, when replaced by Lt Cdr Charles Rosendahl. (*USN*)

The unmarked ZR-3 makes its first American flight on 25 November 1924, when it was flown from Lakehurst to Naval Air Station Anacostia D.C. for its combination christening and commissioning. She was christened into the US Navy as the *Los Angeles* (ZR-3) by Grace Coolidge, wife of President Calvin Coolidge, at NAS Anacostia. (*USN*)

The replacement Zeppelin was first flown over Germany on 27 August 1924, and after completing flight trials began its transatlantic delivery flight on 12 October under the command of Hugo Eckener, arriving at NAS Lakehurst on 14 October 1924 after an eighty-one-hour journey of 4,867 miles. The transatlantic flight was considered a major aviation achievement, and Captain Eckener and his crew were celebrated in a New York City Broadway parade and received at the White House by President Calvin Coolidge. The Atlantic would not be crossed non-stop by air again until Charles Lindbergh's flight in the Spirit of St Louis in May 1927.

The still unnamed ZR-3, commanded by Capt. George Steele, made its first American flight on 25 November 1924 and flown to Naval Air Station Anacostia, near Washington, DC, where it was christened the *Los Angeles* by the Grace Coolidge, wife of President Calvin Coolidge, with a bottle of water from the River Jordan, since Prohibition prevented the use of the much more appropriate, but alcoholic, champagne.

USS *Los Angeles* (ZR 3) Specifications and Performance

Specifications

Air displacement of hull: 2,764,461 cu ft (78,280,818 cu litres)
Gas cells: 14 of various sizes of rubberized fabric
Volume of gas cells: 2,599,110 cu ft (73,598,599 cu litres)
Hull structure: Duralumin
Outer cover: Cotton panels covered with four coats of dope
Length: 658ft 4in (200.7m)
Height (draft): 104ft 5in (31.9m)
Maximum diameter (beam): 90ft 8in (27.6m)
Main frame spacing: 49ft 3in (15m)
Engines: 5 Maybach VL-1(V-12 4-stroke liquid-cooled piston)
Total horsepower: 2,000
Propellers: 2-bladed fixed-pitch, rotatable wooden 12ft (3.7m) diameter
Fuel tanks: 49 (6,487lb), 10 (672lb), and 2 (300lb)
Fuel capacity: 40,000lb (18,143.7kg)
Oil tanks: 3
Weights (95% inflated with helium)
Fixed weights: 91,030lb (41,290.5kg)
Useful lift: 66,970lb (30377.1kg)
Total weight (= gross lift): 158,000lb (71,667.6kg)

Performance

Maximum speed: 75mph (120.6kmph)
Maximum speed endurance: 2,825 miles (4,546kmph)
Maximum speed endurance: 43 hours
Cruising speed: 55mph (88.5kmph)

Cruising speed endurance: 5,770 miles (9,286kmph)
Cruising speed endurance: 119 hours

Crew
Complement: 82 (13 officers and 69 enlisted men)
Flight: 43 (10 officers and 33 men)

Commanders
Capt. George Steele: (USNA 1900) 25 November 1924 to 10 May 1926
Lt Cdr Charles Rosendahl: (USNA 1914) 10 May 1926 to 9 May 1929
Lt Cdr Herbert Wiley: (USNA 1915) 9 May 1929 to 31 March 1930
Lt Cdr Vincent Clarke: (USNA 1915) 31 March 1931 to 21 April 1931
Cdr Alger Dresel: (USNA 1909) 21 April 1931 to 1 February 1932
Cdr Fred Barry: (USNA 1908) 1 February 1932 to 30 June 1932

Chronology
Contract signed: 23 June 1922
Design prepared: 1922
Built by: Luftschiffbau Zeppelin, Friedrichshafen, Germany
Construction Number: LZ-126
Cost to German Government: $713,332
Cost to US Government: $150,000
Completed: August 1924
First flight: 27 August 1924
Transatlantic flight to Lakehurst: 12–15 October 1924
Christened: 25 November 1924 by Grace Coolidge, First Lady
Commissioned: 25 November 1924
Final flight: 24–25 June 1932
Decommissioned: 30 June 1932
Formally stricken: 24 October 1939
Total flights: 331
Total flight time: 4,181.28 hours
Total mileage: 198,400 miles (319,294km)

During the first few months the *Los Angeles* operations were restricted as the Bureau of Airships did not have the necessary helium to operate both the *Shenandoah* and *Los Angeles*. The existing production from the Fort Worth Plant was initially so limited that the Navy could not fill both the *Shenandoah* and *Los Angeles* simultaneously and for a time during 1924–25 when both were operational, the gas from one airship was transferred (deflating it) to the other, so that each was available to alternate operations until 3 September 1925, when *Shenandoah* was lost.

The Council of Ambassadors that approved her sale to the US restricted *Los Angeles* from participating in any militarily useful activities such as Fleet exercises. The *Los*

Angeles was then used as a training airship and as a research and development vehicle, engaged in an assortment of scientific and technical experiments in 1925–31. Until late 1925, the *Los Angeles* acted as a flying laboratory to develop the design and many of the improvements for the *Akron* and *Macon*. On 20 February 1925, she flew a round trip to Bermuda, returning to Lakehurst two days later, and during May 1925 she cruised to Puerto Rico to operate briefly over the Caribbean, During this time she practised mooring between flights to the special mast built on the mooring airship tender *Patoka* (AO-9). Operations in late 1925 and early 1926 were suspended temporarily as the airship required overhaul but when this was complete, operations were again limited due to lack of helium. During mid-1926, she began a series of flights along the Atlantic seaboard to calibrate radio direction stations and conducted numerous training flights from the Lakehurst area over the eastern areas of the US.

Lt Cdr Charles Rosendahl was to become the most experienced and knowledgeable of the six Navy rigid airship commanders and the leading proponent of America's rigid airship programme but would not expedite the use of his hook-on aircraft. (*USN*)

As the *Los Angeles*' commander, George Steele had proved to be a lacklustre leader, often ill and unenthusiastic, causing Moffett to replace him on 10 May 1926. The new commander, Lt Cdr Charles Rosendahl, was to become the most experienced and knowledgeable of the six Navy rigid airship officers and the leading proponent of America's rigid airship programme. During his three years of commanding the *Los Angeles*, Rosendahl was to be a dynamic commander whose enthusiasm for his airship and its mission did much to advance the US Navy's airship evolution, as did his promotion of helium-inflated airships to Congress and the Navy Department for many years onward. However, Rosendahl was not in command for any aircraft hook-on experiments, which were to begin later in the year in which he was relieved.

Rosendahl Replaced by Wiley as the *Los Angeles*' CO

On 9 May 1929, Rosendahl was relieved as commanding officer of *Los Angeles* and assumed duty as the commander of the Rigid Airship Training and Experimental Squadron at NAS Lakehurst. Rosendahl was succeeded by Hubert Wiley, who was to command the airship during the early phases of hook-on experiments, April 1929–April 1930. A 1915 US Naval Academy graduate, Lt Wiley was assigned to NAS Lakehurst on 11 April 1923. He served aboard the USS *Shenandoah* from its first flight and a year later was its mooring officer, but he was not on board when the airship was destroyed. Wiley was then assigned to the *Los Angeles* on 19 January 1925. He was promoted to lieutenant commander on 17 December 1925 but was transferred to NAS Pensacola, Florida. In 1928 Wiley served as the executive officer of *Los Angeles* and then was promoted to command the airship.

Lt Cdr Hubert Wiley had served as the *Los Angeles*' executive officer before succeeding Rosendahl to command that airship during the early phases of hook-on experiments. (*USN*)

The NAF and BuAer Begins Testing the Trapeze System

Navy Fleet capital ships extended their scouting range by catapult launching and then retrieving floatplanes, so when the Navy's gigantic new rigid airships appeared, it was proposed to extend their scouting range by using small scout aircraft able to be launched and retrieved, and then stored inside the airship. In early 1926 the Navy began negotiations with the Goodyear-Zeppelin Company for the design and construction of an operational trapeze to be installed on the *Los Angeles* for the development of airship/aircraft handling equipment and techniques. During 1929, *Los Angeles* was used to test the trapeze system to launch and recover fixed-wing biplanes from rigid airships. The *Los Angeles* would have no internal aircraft hangar accommodation, unlike the later *Akron* and *Macon* airships.

During 1929–35, seventeen Navy aircraft were modified with skyhooks and operated with the *Los Angeles*, the *Akron*, or the *Macon*: one Vought UO-1, six Consolidated N2Y-ls, one Curtiss XF9C-1, one XF9C-2, six F9C-2s, and two Waco XJW-ls. All were expedients; none were specifically designed for that particular service. There was also one glider, a 'spy basket', and several proposed parasite aircraft. For the *Los Angeles* trapeze tests the Navy had acquired a single Vought UO-1 (BuNo. 6491).

Vought OU-1

The OU-1 was the subsequent development of Vought's end of the First World War VE-7s and VE-9s. The OU-1s were unarmed US Navy observation float seaplanes for battleship catapult use and would become the standard Navy observation aircraft for ten years beginning during 1923. Initially designed as a seaplane, the UO-1 was soon classified as 'convertible', using an interchangeable single main float or a wheeled landing gear, and these were designated UO-1Cs. The UO had an airframe basically like that of the VE series but with some modifications such as fuselage streamlining and different powerplants. They were initially powered by the Lawrence J-1 or J-3, later by Wright J-1 or J-3 radial engines, and from 1927 many were re-engined with the Wright J-5. The UO-1 could be converted into a fighter by easily fairing over the front cockpit of the observation plane, mounting machine guns in that area, and upgrading to a 220hp Wright R-790 Whirlwind with a supercharger. These were designated as FU-1s, the final development. The UO-1 (BuAer serial No. 6615) was the last delivery of thirteen of these aircraft procured on contract No. 57207 of 1923 as a standard fleet observation plane. On 26 November 1924, the UO-1 was the first aircraft to be catapulted from a battleship (USS *California*) at night. It was modified with a skyhook at the Naval Aircraft Factory, Philadelphia, in the autumn of 1928, was used in the initial trapeze experiments with the *Los Angeles* and continued at Lakehurst until 1931, when it was displaced by the N2Ys.

Vought OU-1 Specifications and Performance

Specifications
Crew: 1
Length: 28ft 4.5in (8.65m)
Height: 10ft 2in (3.10m)
Wingspan: 34ft 4in (10.47m)
Wing Area: 270 sq ft (25.1 sq m)
Empty Weight: 2,074lb (943kg)
Gross Weight: 2,774lb (1,260kg)
Powerplant: 1 × 220hp Wright J-5 Whirlwind 9-cylinder air cooled radial engine

Performance
Maximum Speed: 122mph (196kmph) at sea level
Range: 410 miles (660km)
Service Ceiling: 26,500ft (8,080m)
Climb to 5,000ft (1,520m): 5 minutes

Armament
Guns: 2 × .30in machine guns

Vought OU-1 on the USS *Los Angeles*

Although no trapeze was yet installed on the *Los Angeles* and no skyhook was installed on the Vought OU-1, the Navy began aircraft-to-airship hook-on feasibility experiments. On 11 June 1927, Lt (Junior Grade) Delong Mills, (USNA, 1920), flew inaugural 'air

Vought OU-1 BuAer No. 6615. (*USN*)

exploration tests' in a standard (no hook) Vought OU-1 (6491). After an 0430 dawn take-off (with two photographers aboard), the UO-1 rendezvoused with the *Los Angeles*, flying a series of passes under the airship's hull to determine the best future location of the trapeze. Upon Capt. Rosendahl's signal, Mills dropped astern, about 800ft behind and about 200ft below the ZR-3, and then began his approach. Soon his upper wing blocked his view, but the airship reappeared as he neared its tail. Mills then began climbing and passed about 30ft below the No. 1 car. By throttling his engine just enough to maintain control but still climb slowly, Mills passed the airship's after-wing cars, after which he was able to maintain the Vought about 10ft below the airship's keel and manoeuvre either ahead and back or up and down. He kept the biplane in close formation at any specific location relative to the airship and continued there for prolonged periods. In all, five separate approaches and simulated hook ons were made and Mills reported that an ordinary pilot could undoubtedly maintain a steady course within 10ft of the airship's hull and complete a hook on, allaying any fears that the airshipmen had of a possible collision.

Although Goodyear designed and built the trapeze and the Vought OU-1's skyhook, its subsequent engineering development can be credited to the Naval Aircraft Factory, Lakehurst personnel, and the BuAer, especially the Lakehurst's experimental officer, Lt Calvin Bolster, who would become a principal force in the trapeze project along with test pilot Lt Adolphus 'Jake' Gorton.

During the summer of 1928, the NAF and the BuAer, working at Lakehurst, initially considered an early model of the Vought OU-1's skyhook that had undergone extensive static tests there. On 1 July 1928, for these tests the *Los Angeles* was hoisted so that a civilian team assisted by the airship's crew could conduct dynamic shed testing of the aircraft attachment gear by employing a railroad flat car equipped with an engaging hook to simulate actual hook-on conditions. It was mounted at the end of a telescoping tube

On 11 June 1927, Lt (JG) Delong Mills flew inaugural 'air exploration tests' in a standard (no hook) Vought OU-1 (6491) flying close to the *Los Angeles*, which had no trapeze installed. (*USN*)

and had a relatively small bearing surface for engagement with the trapeze main guard tube. The position where the hook's movable tube fitted into the main guard tube is shown in the photo at the engineer's left hand (see photo on next page). As the hook contacted the trapeze, the Vought's flight momentum caused the aft section of the hook tube to be drawn out rearward. If movement of the hook exceeded a pre-set maximum of 6.5in, a cam at (B) automatically released the hook. Upon automatic release, the hook flipped in an arc around point (A). When the pressure was off the hook a spring returned it to its 'armed' position. After the Vought was engaged on the trapeze, the pilot could release the hook manually with a lever in the cockpit, acting through control wire (D). If the hook of this early model was manually released it was necessary to descend to the ground and reset the mechanism before flying to the second hook on, which would be a serious problem if the aircraft was far from a landing field or low on fuel. The next hook-on model was fully automatic. Components (E) and (F) adjusted the travel of the hook tube. A lever at the cockpit, acting through wire (G) upon (E) allowed the pilot to lock the telescoping tubes. Component (H) was the steadying point or 'auxiliary hook', one on each wing. After the Vought hooked on to the trapeze, a pair of arms were lowered from the trapeze to engage the open jaws of these hooks. This arrangement provided a three-point grip while the aircraft was being hoisted against the airship hull.

During October 1928, the Navy announced that the *Los Angeles*, then barnstorming in Texas, would 'soon' begin hook-on experiments with the equipment to be installed during 1929. However, the development of this second airship trapeze and aircraft hook-on equipment continued slowly with 'shed [hangar] testing' scheduled at Lakehurst. The next hook-on apparatus model was fully automatic and mostly duplicated the Army's Sperry

The UO-1 (6615) skyhook components being inspected by a Naval Air Factory engineer at Lakehurst. See text for photo legend. (USN)

The Vought's skyhook undergoing shed testing at Lakehurst on the trapeze to be installed on the *Los Angeles* in mid-1929. (*USN*)

Messenger assembly that had completed a successful hook on with the Army blimp TC-5 using a firm and rigid trapeze-type gear. However, it was this automatic feature, and the small bearing area of the hook, which would foil Gorton's first hook-on attempts. Except for a few insignificant operational repairs and adjustments to replicate flight testing, the tests were 'very reassuring', and Goodyear was to begin its construction. Between 1929 and 1935 the skyhook would continue to undergo several major redesigns and modifications.

On 24 June 1929, the trapeze equipment was approved for operations on the *Los Angeles* and a 400lb trapeze and yoke on an 'aircraft landing device' were installed at frame 100, beneath the keel, between the four wing cars. Two days later, the electric overhead cranes were connected at airship frames 25 and 175 and the unmoored ZR-3 was raised about 25ft. Overhead suspensions were secured at frames 100, 110 and 115, and static tests were conducted on the hook-on gear. After completion, the hull was lowered, the cranes and suspensions detached, and the airship secured.

Lt Adolphus 'Jake' Gorton

To conduct the *Los Angeles* hook-on flight phase, the Navy assigned a Vought UO-1 (6615) to be flown by experienced experimental pilot Lt Adolphus 'Jake' Gorton. Gorton, Naval Aviator Number 1,720, had represented the Navy in early air races, beginning with the 1921 Pulitzer. His Navy racing continued in October 1922 with the Curtiss Marine Trophy Race in conjunction with the National Air Races (NAR) in Detroit, which Gorton won at an average speed of 112.6mph. On 8 August 1923, he broke two aviation speed records in one day flying a USN NW-2 over the Delaware River at 177mph, and then at 185.5mph. Gorton was also a member of the Navy's 1923 Schneider Cup racing team but before the race, a piece of the failed propeller pierced his pontoon and he was unable to compete. Besides racing, in 1928 Gorton was a member of the crew that set seven endurance and distance records with a NAF XPN-12 seaplane. Most of his career was as a NAF test pilot, flying various experimental developments, including participation in the first night carrier landings, which were made aboard the USS *Langley*. As a NAF associate, Gorton was assigned to the *Los Angeles*.

Lt Adolphus 'Jake' Gorton, an experienced experimental pilot, conducted the *Los Angeles'* first hook-ons. (*USN*)

The *Los Angeles*/Vought OU-1 Trapeze Tests
3 July 1929 Hook-On Failures

At 0022, 3 July 1929, Lt Cdr Hubert Wiley cast the *Los Angeles* off from Lakehurst shortly after midnight and after an unrelated test he stopped the No. 1 engine and set Nos. 2, 3,

4 and 5 to cruising speed at 04.06 hours, dawn. Nine minutes later, Wiley then requested Lt George Watson, officer of the deck, to bring the ship into the wind and the test began. Unlike aircraft taking off from aircraft carriers, this manoeuvre was unnecessary because both craft were moving in the same medium (air). Gorton swung the Vought OU-1 in on the tail of *Los Angeles* at 2,500ft and lined up a skyhook mounted on his upper wing with the yoke of the trapeze suspended from the airship's frame 100. After six minutes of 'fishing', Gorton touched the trapeze but was not able to hook it. On his next approach, the Vought again touched, remained on the trapeze for only a short time but then slipped off. Gorton's approaches were on a parallel course to ZR-3 and level with the trapeze. To reach the bar, he had to fly through turbulence created by the airship's hull, prop wash from power cars four and five, and eddies from the trapeze itself. Wiley discontinued the test at 04.30 hours and searched for less turbulent air at a different altitude. About twenty minutes later, Gorton approached the trapeze and hooked on for about five seconds but did not remain attached and slipped off due to a structural failure of the hook. At 05.00 hours, the test was discontinued after a total of fifteen approaches, only four of which resulted in any contact with the trapeze and one abortive hook on.

The hook's design had incorporated a similar pressure release feature that was used in the Army's skyhook. It was a safety measure that provided for the hook flipping open and releasing the Vought if the hook was flown against the trapeze with a speed differential of more than 3mph. Gorton barely touched the trapeze and slipped off as this safety element had functioned too well.

After the failed tests, Gorton reported that he still thought that the existing gear was satisfactory, and that successful hook-ons could be made with it, but that the pressure release mechanism in the hook would have to be replaced and redesigned. Since Gorton was an experienced pilot, Lt Calvin Bolster, Lakehurst's experimental officer, agreed with his assessment. Bolster began design modifications to the hook-on apparatus, particularly a redesign of the skyhook safety release. The skyhook was mounted on a spring-loaded tube so that if the pilot struck the bar at excessive relative speed, the hook pulled back and released (Gorton was also furnished with a manual hook release control.) Bolster determined that the correct method was to use a fixed hook on the UO-1 with no automatic release, which allowed the trapeze bar to swing forward under a gradually increasing braking action when struck by the aircraft.

Gorton also believed that an alteration in his flying approach to the trapeze was necessary. During his 3 July attempts, he had made his approaches level with the trapeze and 'fished' with his hook, requiring sensitive stick and rudder control, which was made more difficult by the air turbulence from the *Los Angeles*' hull and propwash. To avoid fishing, Gorton suggested what he termed a 'reverse carrier approach'. During a landing approach to a carrier's flight deck, an aircraft would descend in a stalling attitude, and then stall out on the carrier's arresting gear. On an airship trapeze approach, rather than flying level with the trapeze, he would reverse this and approach the trapeze, closing from about 100ft below and behind and then climbing toward the bar in a stalling attitude, keeping outside the disturbed zone of air until the hook was very near the trapeze, and then stall the plane on to the trapeze yoke.

Again, there were concerns from several veteran airshipmen, who feared that Gorton might not stall out on the trapeze but fly on into the *Los Angeles*, America's only rigid airship. But Gorton reaffirmed to Bolster that he considered the revised hook-on apparatus gear was operational, and he would soon be successful using the reverse carrier approach.

Nonetheless, Lt Cdr Leslie Stevens of the BuAer interceded, believing that the trapeze concept was too complicated and perhaps the airship should have the hook and the OU-1 have a simple, trapeze-like fitting. Stevens proposed that the Vought fly up under the airship, where the pilot would reach up and snatch a hook that trailed from a cable lowered from the airship. He would then place the hook through an eye on his aircraft, cut the engine, and be hoisted aboard the airship, a method that was basically the same as used to retrieve catapulted floatplanes from the water alongside warships. On 15 August, Stevens tested his assumption, piloting a Vought O2U in the *Los Angeles'* slipstream, but he struggled and failed to grab a small sandbag trailing from the airship's frame 100 and the original hook-on concept was undertaken.

20 August Attempts and Success

During the morning of 20 August, after the pressure release feature had been removed from the skyhook, Gorton returned to piloting the UO-1, to attempt his new reverse carrier approach technic. His first hook-on pass was successful, he then missed the trapeze on the second pass, but the third and fourth ended in successful hook ons. After his final hook on, Gorton shut down the engine, and the *Los Angeles* circled left, to determine the effects of the parasite's added weight and drag on the airship's performance. Tests continued the next day in rough air, but Gorton was able to make an immediate hook on. Gorton released and returned to base as Wiley circled in the *Los Angeles*. Gorton delivered the Vought to Lt Cdr Charles Nicholson, who managed BuAer's component of the trapeze project. Nicholson made two unsuccessful approaches before achieving his first hook on, after which he released to make one more hook on before the exercise was halted. The exercise resumed with BuAer's Lt Cdr Leslie Stevens at the UO-1's controls for one more hook on before the *Los Angeles* left for the day. From this point on, the hook on had passed from the experimental stage into actual operation and all future work was directed toward its refinement and simplification.

Lt Cdr Wiley, an airshipman with no previous aircraft experience, was the *Los Angeles'* captain on this successful hook-on flight. In the years directly ahead, Wiley would show an appreciation for the role the hook-on aircraft were to play for the huge rigid Navy airship's future military success. His collaboration with the *Akron* and *Macon* hook-on pilots in the innovations and implementation of some very inventive scouting tactics would establish him as the most successful of the Navy's airship captains.

Nicholson's encouraging report caused Moffett to proclaim these tests a success, but with reservations. Moffett did not believe that a future fleet of airship carriers would be of significance as the number of aircraft carried would always be too small. However, as an airship advocate, Moffett believed that aircraft hook on greatly increased the rigid's usefulness to the Fleet in a reconnaissance role.

On 20 August 1929, Gorton returned to piloting the UO-1, attempting a new approach technic with a redesigned skyhook and was successful on his first hook-on pass. The photo shows the OU-1's engine to be shut down while tests were conducted to determine the effects of the parasite's added weight and drag on the airship's performance. (*USN*)

Los Angeles First Public Demonstration: 1929 National Air Races at Cleveland

On 28 August 1929, the *Los Angeles* was to make a much-anticipated first public demonstration of its hook-on aircraft at an appearance at the greatly expanded and wildly successful National Air Races (24 August–2 September) held over Cleveland, Ohio. More than 100,000 would attend, including many dignitaries and movie stars. Among them were national hero Col Charles Lindbergh, who had single-handedly raised America's consciousness of air travel. Lindbergh performed aerobatics with two pilots of the Navy's High Hat Squadron (including future *Akron* HTA pilot Lt Fred Kivette), Amelia Earhart flew spins in a glider and Dr Juan de la Cierva demonstrated his novel autogiro. The *Graf Zeppelin* was to fly over on the last leg of its around the world flight. Also present on its first public performance was the new ZMC-2 (Zeppelin Metal Clad) 'Tin Blimp', the only successfully operated metal-skinned airship ever built. After watching the thrilling exploits of the top men and women air racers of the day, at about 1700 the *Los Angeles* flew low over the crowd at 55mph, on a heading toward the Cleveland airport.

The New York Times of 29 August 1929, reported:

> A.W. Gorton of the of the Naval Aircraft Factory, Philadelphia contributed to the success of the big Navy airship. Gorton flew a tiny Vought biplane up beneath the dirigible as the airship soared across the field flanked and followed by a convoy of non-rigid blimps and swarms of insect-like planes from nearby Goodyear-Akron. The *Los Angeles* circled and loitered magnificently over the airport, stealing the show. Gorton had to be accurate. On both sides of him hung the bulky gondolas housing two of the ship's Maybach engines. Three times he tried to hook his 'shepherd's crook', a steel contrivance built up about two feet from his upper wing to a lattice-work metal trapeze that hung down seventeen feet from the bottom of the airship's hull, amidship. Three times he made the contact, but before the hook caught firmly it slipped off and the flier swung out into the air in a diving turn.
>
> Wiley then ordered *Los Angeles*' engines Nos. four and five reduced to half speed; and at 1735 Gorton hooked on, cut his engine to idling speed, and the Vought swung down out of the flying position.
>
> Inside the airship, bluejackets, by means of apparatus that is still a Navy secret, pulled the plane snugly against the hull. Wiley then brought the airship with its captive about to pass in review. To add to the spectacle, Calvin Bolster of the Naval Aircraft Factory, without a parachute, dropped down from the airship's hatch onto the Vought's upper wing and swung down into the front cockpit. At 1750, the trapeze was then lowered, and Gorton tripped the hook and dropped off into a dive until flying speed was gained and landed with Bolster, the first passenger disembarked from an airship.

The Times quoted Bolster on his transfer to the Vought:

> It was simple enough. We would have done it before except that hitherto we haven't been able to pull the plane up close. Today I merely climbed though the hatch to

> the top wing, which was only three or four feet below the airship, and that is about all there is to it.

The stunt value of the Cleveland demonstration confirmed that an aircraft had actually 'landed' on the airship, and that this procedure and the transfer of personnel was a relatively simple procedure.

Hook-On Tests Continue During Autumn 1929

No further hook-on experiments took place until October 1929, when on the 8th, Chief Boatswain (Aviation Pilot) E. E. Reber made practice approaches without hook ons, and then on 10 October Chief Aviation Pilot John O'Brien made a hook on and after fourteen minutes in contact, he released. The next day, O'Brien made an additional hook on, remaining captured for five minutes while watched by an eminent audience in the *Los Angeles* control car, including Adm. William Moffett and the Secretary of the Navy Charles Francis Adams, and his official party.

On 14 November, O'Brien secured the Vought after six tries and unhooked after three minutes in contact, whereupon Wiley left Lakehurst and further trials for a flight over Washington, DC. Hook-on exercises continued early the next day when at 0940, O'Brien made an approach and successful attachment. The year's final hook on was flown by O'Brien during the afternoon of 20 November, after eight failed initial tries for the trapeze.

Prufling Glider on the USS *Los Angeles*

The *Los Angeles* carried a mooring officer who would parachute in case a landing had to be made at a place other than an established Navy LTA base. Once on the ground, he was to organise and direct a local landing crew composed of the fire department and police department and would then direct the approach and mooring of the airship. During January 1930, Adm. Moffett considered launching a glider from the *Los Angeles* to transport a mooring officer from the airship to the ground. Moffett approached Navy Lt Ralph Barnaby about his idea. During his nearly thirty-year naval career, Barnaby, holder of the No. 1 Soaring Certificate signed by Orville Wright, became renowned for glider designing, engineering, and piloting.

By 18 January, the Navy's first glider (A 8546), a German RRG Prufling ('tester') intermediate training glider was purchased from the American Motorless Aviation Corporation on contract No. 15507 of 2 January 1930. The single Prufling was never assigned a formal US military aircraft designation. The Prufling measured 18ft long; had a wingspan of 34ft 5in; weighed 231lb empty and had a gross weight of 430lb. The glider was assembled by Barnaby at Lakehurst, while Calvin Bolster fabricated and installed the mounting and release mechanism. No glider hook ons were to be attempted back on the *Los Angeles* after Barnaby's release, only a ground landing.

On 30 January heavy snow postponed the first trial, but the next day was clear and cold. After early morning delays caused by the cold, the *Los Angeles* ascended at 1023, towing

On 31 January 1930 Navy glider specialist Lt Ralph Barnaby flew the Navy's first glider, the German Prufling, from the *Los Angeles*. After six and a half minutes, he would skid to a safe landing on a snow-covered field. (*USN*)

the Prufling glider, which was then attached to special fittings at airship frame 100 and flown aloft. Capt. Wiley flew various courses, escorted by airships J-3, J-4, ZMC-2 and aircraft carrying news photographers, reporters, and observers.

At 1112, reaching Barnaby's requested 3,000ft launch altitude, Wiley stopped Nos. 1 and 2 engines and the dapper Barnaby, wearing navy blues with a sweater and leather flight jacket, helmet, fleece-lined boots, and seat-pack parachute, climbed down an aluminium ladder into the icy cold slipstream. Barnaby wiggled into the tiny cockpit and secured the cockpit cover while the ladder was being drawn up. Wiley then ordered the airspeed restored to a predetermined 46mph to ensure control. Calvin Bolster operated the glider-releasing lanyard, and the freed glider moved aft and climbed as Barnaby pushed the stick forward and quickly passed the two large 18ft propellers spinning nearby out in front and two behind the glider. Barnaby levelled off at about 100ft below the airship and let the glider slow down to its normal gliding speed of 30mph. After six and a half minutes, Barnaby ended his descent, sliding gently on to a snow-covered field. It was not the first manned airship–glider composite flight, as most sources often state. John Montgomery's 17 March 1905 launch of a glider should be credited as the first.

Spring 1930: Wiley Replaced by Lt Cdr Vincent Clarke and Hook-On Tests Continue

On 31 March 1930 Lt Cdr Hubert Wiley was replaced as *Los Angeles* commander by Lt Cdr Vincent Clarke (USNA 1915), who would serve until 21 April 1931. Clarke had been awarded the Navy Cross during the First World War for 'distinguished and heroic

On 31 March 1930 Lt Cdr Vincent Clarke replaced Lt Cdr Hubert Wiley as *Los Angeles* commander and would serve until 21 April 1931. (*USN*)

Lt Cdr Charles Nicholson flew the Vought OU-1 off the *Lexington* and then climbed to the *Los Angeles* for the first such aircraft carrier–airship rendezvous. (*USN*)

action as Commanding Officer of the USS AL-10'. Until better hook-on weather arrived in late spring, Clarke conducted many airship training flights.

May 1930 Presidential Fleet Review

On 8 May 1930, the *Los Angeles* joined in a Presidential Fleet review of battleships, cruisers, and carriers off the Virginia Capes. The carriers *Saratoga* then the *Lexington* began to launch their aircraft. Cdr Nicholson flew the Vought OU-1 off the *Lexington* and then climbed to the airship's altitude, for the first such aircraft carrier–airship rendezvous. As President Hoover watched from the heavy cruiser *Salt Lake City*, the *Los Angeles* proceeded from its position about 5 miles to leeward (away from air operations) and assumed its position to receive the Vought. Aboard the *Los Angeles*, NBC radio announcer George Hicks broadcast the pilot's approach and hook on from his squatting position over the hatch at frame 100: 'He did it – no, no, he didn't! Yes, he did! He's on! He's on!' The Vought was still swinging on its hook when Hicks handed the microphone to Nicholson, who gave listeners a brief exposition on the 'art of hook-on flying'.

Memorial Day 1930: Prufling Glider Release

The last of May's eight ascents occurred during the Curtiss Marine Trophy races at Anacostia on Memorial Day, 31 May, which saw the Prufling glider attached at Frame 120 to leave the trapeze clear. Barnaby, who had contracted influenza, was replaced by volunteer Lt T. G. W. 'Tex' Settle, a very qualified lighter-than-air pilot. In 1929 Settle, with co-pilot Ens. Wilfred Bushnell, won the National Balloon Race. In 1932 he and Bushnell would win the Gordon Bennett International Balloon Race, setting a free balloon distance record that stood until January 2010. Settle had served as the *Shenandoah*'s radio officer and the *Los Angeles*' engineering officer, and after the Navy had rejected his application for heavier-than-air instruction, he completed civilian flight training for his pilot's licence. In 1930, he oversaw the Navy's inspection team at the Goodyear-Zeppelin plant where the *Akron* was under construction. While there, he had been introduced to glider flying by Dr Wolfgang Klemperer, one of Goodyear's engineers and who had been an authority on gliders in Europe and became an accomplished glider pilot.

Before its release, while encountering turbulent air, the glider's rudder came free of its chocks; this caused it to yaw, damaging its starboard wing. Clarke ordered the airship's engines to be slowed so Chief Boatswain's Mate Robert Davis could assess damage to the glider while lowered on a bowline. Despite a 5in hole in the starboard wing, Settle agreed to fly the glider, and the *Los Angeles* cruised on to the Curtiss races. At 1418, 2 miles south-east of NAS Anacostia, Settle climbed into the glider and was dropped for ten minutes of flying and made a perilous but safe landing despite the hole in the wing. After Settle was dropped, the *Los Angeles* then circled while Nicholson, in the UO-1, flew two unsuccessful approaches in very rough air before hooking on to the *Los Angeles*' trapeze before the amazed 15,000 spectators. While USMC Capt. Arthur Page won the Curtiss Trophy in a Curtiss F6C fighter, a special trophy for another racing event, sponsored by Assistant Secretary of the Navy for Aeronautics David Ingalls, was won by

The Memorial Day 1930 Curtiss Marine Trophy races at Anacostia saw the Prufling glider attached to the *Los Angeles*. Lt Ralph Barnaby, who had contracted influenza, was replaced by experienced volunteer Lt T. G. W. 'Tex' Settle, who was released and landed safely. (*USN*)

Lt D. Ward Harrigan. This was to be the first time that Harrigan had seen an aircraft latch on to a trapeze suspended from an airship. About a year later he would be based at Lakehurst flying his own hook ons on the *Akron*, and later would be named as the first HTV squadron leader on board the *Akron* and *Macon*.

Los Angeles Becomes a Hollywood Film Star

During August 1930 the *Los Angeles* would become a Hollywood film star in three-time Oscar-winning director Frank Capra's early film career, $650,000 big budget, *Dirigible*. The Columbia Moving Pictures action-adventure film movie starred Jack Holt, Fay Wray, and Ralph Graves. The film synopsis: 'A French explorer enlists the help of the US Navy in an expedition to the South Pole. There is competition between the airship division and fixed-wing fliers, resolved in triumph and disasters.' In the film the airship would fly an aircraft hooked to its trapeze to within 200 miles of the Pole and the plane would detach, claim the land for America and return. The

During summer 1930 the *Los Angeles* would become a Hollywood film star in the Columbia and Oscar-winning director Frank Capra big budget action-adventure film *Dirigible*. (*Columbia Moving Photos*)

Navy Department authorised Columbia to utilise the *Los Angeles* (flying as the airship *Pensacola*) over many hours of filming at Lakehurst. On 19 August, with its camera equipment installed in the main car, the *Los Angeles* circled over Manhattan while the Columbia camera crew unhurriedly filmed the Island. Clarke unmoored his airship for a second time that day and flew to Philadelphia, where the airship 'arresting gear was tested' over its Navy yard. Columbia spent the next day filming aircraft hook ons, which were a spectacular part of the movie. The movie was described as 'a very realistic film that featured the giant rigid airship, *Los Angeles*'. While some miniatures were utilised for a crash scene and to represent some stunt flying such as doing loops around the dirigible, much of the air action was photographed at Lakehurst. The cinematographer for the film was Elmer Dyer, famous for his aerial films of the 1920s and 1930s, including *Hell's Angels*. The film received lukewarm reviews but was profitable, grossing about $1 million.

25 August 1930: Last Hook-On *Los Angeles* Trapeze Removed for Ten Months

During the morning of 25 August 1930, the *Los Angeles* began manoeuvring for a hook on by Chief Aviation Pilot John O'Brien, who landed at 1002. With the OU-1 'housed' (secured), Clarke cruised towards New York City and while over the inner harbour he circled to allow the J-3 Blimp to photograph the airship carrying the OU-1. Finally, at 1426, Clarke headed back to Lakehurst and August's final hook on occurred during the morning of the 25th, with the *Los Angeles* also dropping three men and seven dummies equipped with parachutes. This exercise was to be followed by a hook on by O'Brien carrying a passenger. After hooking on at 1002, the Vought was then housed and carried towards New York City. Clarke circled over upper New York Bay, then Manhattan escorted by the J-3 for photos. During the early afternoon, Clarke continued circling over upper New York Bay and then Manhattan for more filming until 1426, when Clarke turned the *Los Angeles* for the return to Lakehurst. At 1536, when nearing the Lakehurst mooring, Clarke set four engines to half-speed and the No. 1 stopped, to allow O'Brien to cast off at 1536, carrying a passenger, to land at Lakehurst before the *Los Angeles* arrived. This demonstration was to be the last hook on for nearly ten months. By this time, the fundamentals of aircraft hook-on operations with rigid airships had been resolved using the *Los Angeles* and the venerable UO-1.

The *Los Angeles* then spent mid-November to mid-January 1931 undergoing maintenance and repairs, the last half of January in post-repair trials, February in the Caribbean, and upon its return to Lakehurst only flew seven times in March and April. Meanwhile, its trapeze was at the Naval Aircraft Factory for modifications and was not reinstalled until late May 1931. Procurement of operational aircraft for the large *Akron* and *Macon* was still in the future, and the types to be used had not yet been decided. It would not be until May 1931 that another flurry of eight *Los Angeles* hook-on trials would occur, with O'Brien being joined by newly selected pilots.

Organisation and Training of the Heavier-Than-Air Units

The organisation and training of the heavier-than-air units to fly from the airships, *Akron*, and *Macon*, which were being readied for operations during September 1931 and June

1933, respectively, caused the Bureau of Navigation (then responsible for Navy personnel) to call for HTA pilots to volunteer for hook-on trials. The response saw forty-one pilots apply from only the Scouting Force.

Lt Daniel Ward Harrigan

Lt Daniel Ward Harrigan, US Naval Academy Class of 1922, was the first pilot to receive orders 'to proceed to NAS Lakehurst to assist in the development of aircraft operations in connection with airships'. All subsequent HTA pilot assignments would also be US Naval Academy graduates since the USNA was the main supplier of regular Navy officers in the 1920s and 1930s. After four years of sea duty, Harrigan attended flight training at Pensacola, where he received his wings in 1927. From Pensacola he was ordered to additional training with the pilots who were to form the squadrons of the uncompleted carriers *Lexington* and *Saratoga*. As a member of the Experimental Landing Unit, he developed landing techniques to be used on board the new carriers and would be the first pilot of the Pacific Fleet Air Squadrons to land aboard the *Lexington*. After serving two years with Fighting Squadron Five, Red Rippers, aboard the *Lexington*, he was assigned as a flight instructor at Hampton Roads, which quickly bored him. The 30-year-old Harrigan reported to NAS Lakehurst in February 1931 and became intrigued by the future tactics and military use of hook-on aircraft and the practicability of the trapeze gear.

Lt Howard 'Brigham' Young

Several months later a second pilot, Lt Howard 'Brigham' Young, joined Harrigan. After graduating from the USNA in 1923, Young joined the USS *Florida* and then Battle Fleet, USS *California*. He then was stationed at NAS Pensacola, Florida, completing flight training, and was designated Naval Aviator on 24 April 1926. Young was assigned to Observation Squadron 2 based on the carrier USS *Langley* for two years and transferred to Fighting Squadron 2 in June 1928. Between August 1929 and June 1931, he again served at NAS Pensacola, after which he had LTA training at the Naval Air Station, Lakehurst, New Jersey. He then entered heavier-than-air training in September 1932, qualifying as a Naval Aviator on 28 September 1932. He was then assigned to the HTA Unit attached to airship *Akron*.

Prior to Harrigan's arrival at Lakehurst in February 1931, hook-on flying was completed periodically by Jake Gorton and other pilots from the Naval Aircraft Factory who were mostly concerned with the basics of the equipment and the 'art' of flying to the trapeze. Harrigan's arrival as a full-time pilot with the *Akron* was a good choice as he was dedicated to testing and perfecting the use of the trapeze for future use in military operations. During the summer of 1932, after more *Akron* hook-on pilots arrived, Harrigan instilled his commitment to the hook-on project in them so that each pilot enthusiastically contributed to the development of the trapeze technic.

HTA Unit flight operations lagged in getting under way when Harrigan arrived at Lakehurst. The old Vought UO-1 (6615) was still present and the first of the six Consolidated N2Y-1 trainers (8605), which had recently been equipped with a hook,

Pilots Lts Howard Young (L) and Daniel Ward Harrigan (LC) and Lt Calvin Bolster (RC), Lakehurst's experimental officer, led the way in conducting practice N2Y-1 hook ons. Greeting the three is Cdr Philip Seymour, the Lakehurst Air Station's Executive Officer. (*USN*)

would arrive during March. The *Los Angeles* had flown to Panama, on manoeuvres with the Fleet, and to lighten it for the long flight the trapeze had been removed in December 1930 and was at the Naval Aircraft Factory for modifications. In the interim, Harrigan, with nothing to hook on to, arrived at the Naval Aircraft Factory to test the new Curtiss XF9C-1 Sparrowhawk prototype, serial 8731.

Since the trapeze was not to be reinstalled on board the *Los Angeles* until June, Harrigan and the newly arrived Young attended the LTA course with Class VIII training in free balloons and non-rigid airships, qualifying as balloon and blimp pilots.

Consolidated Fleet N2Y-1 on the USS *Los Angeles*

Obtaining the next-generation hook-on aircraft was under the authority of BuAer's Plans Division, the most influential policy organisation outside of Adm. Moffett's office. The division was headed by future Second World War carrier admiral Cdr Marc Mitscher, who was not a rigid airship advocate but managed to secure six Consolidated N2Y-1 training planes from Pensacola, and was offered any discarded suitable temporary or experimental aircraft, such as the Berliner-Joyce XFJ-1, Fokker XFA-1, and Curtiss XF9C-1. Airship advocates believed that the N2Y-1s would serve temporarily on the *Los Angeles* and later only temporarily on the *Akron* and *Macon* as operational aircraft. The other temporary fighter types offered would be employed only to collect data for a specially designed, high-performance hook-on aircraft, to be built and operated in the future.

The N2Y-1 was a Fleet Model 1 civilian trainer derivative, all of which were conventional biplanes with staggered, equal-span wings, and fixed-tailskid undercarriage. Accommodation was provided for two crewmen seated in tandem, originally sharing a single open cockpit, but in most later models they were seated in separate open cockpits. The fuselage was of typical contemporary construction with the wings consisting of a wooden spar with duralumin ribs, and the entire aircraft was fabric covered. The prototype's 110hp Warner Scarab was replaced by 115hp Kinner engine.

A small number of US-built Fleet Model 1s were purchased by the US military, including several to be evaluated by the AAC as the PT-16. One initial prototype aircraft, a Fleet I two-seat biplane trainer, was tested by the US Navy in 1929 as the XN2Y-1 (BuNo. 8019). A contract lot of six N2Ys (Nos. 8600–8605) were originally procured from the Fleet Aircraft Corporation on contract No. 16684 of 17 March 1930 for delivery to be made to NAS Pensacola in mid-1930. The Navy would then send them to the Naval Aircraft Factory for hook-on modification and then return them to Lakehurst for testing on the *Los Angeles.* Afterward they were intended to serve temporarily as scouts for *Akron* and *Macon* airships until a more suitable operational hook-on aircraft (the Curtiss XF9C-1 Sparrowhawk) was procured.

These N2Y-1s were equipped with 'skyhook' gear mounted over their upper wings to permit operation from the dirigibles' trapeze gear as training for future Sparrowhawk pilots for in-flight launching and recovery. The two-seater N2Y-1s were also to act as service aircraft, flying passengers to the en route airships. A later N2Y-1 configuration was to have its upper fuselage sheet metal covering removed to accommodate a litter for patient evacuation from the airship.

Meanwhile, the *Los Angeles* spent mid-November 1930 to mid-January 1931 in maintenance and repairs, the last half of January in post-repair trials, February in the Caribbean, and upon its return to Lakehurst only flew seven times in March and April. Meanwhile, its trapeze remained at the Naval Aircraft Factory for modifications, and it was not until 26 May 1931 that a crew of civilian workmen reinstalled the trapeze at Lakehurst. It was late May 1931 when the first (of six) hook-equipped N2Y-1 trainers (8605) finally arrived at Lakehurst, replacing the aging UO-1. However, on 3 June, the trapeze required further modification by the Naval Aircraft Factory staff at Lakehurst, delaying the first hook-on trials.

Also, it was not until 1931 that the Department of State was able to obtain approval for the *Los Angeles* to participate in military exercises. So, from 1925 to 1931, the *Los Angeles*, as the Navy's only rigid airship, was unable to validate her scouting role for the Fleet. Meanwhile, there was a growing number of Navy Department and BuAer officers that considered the rigid airship as unnecessary or unqualified for naval operations. During the six-year interim, the Navy's aircraft carriers and heavier-than-air aviators continued to gain experience, acceptance, and demonstrated their utility in Fleet operations.

Consolidated Fleet N2Y-1 Specifications and Performance

Specifications
Crew: 2
Length: 20ft 9in (6.32m)
Height: 7ft 10in (2.39m)
Wingspan: 28ft (8.53m)
Wing Area: 195 sq ft (18.1 sq m)
Empty Weight: 1,063lb (48kg)
Gross Weight: 1,820lb (826kg)
Fuel Capacity: 55 US gallons (46 Imp gal; 210 litres)
Powerplant: 1 × 110hp Kinner K-5 5-cylinder radial engine

Performance
Maximum Speed: 113.5mph (182.7kmph)
Cruise Speed: 88mph (142kmph)
Service Ceiling: 12,200ft (3,700m)
Rate of Climb: 730ft/min (3.7m/s)

Six N2Y-1s (Nos. 8600–8605), Fleet Model 1 civilian trainer derivatives, were contracted to replace the aging Vought UO-1 for training future F9C-2 Sparrowhawk pilots for airship in-flight launching and recovery. (*USN*)

Cdr Alger Dresel Relieves Lt Cdr Vincent Clarke as *Los Angeles* CO

On 21 April 1931 Cdr Alger Dresel relieved Lt Cdr Vincent Clarke as *Los Angeles* CO. The 16-year-old Dresel was appointed to the Naval Academy in 1905. After graduation, Dresel served aboard the battleship USS *Wyoming* until 1916 and was given command of the convoy escort destroyer USS *Paulding*. In 1920, Dresel was assigned to the Bureau of Navigation for four years and subsequently commanded the destroyers USS *Borie* and *Villalobos*. In 1929, Dresel underwent instructions for flying LTA aircraft at NAS Lakehurst. From that point Dresel would serve as the commander of all three ZRS airships: assigned to command the *Los Angeles* from 21 April 1931 to 1 February 1932, the *Akron* From 22 June 1932 to 3 January 1933, after which he was assigned to command the *Macon* from 23 June 1933 to 11 July 1934.

On 21 April 1931, Cdr Alger Dresel replaced Lt Cdr Vincent Clarke as the *Los Angeles* captain and, like Cdr Wiley, would later serve as the *Macon*'s captain. (*USN*)

9 June 1931: First Hook-On in Ten Months

The last hook-on trial for the *Los Angeles* was on 25 August 1930 as the airship was flown to Panama on manoeuvres with the Fleet. To lighten it for the long flight, the trapeze had been removed in December 1930, was sent to the Naval Aircraft Factory for modifications and not reinstalled until 26 May 1931.

On 9 June 1931, R. Adm. William Moffett, head of the Navy's Bureau of Aeronautics; David Ingalls (the Navy's only fighter ace of the First World War, with six credited victories); and Roy Howard of the Scripps-Howard News Syndicate observed this first hook-on demonstration and the first under new *Los Angeles* skipper Cdr Alger Dresel.

After being schooled in trapeze technique by John O'Brien, Lt Ward Harrigan flew his first successful N2Y-1 hook on followed by nine more consecutive ones as Dresel circled the *Los Angeles* over Lakehurst. Two of his successful hook ons were recorded on motion picture film for training purposes. Afterwards, in his post-flight report, Harrigan reported that he 'had had few difficulties' and was surprised to find how easy it was to hook the N2Y on to the *Los Angeles*' trapeze.

Hook-on pilots would come to agree that a landing on the trapeze was easier because the airship and aircraft were moving in the same medium (air), so their relative speeds were approximately zero, allowing the pilot to concentrate on getting the hook onto the trapeze yoke. During a conventional carrier landing, however, the runway (the sea) was a fixed surface while the carrier's flight deck was a surface in motion relative to the sea. For a trapeze hook on, there were no icy or wet runways, or missing the carrier's arresting gear.

The N2Y-1 pilot manoeuvring towards the trapeze hook-on bar for attachment. After a successful hook on, the N2Y dropped away for another practice run or to return to land at Lakehurst. (*USN*)

If a pilot stalled out in his approach to the trapeze, he usually had the benefit of 1,500ft of altitude in which to recover, which was non-existent in a stall during a conventional landing.

After these hook ons, the *Los Angeles* would make only two flights while mooring along the north-east coast until it returned to Lakehurst on 15 July. On 27 July, the King and Queen (the *Los Angeles'* first woman passenger) of Siam (Thailand) and their royal entourage observed hook-on demonstrations as official *Los Angeles* visitors. Harrigan hooked on to the airship at 1110 at 300ft off the coast en route to New York and released five minutes later. On 18 August, Harrigan was joined by Lt Howard Young, who was making his first hook-on flight. At about 0930, the two pilots began alternating approaches in their N2Ys at the newly improved trapeze designed by Lt Calvin Bolster. As the *Los Angeles* navigated various courses at 1,800ft, paralleling the beach 2 or 3 miles off the Barnegat Inlet on the New Jersey coast, Harrigan easily made three hook ons while rookie Young also had no problems during eight successful landings.

The next hook-on practices were conducted during the mid-morning of 8 September, off Brigantine Island, located east of Atlantic City. *Los Angeles'* Commander Dresel followed the Atlantic coast, while thousands of Atlantic City Boardwalk sightseers watched sixty-four hook ons that were completed between 0905 and 1054. Afterwards the *Los Angeles* turned towards the USS *Patoka*'s mooring mast for refuelling off Newport. The *Patoka* was a replenishment oiler, serving as a tender for the airships *Shenandoah*, *Los Angeles*, and later the *Akron*. The *Los Angeles* remained moored to the *Patoka*'s mast overnight before leaving at 1048 on the 9th, following a northward course along the shore, where the two N2Y pilots made three hook ons, ending before noon.

During the morning of 18 September hook-on practice was conducted over Lakehurst in a brisk north-east wind, and with the airship cruising at the low hook-on speed of 53mph, three hook ons were successfully completed. When the day's practice ended, forty more hook ons at normal hook-on speeds were completed successfully.

By the end of September, Harrigan and Young decided to initiate nighttime hook ons but at that time the N2Y-1s were not equipped with navigation lights, so their pilots carried flashlights in their cockpits intending to aim their beams forward to display the location of the trapeze yoke in the darkness. To illuminate the trapeze, the mechanics in the *Los Angeles'* Nos. 2 and 3 power cars were supplied with flashlights to aim forward at the yoke. Later, aboard the *Akron*, a headlight scavenged from a Model-A Ford was used to illuminate the trapeze. At 0824 on 29 September, the *Los Angeles* cruised toward Lakehurst and moored at 1723, where she lingered on the mast for sixty-seven minutes to disembark passengers and replenish water ballast and fuel. Once airborne, she flew eastward to rendezvous with Harrigan and Young over the Atlantic near Barnegat. At 1940, the first N2Y approached the *Los Angeles'* crudely lit trapeze yoke, at which crewmen aimed flashlights from the cabin. After twelve hook ons were completed by 2030, the two pilots reported that the poor lighting was barely adequate and needed improvement but also reported that the calmer night air made for easier hook ons. Two weeks later, on 13 October, over the Jersey coastline, Young flew his N2Y to complete twenty-eight trapeze hook ons, surely qualifying him as a hook-on expert. These were to be the last *Los Angeles* hook ons by N2Ys.

Fleet Problem XI April 1931

The concept of the aircraft carrier as an independent and offensive weapon was becoming established among senior officers in the Navy during the Fleet Problem IX of 1929 and during the following year in Fleet Problem X, when the Fleet tested the carrier strike force concept in which 'aviation scored heavily against battleships'. The next year, during Fleet Problem XI in April 1931, the *Los Angeles* finally received approval to participate in military exercises. With David Ingalls again on board, the *Los Angeles* flew to join the Fleet in the Panama Canal Zone. During the exercise, the *Los Angeles* managed to locate the enemy's main body and report its location before being hypothetically destroyed by aircraft from the enemy carrier *Langley*. However, the *Los Angeles*' first reliable report of the enemy main body was received and made possible a successful attack later in the day by the *Lexington*'s aircraft. Nevertheless, after the *Los Angeles*' destruction, Adm. William Pratt removed her from the exercise with the terse message: 'You are sunk … Pleasant voyage.'

The New York Times subsequently (25 February 1931) published; an article entitled 'NAVAL MEN DOUBT AIRSHIP WAR VALUE; Experiences of *Los Angeles* in Manoeuvres Strengthen Beliefs Long Held. SCOUTING UTILITY DENIED Dirigible Quickly "Destroyed" but Experts Stress Contact Made and Foresee Better Defense. Experts Defend Airship. Sees Little Naval Utility.' This elicited a response from Assistant Secretary Ingalls, which stated that the performance of the *Los Angeles* 'definitely established the advisability, or rather the necessity, of the continued development and maintenance of lighter-than-air by the United States Navy'.

The *Los Angeles* is Decommissioned and the *Akron* is Commissioned

Despite Ingalls' positive assertion, the rigid airship received intense internal criticism from senior naval officers. Adm. Frank Schofield, the Commander in Chief, United States Fleet (C-in-CUS), considered that 'rigid airships' appeal to the imagination is not sustained by their military usefulness … [and] their expense was out of proportion to any benefit they could provide the Fleet'.

Airship advocate Adm. Moffett, countering this upper echelon opposition, stated:

> To a comparatively small group who have had experience with airships or who had studied their possibilities, the performance of the *Los Angeles* was gratifying. To a much larger group, and this group includes a great many who have given no consideration, or only cursory consideration, to airships, the *Los Angeles* merely confirmed pre-conceived opinions that airships either are no good or are of so little practical use that their existence is not justified.

With the *Akron*'s commissioning on Navy Day, 27 October 1931, the continued expense of maintaining the *Los Angeles* no longer seemed necessary and consequently the Navy Department decommissioned it in 1932 'in order to effect economies'. With the *Akron* nearing completion, Adm. Pratt felt obliged to write an article endorsing the new rigid airship, claiming that 'Undefended, slow, obsolete, the destruction of the *Los Angeles* would be expected on making tactical contact with combatant ships. It is quite another matter to attack a modern armed airship.' The mission of demonstrating the value of the rigid airship to the Navy upper echelons passed to the *Akron* and *Macon*.

Chapter Five

Akron (ZRS-4) and *Macon* (ZRS-5): An Overview

Prelude

From the mid-1920s, with Japan rising as a Pacific threat, the Navy began to explore the strategic employment of very large, long-range rigid airships for scouting in advance of the Fleet over the immense Pacific Ocean to protect its territorial responsibilities in Guam and the Philippines.

However, it would be the spectre of the Army assuming control of the rigid airship programme that would then play the pivotal role in the Navy's decision to continue its own development. Senior Navy leadership was fearful that if the Army secured rigid airships, the Navy could lose its claim to shore bases, long-range seaplanes, and possibly have its fledgling aircraft carrier programme contested. This perception had been substantiated in 1926 by Maj. Gen Mason Patrick, the Chief of the Army Air Service, before the Joint Army Navy Aeronautical Board. Patrick demanded that the board approve that Army aircraft be assigned to coastal defence and to be allowed 'to fly over water to the limit of their practical operating radius'. While Patrick was envisaging long-range patrol bombers rather than rigid airships, Adm. Moffett vigorously opposed Patrick's proposal. The Board did not grant Patrick's proposal and the Navy's *Akron* and *Macon* rigid airship fleet programme was revived. Thus, the continuation of the Navy rigid airship programme ultimately was not because of any prevalent confidence in their military value, but because of a prevailing belief among senior naval leadership that, in a time of restricted funding and interservice rivalry, the Army posed a threat to the Navy, and naval aviation.

In 1926, as part of the 'Five Year Procurement Programme', the Navy obtained authorisation to contract the construction of two exceptionally large helium-filled scouting airships with design studies to include the carrying and recovering of aircraft. A competition resulted in a contract to the Goodyear-Zeppelin Company of Akron, Ohio, in 1928 for construction of two similar airships, designated ZRS-4 and ZRS-5, that were eventually named the *Akron* and *Macon*. The designation ZRS was used by the Navy to distinguish ships or aircraft as to type and mission, so this indicated Z for Zeppelin airship, R for reconnaissance, and S for scouting.

Dr Karl Arnstein and Paul Litchfield

During 1924, Paul Litchfield was promoted to Vice President of the Goodyear Company and that same year he established a joint venture with the German Luftschiffbau Zeppelin Company and formed the Goodyear-Zeppelin Corporation, Akron, Ohio. As part of the Goodyear-Zeppelin arrangement, Luftschiffbau Zeppelin was to send technical experts to Akron to train Goodyear employees in the design and construction of

Karl Arnstein, one of the most important airship engineers and designers in Germany during the First World War, would emigrate to America to lead the Goodyear-Zeppelin Company in developing the plans that became the USS *Akron* and USS *Macon*. He is shown posing with an RM-7A, an earlier model of the ZRS-4 *Akron*, being built in the background. (*Goodyear/USN*)

airships. Litchfield stipulated that the Zeppelin Company's chief designer, Karl Arnstein, also be included in that group, and in November 1924 he arrived in Akron along with a team of twelve hand-picked Zeppelin engineers. It was under Arnstein's leadership that Goodyear-Zeppelin developed the plans that became the USS *Akron* and USS *Macon*. In 1926, Litchfield became the president of the Goodyear-Zeppelin Corporation and expedited Goodyear's leadership into airship design and manufacture that flourished during the Second World War and continues to this day.

Akron and her sister ship *Macon* were developed by the Navy beginning in 1929 at the newly completed Goodyear-Zeppelin Airdock in Akron. Their design and construction were managed by Dr Arnstein. Born in Prague, he had worked on Luftschiffbau-Zeppelin's designs during the First World War. However, because of discrimination due to his Jewish faith, Dr Arnstein was eager to immigrate to America in 1924 to become the Vice-President of Engineering at Goodyear-Zeppelin. Arnstein's Goodyear-Zeppelin designs were markedly different from the conventional Zeppelin designs he had worked on at Friedrichshafen under the direction of the conservative Ludwig Dürr, the Zeppelin Company's chief designer since 1906. Arnstein was now free to develop new designs and techniques for the *Akron* and *Macon*. During his career he was granted thirty-five US aviation-related patents, developed stress analysis methodologies that were incorporated into future airships, bridges, and aircraft materials and designed the mammoth Goodyear Airdock. From 1940 until retirement in 1957, Dr Arnstein headed the Goodyear Aircraft Corporation Engineering Department.

The huge Goodyear-Zeppelin Airdock, still in existence at Akron, Ohio, measures 1,175ft long, 325ft wide, and 211ft high, and has 364,000 sq ft of floor space. It remains the largest structure in the US without internal support. (*Goodyear/USN*)

Akron and *Macon* General Description

The *Akron* and *Macon* sisterships truly were 'Queens of the Skies', measuring 785ft long with a 133ft diameter and a height of 146ft. The *Macon* was only 71ft shorter than the RMS *Majestic*, the largest sea-going passenger vessel afloat at the time, and dwarfed the late twentieth century's Queen of the Skies, the Boeing 747, being three times longer

The USS *Akron* seen over New York City. The *Akron*'s first flight was on 25 September 1931, it was commissioned on 27 October 1931 and took its first aircraft aboard on 3 May 1932. (*USN*)

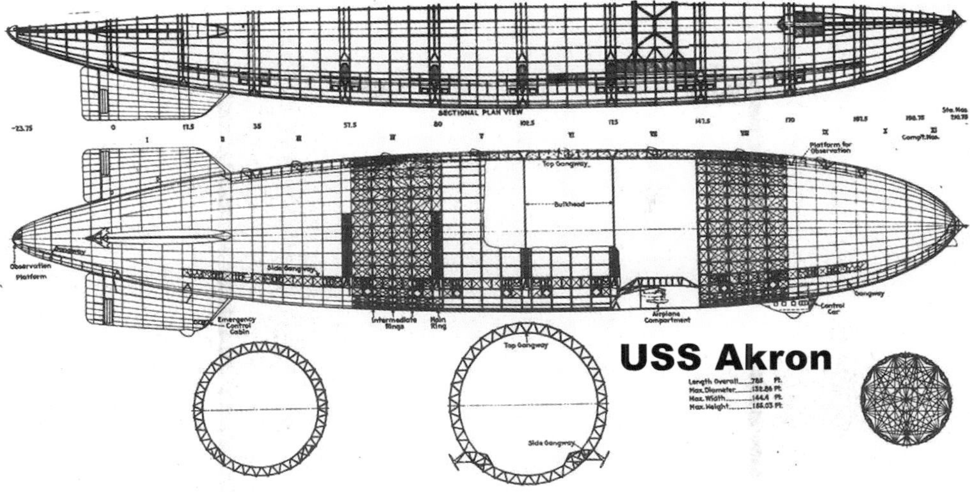

and much wider in girth. Although only 9ft longer than its contemporary, the 776ft-long *Graf Zeppelin,* it had almost twice the gas capacity (6,850,000 cu ft vs 3,708,040 cu ft) due to its 35ft diameter. The construction of the two US airships each required 25,000 individual parts, 6.5 million rivets, and 1,500 miles of wire to fasten their Duralumin airframe together. The outer hull was covered with 7 acres of fabric that was sewn tightly together with 1,000 miles of thread and painted with four coats of acetate dope, the last two containing aluminium powder that gave the airship its silvery lustre that was to reflect heat. The structure of these airships represented 83 tons (166,000lb), whereas the gross weight at take-off was 200 tons (400,000lb) at cruising trim. The vertical and horizontal stabiliser surfaces each weighed 2 tons and they measured 105ft fore and aft, 40ft from the root to the tip, and 12ft thick at the widest point of their aerofoil shape. The elevators and upper rudders were approximately 42 × 16ft and 5ft thick. The lower fin contained a separate set of flight controls for emergency use.

Akron and *Macon* as Aircraft Carriers

Both airships were designed to transport small single-engine biplane parasite scouting aircraft that could be launched and retrieved in flight to significantly increase the Fleet's search area. During the First World War a German Zeppelin had visual range of 30 miles and could search a path 60 miles wide, so while cruising at 45mph during a maximum of twelve hours of daylight it could search approximately 32,000 square miles daily. However, the *Akron* or *Macon*, flying at 60mph, and utilising two of its scouting aircraft, each flying out 60 miles on each search beam, the airship increased its visual search range from 60 miles to 180 miles and so could search approximately 129,000 square miles during the same twelve hours. The Navy projected ten airships carrying retrievable scouting aircraft, based in Hawaii, setting out in two relays of five, could form a reconnaissance area nearly 1,200 miles wide, and within six days arrive off the Japanese coast. Normally, it would require forty Navy cruiser surface ships eighteen days to cover the same area and distance.

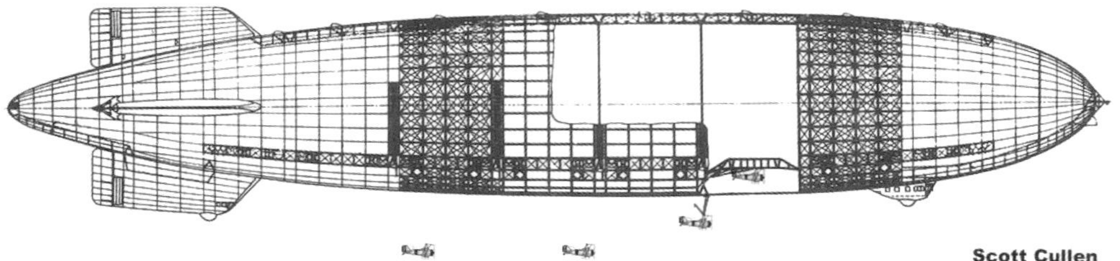

The USS *Macon* seen over New York City. The *Macon*'s first flight was 21 April 1933, it was commissioned on 23 June 1933, and took its first hook-on aircraft aboard on 6 July 1933 (*USN*)

Akron and *Macon* Specifications and Performance

Specifications

Air displacement of hull: 7,401,260 cu ft (209,580,344 cu litres)
Volume of gas cells: 6,850,000 cu ft (193,970,399 cu litres)
Gas cells: 12 gelatin-latex fabric, each containing 541,660 cu ft of helium
Length overall: 785ft (239.3m)
Total height from ground: 146.5ft (44.7m)
Maximum diameter: 132.9ft (40.5m)
Outer covering: 33,000 square yards (27,592 sq m) cotton cloth with coats clear dope
Hull structure: Duralumin 17-SRT

Number of main keels: 3
Number of main frames: 12
Main frame spacing: 73.8ft (22.5m)
Number of intermediate frames: 33
Engines: 8 German Maybach VL-2, (12 cylinders, V-type, fuel injected, water-cooled)
Total horsepower: 4,480
Propellers: *Akron*: Two-bladed fixed-pitch, rotatable wooden 16.33ft diameter *Macon*: Three-bladed variable-pitch, rotatable metal 16.33ft diameter
Maximum fuel capacity: 126,000lb (57,153kg) in 110 tanks
Oil capacity: 2,400lb (1,088.6kg) in 8 tanks
No aircraft accommodated in hangar: 5

Armament
Guns: 8 × .30 calibre machine guns

Weights (95% inflated with helium)
Fixed: *Akron*: 250,356lb (113,160kg) *Macon*: 242,356lb (109,931kg)
Useful: *Akron*: 152,644lb (69,238kg) *Macon*: 160,644lb (78,867kg)
Total weight (gross lift): 403,000lb (182,798kg)

Performance
Speed and endurance (*Macon* 95% inflated with helium):
Maximum speed: 87mph (140kmph)
Standard speed: 75mph (121kmph)
Standard speed endurance: 4,855 miles (7,813km)
Standard speed endurance: 75 hours
Cruising speed: 63mph (101kmph)
Cruising speed endurance: 5,940 miles (9,560km)
Cruising speed endurance: 108 hours

Airship Crew
Complement: 91 (16 officers and 75 enlisted men)
Flight: 60 (10 officers and 50 enlisted men)

Aircraft Crew
Pilots: 4
Mechanics: 15

***Akron* Commanders**
Lt Cdr Charles Rosendahl (USNA 1914) 27 October 1931 to 22 June 1932
Cdr Alger Dresel (USNA 1909) 22 June 1932 to 3 January 1933
Cdr Frank McCord (USNA 1910) 3 January 1933 to 4 April 1933

***Macon* Commanders**
Cdr Alger Dresel (USNA 1909) 23 June 1933 to 11 July 1934
Lt Cdr Hubert Wiley (USNA 1915) 11 July 1934 to 12 February 1935
***Akron* and *Macon* Chronology**
Construction authorised by Congress: *Akron*: 24 June 1926/*Macon*: 24 June 1926
Contract signed: *Akron*: 6 October 1928/*Macon*: 6 October 1928
Cost: *Akron*: $5,375,000/*Macon*: $2,450,000
Built by: Goodyear-Zeppelin, *Akron*, Ohio
Hull Number: *Akron*: ZRS-4/*Macon*: ZRS-5
Laid down: *Akron*: 31 October 1929[2]/*Macon*: 1 May 1931

Christened
Akron: 8 August 1931 by First Lady Lou Henry Hoover/*Macon*: 11 March 1933 by Jeanette Moffett, wife of R. Adm. William Moffett
First flight: *Akron*: 25 September 1931/*Macon*: 21 April 1933
Commissioned: *Akron*: 27 October 1931/*Macon*: 23 June 1933
First aircraft aboard: *Akron*: 3 May 1932/*Macon*: 6 July 1933
Destroyed: *Akron*: 4 April 1933/*Macon*: 12 February 1935
Formally stricken: *Akron*: 30 April 1933/*Macon*: 26 February 1935
Total flights: *Akron*: 73/*Macon*: 54
Total flight time: *Akron*: 1,695.8 hours/*Macon*: 1,798.2 hours

***Akron* Dirigible vs Naval Surface Cruiser**
Cost of Construction: *Akron*: $2.45 million vs $18 million
Service Life: *Akron*: 10–15 years vs 20–25 years
Cost of Maintenance/Operation: *Akron*: $400,000/year vs $1 million/year
Pay of Crew: *Akron*: $225,000 /year vs $650,000/year
Crew: *Akron*: 65 men/15 officers vs 550 men/55 officers
Maximum Speed: *Akron*: 83mph (133kmph) vs 37mph (60kmph)
Cruising: *Akron*: @ Cruising Speed 10,360 miles (16,575km) vs 11,500 miles (18,500km)
12-Hour Daylight Scouting Area: *Akron*: 26,400 square miles (68,372 sq km) vs 4,800 square miles (12,500 sq km)
Area of Scouting Visibility: *Akron*: 20 miles (32km) vs 10 miles (16km)
Aircraft Carried: *Akron*: 4 Trapeze Aircraft vs 4 Catapult Seaplanes

Armament
Akron: 6 × .50 cal. Machine Guns vs 9–10 × 8 and 8–10 AA guns
Note: $1 in 1932 = $22.21 in 2025

2. Adm. William Moffett installed the first symbolic gold rivet in the airship's frame.

Chapter Six

The Search for New Hook-On Aircraft for *Akron* and *Macon*

Trials on the *Los Angeles* had shown that the OU-1 and N2Y were inadequate as a hook-on aircraft to be retrieved and then stored in the hangars and flown from the new *Akron* and *Macon* airships under construction, so the Navy looked for a substitute.

1930 BuAer Design 96 Specification

The 1930 BuAer Design 96 Specification was issued to the aircraft industry for proposals for a lightweight shipboard fighter. Two types competed: the General Aircraft XFA-1 and the Curtiss XF9C-1. These were officially initiated as 'small carrier-based fighters', but probably were actually designed as 'small airship-based fighters'. This classification was due to political and budgetary considerations; if these aircraft had been specifically classed as 'airship fighters', their development costs could have been deducted from the limited airship budget. They were designed to be small enough to be stored in the airship's hangar and all had fuselage-mounted upper wings, which was the optimum biplane configuration for airship hook-on flying. On 10 May 1930, contracts were awarded for preliminary design work on a single aircraft each to Curtiss and General Aircraft and, because of the specificity of the Navy requirements, the XFA-1 was to be very similar to the XF9C-1.

General Aircraft XFA-1

General Aircraft, the company created by the American Fokker Aircraft Corporation and General Motors 1930 merger, began its design work on the XFA-1 soon after the Navy's release of Design Specification 96. However, the merger stifled its progress, and the XFA-1 was not ready for Navy testing until 1932. The XFA-1 was a staggered biplane with its upper wing gulled into the fuselage. It employed all-metal construction and metal laminate skin except for fabric on its wing and tail surfaces. It was powered by a 400hp Pratt & Whitney R-985A Wasp Junior engine. The proposed armament was to be two fuselage-mounted .30in (7.62mm) machine guns. Initial flight testing revealed poor flying characteristics including longitudinal instability, a problem common to the other small fighters of the time, and over-sensitive controls. To rectify the problem, General Aircraft increased the area of the tail surfaces and initiated other changes but discovered that these only worsened the problems. More modifications accomplished nothing to alleviate the problems and the XFA-1 was ultimately classified as unsafe, with testing terminated. However, by this time the Navy had already selected the Curtiss XF9C-1.

General Aircraft XFA-1. (*USN*)

General Aircraft XFA-1 Specifications and Performance

Specifications
Crew: 1
Length: 22ft 2in (6.75m)
Wingspan: 25ft 6in (7.77m)
Height: 9ft 3in (2.81m)
Wing area: 175 sq ft (16.25 sq m)
Empty weight: 1,837lb (833kg)
Gross weight: 2,508lb (1,138kg)
Powerplant: 1 × 450hp P & W R-1340-C 9-cylinder air-cooled radial piston engine

Performance
Maximum Speed: 170mph (274kmph)
Range: 518 miles (834km)
Service Ceiling: 20,200ft (6,157m)
Rate of Climb: 1,470ft/minute (7.47m/s)

Armament
Guns: 2 × .30in (7.62 mm) machine guns

Curtiss XF9C-1

Procurement and Delivery

A single Curtiss XF9C-1 was procured under contract 17901 dated 30 June 1930. Its BuNo. A-8731 designation was omitted at the time of the manufacture, and for flight purposes it carried the Bureau of Air Commerce Number 968M. The XF9C-1 contract called for it to be delivered to Anacostia for testing within 175 days of the signing date. The total cost was $74,750; the design work $20,000, miscellaneous data $3,000, final and corrected data and drawings $12,000, and $39,750 for the aircraft itself. It was designed and built at the Long Island Curtiss plant in Garden City under the direction of project engineer George Page. The XF9C-1 was originally designed because the Navy wanted to place more aircraft on its aircraft carriers; either by building a smaller type or one with folding wings. It was even suggested that aircraft were to be stowed on carrier decks by stacking them at 45 degrees! The Navy took delivery of the XF9C-1, which was painted light grey with yellow upper wings and horizontal tailplanes, at Anacostia, DC, on 27 March 1931. It was tested, found to be satisfactory and was to become the standard hook-on aircraft.

The Aircraft

The notable initial components that distinguished the XF9C-1 prototype from the final F9C-2 procured aircraft were the position of the upper wing, the full-faired cantilever landing gear, high-pressure tyres, small hard rubber tail wheel, balanced rudder, and the location of the carrier arresting hook. Later, on the XF9C-2 the landing gear was modified into a slimmed-down tripod type, faired with swaged brace wires to reduce drag, and was equipped with low-pressure tyres. The aircraft was powered by a 421hp, air-cooled, R975-C Wright radial engine equipped with a supercharger and spun a two-blade, 96in diameter metal propeller. The E-3 version of this engine would power the production F9C.

XF9C-1 Sparrowhawk Specifications and Performance

Specifications

Crew: 1
Length: 20ft 3in (6.2m)
Height: 10ft 6in (3.2m)
Wingspan: Upper wing 25ft 6in (7.8m)
Lower wing: 23ft 3in (7.1m)
Wing Area: 172.79 sq ft (16.053 sq m) biplane gull-wing
Empty Weight: 1,836lb (833kg)
Gross Weight: 2,502lb (1,135kg)
Useful Load: 666lb (302kg)
Per cent Useful Load: 26.5 per cent
Powerplant: 1× Wright R-975-C Whirlwind 421hp, radial, 9-cylinder, air-cooled
Propeller: 8.5ft (2.6m) diameter, wooden, two-bladed variable pitch
Fuel Tanks: Main fuel tank 63 gallons (240 litres)
Oil Tank: 5 Gallons (18.9 litres)

Performance
Maximum Speed (@ 4,000ft): 176.5mph (284.0kmph)
Maximum Speed (@ 16,000ft): 152mph (245kmph)
Stalling Speed: 60mph (97kmph)
Service Ceiling: 22,600ft (6,888m)
Initial Rate of Climb: 2,150ft/minute (655m/min)
Climb in 10 minutes: 13,800ft (4,206m)
Wing Loading: 16lb/sq ft (78kg/sq m)
Power Loading: 5.9lb/hp (2.68kg/hp)
Normal Radius (@ 125mph cruising speed): 190 miles (306km)

XF9C-1 Flight Testing For Carrier Operations
For testing the aircraft was weighed and instruments for recording flight performance were installed. The initial trials were fulfilled by Curtiss civilian test pilots and on 3 April 1931 one of these demonstrated the aircraft for Navy acceptance. It performed 'satisfactorily' and was accepted for test by Navy test pilots for carrier operations. The Navy performance tests of the XF9C-1 as a carrier fighter were handled by the Flight Test Section at Anacostia on 18 May 1931. The ordnance tests were then commenced, during which 'certain installation features that necessitated redesign or modification of certain components were noted'. The mid-June arresting gear tests at Hampton Roads determined that if the XF9C-1 was to be suitable for carrier duty certain changes were mandatory.

The Curtiss XF9C-1 (BuNo. 8731) was originally designed as a carrier aircraft due to its small size, as more of these aircraft could be accommodated on a carrier flight deck than the existing types. (*USN*)

The XF9C-1 flight test results for carrier operations were included in Navy Report NASA-91, dated 1 July 1931 and issued by the Flight Test Section, NAS Anacostia, DC, under the authority of the President of the Board of Inspection and Survey (BIS), US Navy. This report stated:

> The Curtiss single place carrier fighter, Model XF9C-1, tested, first to determine whether the contract guarantees had been compiled and second the suitability of this aircraft as a service type for carrier operations. The complete flight performance tests were conducted on the XF9C-1 carrying the normal fighter useful load in compliance with the design specifications. The fixed machine guns were fired in the air at high speed and on the ground ... The emergency flotation gear was ground tested. The carrier arresting tests were conducted by the Experimental Division, Naval Air Station, Hampton Roads, Virginia.
>
> The Curtiss XF9C-1 carrying the normal useful load required as a carrier fighter complied with all revised contract guarantees ... and was found under all service load conditions to be in all respects to be a satisfactory military carrier fighter airplane in correct flying balance, controllable and stable in the air and on the ground, and suitable for the purpose intended, except as noted hereinafter.
>
> The Board recommends that the XF9C-1 with the necessary modifications incorporated as listed under RECOMMENDATIONS, be accepted as an experimental type, but considers that its suitability as a service type is dependent on the practicability of correcting the four major items of design as listed.

So, after the contractual guarantees had been complied with and testing reports evaluated the XF9C-1 as a potentially good carrier fighter considering its size and the engine power with satisfactory and suitable fighter qualities, the aircraft was not recommended as delivered because of objections to certain structural features that would have to be modified in order to enjoy unqualified acceptance for carrier operations.

Among the major problems disqualifying the XF9C-1 for carrier use were:

1) The wing and power loadings were so high that the aircraft's performance was 'somewhat inferior to existing fighter types in service aboard carriers' and made it unsuitable for carrier landings.
2) The shoulder height of the upper wing's placement seriously interfered with the pilot's vision in normal straight-ahead flight. Direct vision over the nose was obscured except during high-speed flight and interfered during carrier landing approaches.
3) The gunsight's cone of vision was obstructed by the engine and the anti-drag ring.
4) The aircraft's landing angle made it impossible to make a three-point landing at minimum speed and to maintain satisfactory aileron control during carrier landings.
5) The poor design and location of the arresting gear hook caused a tendency for the landing aircraft to tip over on its nose.

XF9C-1 Modified for Airship Hook-On Operations

Because the XF9C-1 was purchased as a single experimental type and was found unsuitable for carrier duty, it was not placed into production. Consequently, during September 1931, the NAF began modifications on the XF9C-1 to equip it for airship hook-on operations at Lakehurst. To expedite the initial trials with the *Los Angeles*, installation of the aircraft's electric starter and other important airship use modifications were deferred, and only the installation and the static strength and release testing of the hook-on mechanism were to be completed. However, the carrier-landing arrester gear remained.

XF9C-1 Hook-On Testing

During October, Lt Ward Harrigan arrived at the Naval Aircraft Factory to deliver the skyhook-equipped XF9C-1 to Lakehurst for its hook-on trials. It was at Lakehurst that the aircraft received the name Sparrowhawk as Hawk was a name common to many Curtiss aircraft, most of them fighters (i.e. Hawks I–IV, Goshawk, Seahawk, Mohawk, Tomahawk, Kittyhawk, and Warhawk). The name Sparrowhawk seemed suited as it is a small bird of prey with short, broad wings.

The Curtiss XF9C-1 tests for the new hook-on apparatus installation were for static strength and release testing of the mechanism. The carrier-landing arrester gear remained. (*USN*)

23 October 1931: First XF2C-1/*Los Angeles* Hook-Ons

After taking delivery of the XF9C-1 from the Naval Aircraft Factory earlier that month, during the early morning of 23 October 1931, the *Los Angeles* unmoored and flew east over Barnegat Bay and dropped its trapeze. Meanwhile, Harrigan took off from Lakehurst and approached the airship just before 0900 to attempt the aircraft's first ever hook on. At 0926, flying at 68mph, he hooked on and then followed with four more successful

1Lt George Calnan determined that the only way to free the jammed XF9C-1 was to climb down the lattices of the *Los Angeles'* trapeze girders on to the hook-on yoke and pound it with a wrench until the hook was released. Calnan was a 1920 Naval Academy graduate and Olympic fencer, serving on both the *Los Angeles* and then the *Akron*, on which he would perish in the airship's crash. (*USN*)

attempts and returned to Lakehurst. After Harrigan's successes, at 1011 Lt Howard Young arrived, piloting the XF9C-1 to more two successful hook ons but on his third the hook was not released. The XF9C-1 was equipped with the same system as the N2Y-1 trainers, but since it was a heavier aircraft its weight stretched the actuating cable between the pilot's release lever in the cockpit. The hook's releasing gear mechanism then could not be pulled through its complete action, stranding Young's aircraft below the airship's keel. Dresel could not land the *Los Angeles* and flew his airship at half-speed on various courses in the vicinity of the air station while Young, from his cockpit, struggled unsuccessfully to free the hooking mechanism. 1Lt George Calnan determined that the only way to release Young's plane was to climb down the lattices of the trapeze girders to the hook-on yoke to attempt to free the jammed aircraft. Dresel stopped Nos. 4 and 5 engines and slowed Nos. 1, 2 and 3 to cruising speed. Calnan climbed down to a point over the faulty yoke and after ten minutes of pounding it with a wrench it opened. After thirty-five minutes of being hung up, the Sparrowhawk fell free and returned to Lakehurst. Meanwhile, after a new release wire was quickly installed on the airship, Harrigan flew to meet the *Los Angeles* over Jersey City's municipal airport, where the Navy had scheduled a ten-minute trapeze exhibition at 1335, after which the *Los Angeles* headed for Lakehurst.

Three days later, on 26 October, Harrigan was flying the XF9C-1 cross-country towards western Georgia to rendezvous with the *Los Angeles* on its 300th flight for a Navy Day exhibition over Atlanta. During the afternoon of 27 October, over College Park, he made a pair of full-speed hook ons, which were to be last ones anywhere for seven months as the *Los Angeles* would have its trapeze removed and sent to the Naval Aircraft Factory to be cannibalised for parts used in the construction of the *Akron*'s trapeze. The NAF had been contracted to construct the *Akron*'s trapeze in late December 1931 with completion and installation due for February 1932. The *Akron* would not have its trapeze installed until the last week of January 1932 and did not receive any of its aircraft until the first week of May.

On 3 May 1932 the first flight tests of the XF9C-1 were conducted aboard the *Akron* after the airship had undergone repairs to her damaged fin and the completion of her trapeze installation during March and April. Harrigan and Young, two very experienced pilots, had no real difficulties during their XF9C-1 hook ons but had recommendations mainly intended to improve the aircraft's overall performance, its handling during the hook-on procedure, and improvements to the new *Akron* hook-on apparatus:

1) Install the type of hook-on device which would provide the best tripping leverage preventing the accidental tripping of the cam tripping gear.
2) The hook-on device locking spring required strengthening to maintain the cam in the fully locked position.
3) Remove or fair all sleeves and obstructions along the upper surface of the hook-on guard tube as the sleeve near the landing hook tended to stop the trapeze bar from latching properly in the hook, causing the pilots to apply additional throttle control to complete each airship hook on after this sleeve was connected to the bar.
4) Replace the auxiliary hook control levers.
5) The spring balance tension mechanism that assisted longitudinal trim was to be replaced by a pair of trim tabs on the elevators.

Curtiss XF9C-2

The Curtiss XF9C-1 was always considered a spare aircraft by the HTA Unit and not one of the regular 'squadron hookers'. After the loss of the *Akron* and at the time the *Macon* flew west in 1933 it was transferred to NAF, where its skyhook was removed and it was used in utility service until surveyed in 1936.

Since the XF9C-2 was originally owned by Curtiss, not US Navy, it was given the civil registration NX986M and did not carry a Navy serial. The photo shows the aircraft after purchase by the Navy as F9C-2 BuNo. 9064. (*USN*)

Curtiss was motivated by BuAer Detail Specification No. SD-169-2 of 20 July 1931, which designated an improved version of the XF9C-1, and by the possibility of it becoming a production hook-on aircraft. By mid-August 1931, BuAer and Curtiss engineers mutually reviewed the F9C-2's preliminary specification and identified general improvements to the aircraft's design for resolution. Due to the XF9C-1's testing deficiencies, Curtiss, on its own volition and using its own funds, constructed a one-up follow-on prototype aircraft, the XF9C-2, incorporating the required improvements and within ninety days – on 1 November 1931 – the dark blue XF9C-2 was delivered.

To reduce future production costs, Curtiss decided to complete the XF9C-2 with as many of the production changes as possible, but without the hook-on mechanism that required further development. The XF9C-2 differed somewhat from its XF9C-1 predecessor. Its cockpit visibility was improved by raising the upper wing 4in, which gave the aircraft a more distinct 'gull-wing' configuration. This change necessitated new wing-strengthening members, in addition to those necessary to carry the loads of the new skyhook mechanism. Its balanced rudder was eliminated, and its vertical stabiliser was lengthened by 8in. The original XF2C-2 landing gear was that of the XF2C-1. After further testing, this gear was determined to be impracticable and was abandoned for a conventional tripod-type landing gear, which was lengthened to allow an increase of propeller diameter from 96 to 102in. Streamlined, spiffy spats covered high-pressure tyres. The rudder-brake pedal layout was replaced by a hanging pedal design with toe-operated brakes. The XF9C-1's original 421hp Wright R-975-C engine was replaced by a 438hp Wright R-975-E3 on the XF9C-2. The XF9C-1's heavy fuselage structure necessary to withstand the shocks of carrier landings was, unfortunately, retained. During September 1931 trials, test pilots reported that the aircraft could have ground loop problems and while investigating that possibility the aircraft did, in fact, encounter such a severe ground loop that its main gear collapsed and an outer wing panel was damaged. As a remedy, a steerable tail wheel was added to production aircraft. Also, the tail wheel assembly received serious battering when landing and taxying, and a shock absorber was recommended. These changes increased the weight by about 250lb. It should be noted that as the XF9C-2's empty and loaded weight increased with its development as a military aircraft, its performance fell below that of other fighters of the time. There was a consequent loss in performance and manoeuvrability at altitude. However, these aircraft were greater in weight and larger in size than the XF9C-2, whose smaller size and weight would make it suitable as an airship fighter.

On 12 November 1931, after repairing the ground loop damage, the XF9C-2 was considered ready for demonstrations and Navy trials. A day later, the aircraft was ferried to NAS Anacostia by Curtiss test pilot William Crosswell, during which he reported excessive engine vibrations at high speeds. These engine vibrations continued, postponing further testing, and preventing Navy pilots from conducting preliminary trials, including firing tests of the revised gun installation. The XF9C-2 was then sent to the Wright Aeronautical Company for replacement of its vibrating Wright R-975-E3 engine before the tests could continue.

The Contractual Evolution of the XF9C-2 into the F9C-2

During September 1931, the lone Curtiss-owned XF9C-2 prototype was placed on the civil register as NX-986-M, and on 12 October 1931 the Navy awarded contract No. 24020 to Curtiss, in a token one-dollar agreement to cover the prototype's demonstration testing. Two days later, Curtiss received an order for six production F9C-2s, BuNos. 9056 to 9061, with the first F9C-2 scheduled to be delivered by 1 March 1932. Six aircraft were selected based on the airship's designed hangar capacity of four, plus 50 per cent (two) spares.

Curtiss's tests would lead directly to the Navy production Curtiss F9C-2, with NX-986-M the prototype and test vehicle for the remainder of these airship fighters. There was no major difference between the prototype and the Navy production F9C-2s except that the former was the test version and was finally modified to production standard and served with the other airship fighters. Curtiss, envisioning additional Navy contracts, had F9C-3 and -4 designs on the drawing boards, which were labelled as 'carrier fighters' but reportedly did have skyhooks added.

Ultimately, the Navy purchased NX-986-M from the Curtiss company under contract No. 29095 dated 9 November 1932 and its XF9C-2 designation was made official, the aircraft being allocated BuNo 9264. With the XF9C-2 the Navy now possessed a fighter with a suitable basic design and the correct dimensions and performance to meet the requirement for an operational parasite airship aircraft, which would be carried by both *Akron* and the future *Macon*. The aircraft was sent to the Naval Aircraft Factory Philadelphia for installation of a skyhook and was then delivered to Lakehurst on 10 January 1933.

Curtiss F9C-2 Sparrowhawk

F9C-2 Contracts

The six F9C-2s (Nos. 9056–9061) were purchased on contract No. 24021 of 14 October 1931, as direct follow-ons to the two X-prototypes. Once the F9C-2 contract was authorised, resolution of the design details progressed quickly. The first, 9056, flew on 14 April 1932 and was fully tested by the end of July. By September (within twenty-seven months of the XF9C-1 prototype contract signing and eleven months from the production contract) all six F9C-2 production models were in the Navy inventory. (Note: The Navy purchased the aircraft as the F9C-2, but it is referred to as the F9C in some sources.)

F9C-2 Contract Costs

Six aircraft at $22,965 each	$137,790
Spare parts	$34,448
Design information	$9,234
Miscellaneous data	$1,765
Ferrying first article to Lakehurst	$1,000
Final corrected data and drawings	$7,211
Total Cost	$191,448

These contract figures were negotiated during the 1930 Depression era when funding was so short that BuAer spent weeks haggling with Curtiss over the price of $9.25 per aircraft to paint 'U.S. Navy' on the undersides of the lower wing of each aircraft. The Navy ultimately decided that $55.50 was too costly!

First Production Model F9C-2 Demonstration Tests

On 14 April 1932, the first production F9C-2 (BuNo. 9056) was flown at the Curtiss Buffalo plant by Curtiss test pilot William Crosswell. When first flown, this aircraft was equipped with the single-leg XF9C-1 type undercarriage, but this was soon changed to the earlier XF9C-2 tripod type, and the other F9C-2s were completed to the same design. The original high-pressure tyres of the XF9C-2 were replaced by low-pressure types, with the wheels now enclosed in uncovered, open-sided fairings. To increase the F9C-2's operating range, a 30-gallon auxiliary fuel tank was projected to be carried under the fuselage by removing the landing gear. The six F9C-2s were ordered with a standardised 'skyhook' and prop guard.

On 3 May, the first production model F9C-2 BuNo. 9056 was delivered to NAS Anacostia, where it was scheduled to complete its flight test programme. On 6 May 1932 the F9C-2 was prepared and flown to the Curtiss Buffalo plant to be demonstrated by the Curtiss test pilot before the Inspector of Naval Aircraft (INA). This one-hour demonstration flight included a terminal velocity dive to an indicated air speed of 275mph

On 14 April 1932, the first production F9C-2 (BuNo. 9056) was first flown at the Curtiss Buffalo plant and was delivered to NAS Anacostia on 3 May, where it was scheduled to complete its flight test programme. (*USN*)

All F9C-2 pilots were qualified and checked out on carriers because they never knew when they might have to land aboard one. Due to the small size of the landing gear, small, upturned, flange-type fairings were installed forward of the wheel spats to prevent the carrier arresting wires from snagging the F9C's landing gear and tipping the aircraft on its nose. (*USN*)

at 9,000ft, during which the pull-out revealed that 9.8g was experienced. The guns were operable but were not loaded. On 10 May 1932 the F9C-2 was demonstrated at Anacostia by the Curtiss test pilot, who flew it in all established routine flight manoeuvres except the outside loop. On 13 May at the Naval Proving Ground, Dahlgren, Virginia, the F9C-2 was again demonstrated by the Curtiss test pilot in aerobatics and terminal velocity dives. Two tail spins of ten turns each, one to the right and one to the left, were performed. Recovery from the right spin was made in three quarters of a turn, whereas the left spin required approximately one full turn. On the same day four test dives were performed in compliance with the Navy's aircraft contract performance guarantees, after which the aircraft was accepted by the Navy. The overall performance tests were then performed from 15 to 31 May.

Gunnery and ordnance tests were undertaken on 9 to 13 June and the radio tests were completed on 10–11 June, after which the F9C-2 was transferred to the aircraft carrier arresting gear facility at Hampton Roads, Virginia, until 20 June. All F9C-2 pilots were to be qualified and checked out on carriers because there was always the possibility that a carrier landing would be necessary. Due to the small size of the landing gear, small, upturned flange-type fairings were installed forward of the wheel spats to prevent the carrier arresting wires snagging the landing gear and tipping the aircraft on its nose before the arresting gear caught. Later Sparrowhawk photos show them without arresting gear.

After these tests the following improvements were suggested to the aircraft:

1) Improve the pilot's seat adjustment for use in the air.
2) Install additional attachments for the securing of the pilot's seat.
3) Modify the shape and padding of the forward section of the cockpit coaming to have the upper instruments visible from the normal position of the pilot's eyes.
4) Provide an exhaust collector ring.
5) Test the strength of the radio antenna brackets on the upper wings while flying at terminal velocity with the antenna installed.
6) The tail wheel shock absorber required more capacity.

These changes could be easily corrected during production of the five forthcoming F9C-2s.

F9C-2 Arrives at Lakehurst for Hook-On Tests

After the arresting gear tests were performed on 20 June, the F9C-2 was found not to meet current Navy carrier and fighter requirements but was considered at the time to be the best aircraft available for airship operations. From the available literature, it seems that the aircraft, 9056, was initially delivered for initial performance and carrier testing without its hook-on apparatus installed. The latter began on 28 June 1932. For these tests the aircraft was flown from Lakehurst to Anacostia with the primary purpose to determine if the contractor's guarantees had been fulfilled and then 'to determine the operation of the airship hook-on device and the overall suitability of a service type airship fighter'. Since there were no standards to determine if the F9C-2 was suitable as airship fighter, any satisfactory performance would recommend it for its new role.

Upon its arrival at Lakehurst, 9056 was equipped with its hook-on device and was connected to a trolley inside the airship hangar that transported it under the *Akron* to be attached to the trapeze an then be lifted into one of the four stowage positions inside the airship.

On 29 June 1932, flight tests began and nine hook-ons on the *Akron*'s trapeze were performed by Lt Harrigan during 1.35 hours of flight time while Lt Young performed thirteen hook ons during 1.50 hours in the good conditions encountered during their tests. It would be 12 September 1932 when the next two F9C-2s were completed and ferried from Buffalo to Lakehurst, with the remaining three following on 21 September.

F9C-2 Deficiencies Found in the Initial Hook-On Tests

Because the F9C-2 was not originally designed for hooking on to an airship, the Harrigan/Young hook-on tests found that it had several of the same old and some new deficiencies as other hook-on aircraft. As a naval Fleet reconnaissance aircraft, the F9C-2's gull wing interfered with good downward observation, while its oil cooler interfered with good forward vision. Adding the skyhook caused the gunsight to warp out of alignment after several 'belly bumps', as landings on the airship were called. The cockpit was too small for convenient placement of the radio key and there was no place for the navigation/scouting board, which had to be mounted on the control stick. The compass had to mounted on the port wing, outboard of the cockpit hand grip. The cold open cockpit was made even smaller when pilots wore winter flying suits. Exposed service crews did find that access to the fuel and oil tank fillers was satisfactory when the aircraft was attached to the trapeze.

A problem occurred while approaching the trapeze at stalling speeds, when the pilots found that extra right rudder was necessary as a small change of the rudder angle caused an abnormal amount of yaw, which was compensated by raising the left wing. This directional instability was corrected on the production models by adding an 8in-wide section to the vertical stabiliser and a 3in sheet metal strip to the rudder.

The Report of the Board of Inspection and Survey

After the demonstration flight tests, radio tests, and the seemingly mandatory carrier arresting gear tests, the Board of Inspection and Survey (BIS) ordered the F9C-2 to be tested to verify the operation of its airship hook-on apparatus and for its suitability as a 'service type' airship fighter. The three flight officers comprising the original July 1931 BIS, which advised against the F9C-2 for carrier duty unless (too) many recommended changes were made, were replaced. The Board assembled a Sub-Board of Inspection and Survey to evaluate airship hook-on trials and the performance of the hook-on device. This new Sub-Board under Anacostia Flight Test Officer Lt Cdr Gerald Bogan advised that the Curtiss F9C-2 had complied with all performance guarantees:

> This aircraft carrying these items of normal useful load specified for an airship fighter, under all service load conditions, was found to be in all respects a satisfactory military airship fighter aircraft in correct flying balance, controllable and stable in the air, and on the ground, and suitable for the service intended except as previously noted.

The Sub-Board recommended that the Curtiss F9C-2, 'with the prescribed modifications incorporated as listed under all previous recommendations, be accepted as a service type for airship operations'. It should be noted that other than directional instability during the hooking-on procedure, the Curtiss F9C-2 was accepted with only a few minor recommended changes as many of the previous recommended changes for the XF9C-2 had been accomplished, with the basic aerodynamic design and the hook-on apparatus and procedure validated.

The F9C-2 Sparrowhawk Described

The F9C-2s were the first aircraft of the single-seat carrier fighter type constructed at the Garden City, New Jersey, plant of the Buffalo-based Curtiss Aeroplane and Motor Corporation. Originally designed as a carrier fighter aircraft, the Curtiss Company described it as 'more or less intended to comply with the 1930 Bureau of Aeronautics Design No. 96'. The F9C-2 Sparrowhawk fighter was a single seat, all-metal semi-monocoque fuselage biplane. Its fabric-covered, duralumin, staggered wings had the lower wing at the base of the fuselage and the upper wing just above the fuselage, with a very slight gull-wing effect in the centre. The single-fin empennage was all metal, with duralumin sheathing. There was an arresting landing hook attachment mechanism extending from the rear fuselage used when landing on the deck of an aircraft carrier to catch an arresting wire.

F9C-2 Sparrowhawk Biplane Gullwing Specifications and Performance

Specifications
Crew: 1
Length: 20ft 7in (6.2m)
Height: 10ft 6in (3.2m)
Wingspan: Upper wing 25ft 6in (7.8m)
Lower wing: 23ft 3in (7.1m)
Wing Gap: 3ft 10in (1.17m)
Wing Area: Upper wing: 104.5 sq ft (9.7 sq m)
Lower wing: 68.3 sq ft (6.35 sq m)
Total: 172.79 sq ft (16.053 sq m)
Aileron area: 19 sq ft (1.77 sq m)
Wing Chord: Upper wing: 4ft 8in (1.42m)
Lower wing: 3ft 4in (1m)
Empennage: Horizontal Stabiliser: 9ft 3in (2.82m) long/17 sq ft (1.58 sq m)
Elevator: 11 sq ft (1 sq m)
Vertical Stabiliser: 2ft 7in (0.79m) high/15 sq ft (1.39 sq m)
Rudder: 6 sq ft (0.56 sq m)
Empty Weight: 2,089lb (948kg)
Gross Weight: 2,776lb (1,259kg)
Useful Load: 681lb
Per cent Useful Load: 24.6 per cent
Powerplant: 1 × 438hp Wright R-975-E3 Whirlwind 9-cylinder, air-cooled, radial piston
Propeller: 8.5ft (2.6m) diameter, wooden, two-bladed variable pitch
Fuel Tanks: Main fuel tank: 63 gallons (240 litres)
External (replacing landing gear): 30 gallons (114 litres)
Oil Tank: 5 Gallons (18.9 litres)

Performance
Maximum Speed (@ 4,000ft): 176.5mph (284.0kmph)
Maximum Speed (@ 4,000ft) with undercarriage removed: 200mph (322kmph)
Maximum Speed (@ 16,000ft): 148mph (238kmph)
Landing Speed: 63mph (101kmph)
Stalling speed: 60mph (97kmph)
Service Ceiling: 19,200ft (5,900m)
Initial Rate of Climb: 1,700ft/minute (8.6m/s)
Climb in 10 minutes: 11,300ft (3,444m)
Wing loading: 16lb/sq ft (78kg/sq m)
Power loading: 6.4lb/hp (2.9kg/hp)
Normal radius (@ 125mph cruising speed): 176 miles (283km)
Radius (with external fuel): 255 miles (410km)

Fuselage

This was of the semi-monocoque, all-metal type constructed of aluminium alloy and consisted of two parts: a forward section that housed the engine mount, oil tank, fuel tank, wing attachment points and landing gear, and a rear part that contained the cockpit, instrumentation, oxygen, and radio equipment, and empennage attachment. The fuselage

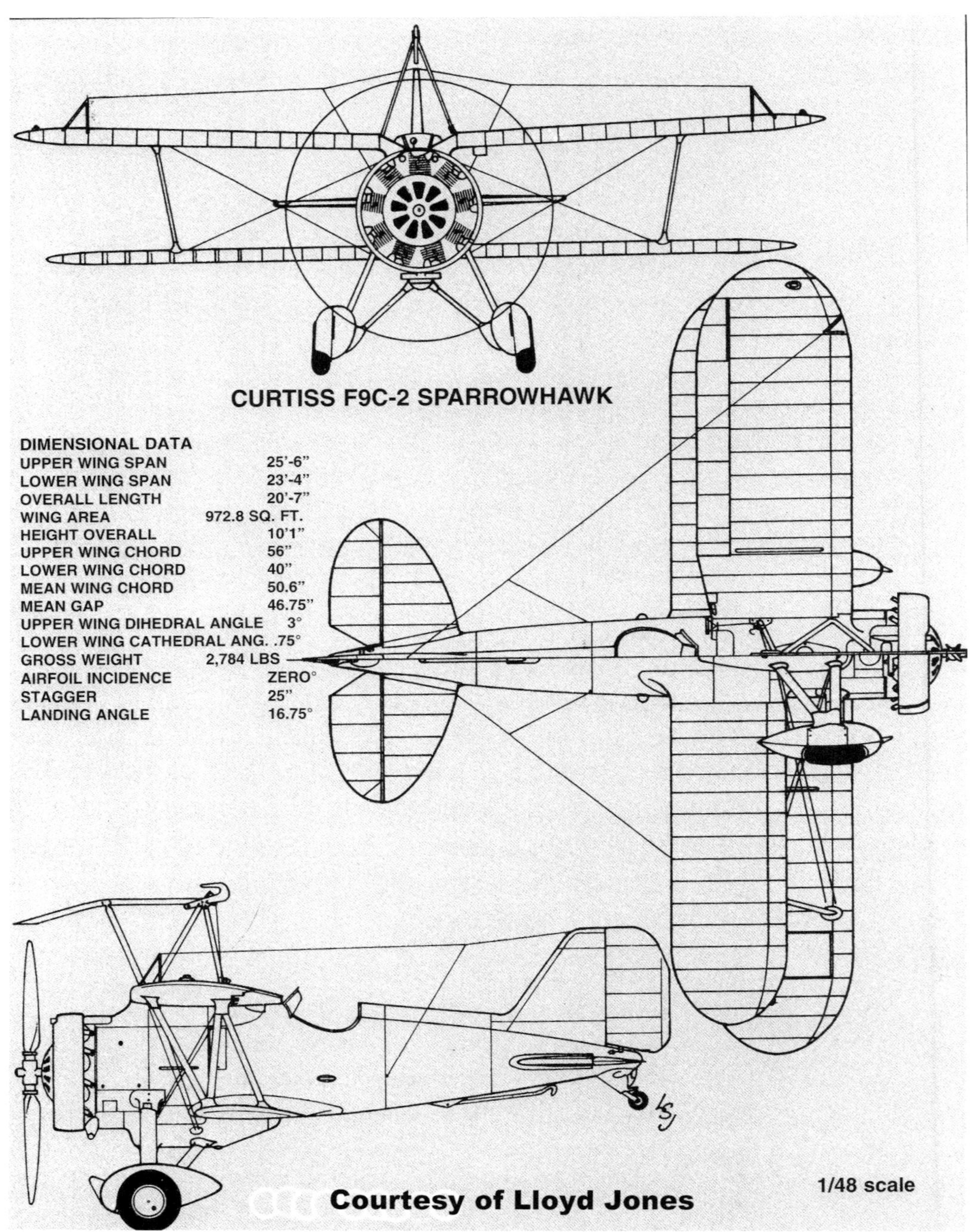

structure was constructed of transverse open bulkheads, short longerons, stringers and skin, all fabricated from 17ST aluminium alloy. The main bulkheads to which the wings and fuselage were attached were of heavy-gauge box construction. The fuselage required strengthening to carry the raised gullwing upper wing load. The remainder of the bulkheads were of 0.5in J section. The flange was 7/16in and of various depths corresponding with the strength requirements. The longerons were hat sections, 0.5 × 1 × 1in with 1in flanges. The upper longeron was located between bulkheads 2 and 6 and the lower longerons between bulkheads 2 and 3. The stringers were of .032in J-section 7/8in deep, 7/16in flat flange, and 0.375in curved flange. The skin of the fuselage varied in thickness. Between bulkheads 2 and 5 it was .025in thick, and .020in between bulkheads 5 and 12, except for a short section on the underbody between bulkheads 5 and 8. Curtiss static tested the fuselage by using sandbags to create high angle of attack conditions to 80 per cent of the design load. This type of static testing disclosed that no part of the fuselage was stressed beyond the elastic limit of the aluminium alloy. The lower fuselage structure served as an attaching point for the drag wires braces along with the terminal point of attachment for the landing gear.

Wing Structure

The F9C-2's biplane gullwing consisted of a 25.5ft-long upper wing and a 23.25ft-long lower wing with a combined wing area of 172.79 sq ft. On the production F9C-2s the upper wing was raised 4in to improve forward vision over the nose and through the gunsight. The wings were constructed of aluminium alloy tubes and structures, with single steel tie rod bracing. Fabric with rib stitching covered the upper and lower wings, including the ailerons. The leading edges of both wing structures were covered with sheet aluminium alloy back to the aft edge of the forward wing spars. Each upper and lower wing consisted of two outer panels joined to a centre-section structure, with a single pair of streamlined steel tubing interplane struts braced with two sets of double flying wires and the standard set of landing wires.[3] One set of flying wires continued from the forward end of the lower fuselage structure to the upper aft wing spar at the attachment of the interplane struts. The other set of flying wires continued from the aft end of the lower fuselage to the upper forward wing spar at the interplane strut. The landing wires ran from the lower forward wing spar at the interplane strut to the bulkhead, to which was attached the aft upper wing hinge fitting. The wires were a swaged streamlined section and were adjustable in length, with their terminals concealed within the wing.

The three-hinge, fabric-covered aluminium alloy frame ailerons were only located on the upper wing and were of the Frise type (an aileron contoured to reduce undesirable yaw) and operated by torque tubes. The ailerons were aerodynamically balanced at 35 degrees up and 20 degrees down. The clearance ahead of the leading edge of the aileron was designed to act as a slot to increase the wing lift and to augment the wing lift at stalling

3 The wing structure of biplanes needed separate wires to bear the upward and downward loads on the wing. The 'flying wires' carried positive lift loads, and 'landing wires' managed inertial droop loads on landing and negative lift in inverted flight or in a downward wind gust.

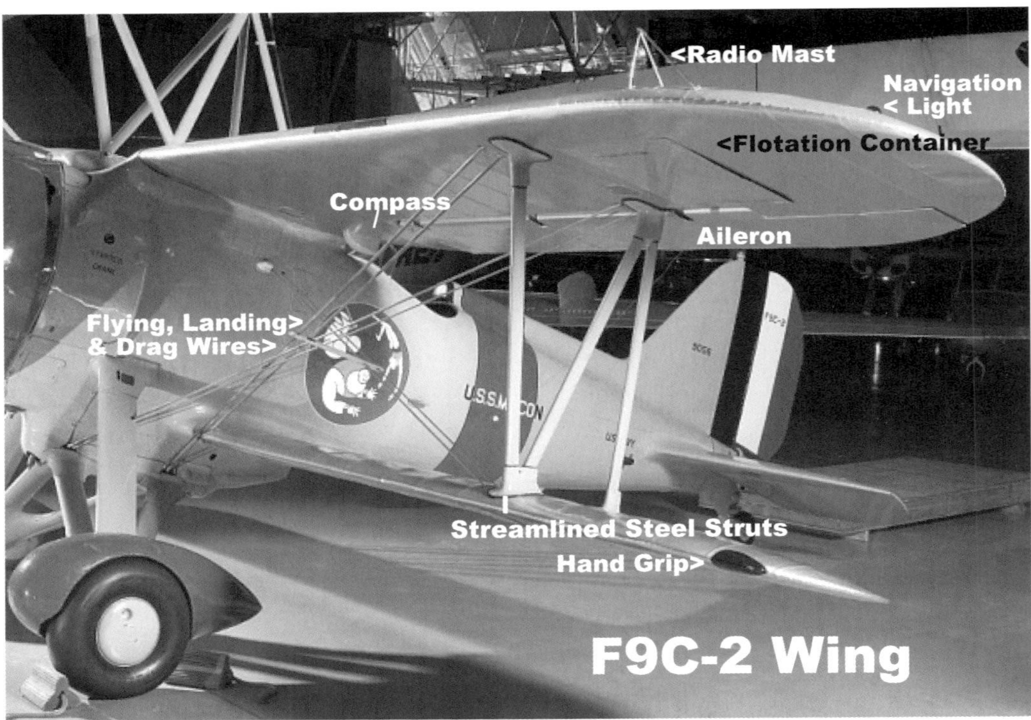

angles, thus making aileron control effective at the low speeds required for approaching the airship trapeze for hook on.

Tail Structure

The horizontal and vertical stabilisers were constructed of an aluminium alloy with a smooth sheet covering attached by rivets and they were an integral part of the fuselage. The elevators were of aluminium alloy framework covered with fabric with the front spar continuous but detachable at the centreline of the fuselage for disassembly. The balanced rudder was fabricated of aluminium alloy and covered with smooth sheet covering attached by rivets. Rudder movement was 35 degrees right and left. The original tail structure caused directional instability and

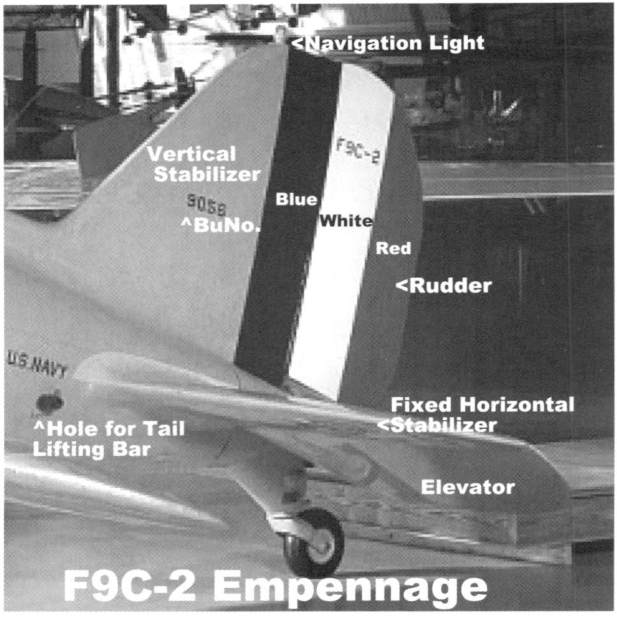

made hooking on to the trapeze and accurate gunnery difficult. This was corrected on production aircraft by adding an 8in section to the vertical stabiliser and a 3in metal strip to the rudder.

Landing Gear or Not

The tail-dragger aircraft had a heavy-duty, three-strut, steel main landing gear with a tail wheel. The narrow-span 6ft 5in main wheels were covered by streamlined spats that covered high-pressure (25psi maximum) 7.5 × 10in semi-balloon tyres. The brakes were cable actuated. The main gear had oil shock absorption suspension able to withstand jolting carrier arrested landings. The main landing gear wheel pants/spats were outfitted with curved fins, called overriders, fixed to their forward midline to prevent the arresting gear wires jumping up and over the pants into the gear struts during carrier landings.

During testing the tail wheel assembly collapsed twice and was revised, with a hard rubber tyre replacing the pneumatic one. The tail wheel was self-steering within the limits of the rudder movement.

When operating from the airship, a F9C-2 had no need for a landing gear as it would be hoisted aboard for fuel and armament replenishment or storage. Therefore, it had been

XF9C-1 early landing gear. (USN)

When operating from the airship, a F9C-2 had no need for a landing gear as it could be hoisted aboard the airship for fuel and armament replenishment or storage. (*USN*)

recommended that the Sparrowhawk, once aboard the airship, have its fixed landing gear removed, which would delete 250lb and allow the installation of a 30-gallon auxiliary fuel tank in its place. A stated initial main objective was to demonstrate the 'flying aircraft carrier's open-ocean search potential using parasite aircraft'. The addition of the 30-gallon fuel tank would increase the F9C's operating range from 175 to 255 miles with an hour and a half of endurance and the reduced drag increased its speed from 176 to 200mph. The *Macon*'s HTA Unit maintenance crew, led by Chief Aviation Machinists Mate William Cody, would become quite proficient at removing and reinstalling Sparrowhawks' landing gear for the belly fuel tank in forty-five minutes. This tank could not be used immediately, since the aircraft's own fuel system returned unused fuel to the main tank that would have no room if full. Early in 1934 operations, the long-recommended permanent removal of the landing gear (making the exterior fuel tank more practical) was finally undertaken.

Cockpit

The single open cockpit was cold and snug, especially when 6ft pilots like Harrigan, Trapnell, Miller, and Kivette were wearing the much-needed heavy flight clothing. The aerobatic F9C-2's flight characteristics demanded the pilot's full attention and many of the features of the cockpit layout were inadequate to that purpose. A small thick, low Plexiglas windscreen that was penetrated by the tubular gunsight was located behind the hump of the upper wing. Forward vision from the cockpit was impeded by the area between the Nos. 8 and 9 cylinders and was remedied by relocation and removal of exhaust pipes, redesign of the windshield frame, and raising the upper wing 4in. Downward vision was impeded by the lower wing location and was a reason for the type's elimination as a carrier aircraft.

The following flight instruments were provided: inclinometer, aneroid altimeter, airspeed indicator, turn and bank indicator, clock mount, and magnetic compass. The following engine instruments were provided: tachometer, oil pressure gauge, oil thermometer, fuel pressure gauge, and fuel quantity gauge. The instruments in the upper part of the instrument panel were difficult to read from the normal position of the pilot's eyes because

Cockpit instrument layout. (*USN*)

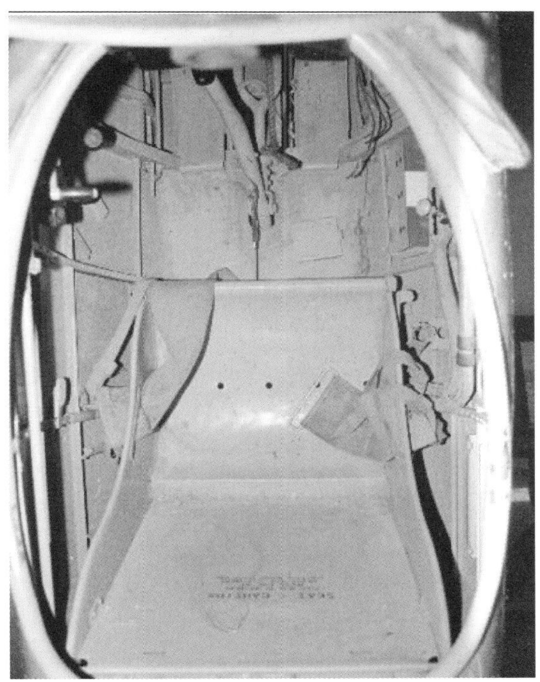
F9C-2 pilot's seat and seat belt looking from above. (*USN*)

of the shape of the forward part of the cockpit coaming and attached padding. There was a leather crash pad surrounding the instrument panel.

The surface controls were operated by a joystick and the original non-adjustable pedal controls for the rudder were replaced with the adjustable hanging type. For elevator control a bungee was installed to compensate for a fixed stabiliser during minor variations in longitudinal trim. The ailerons, operated by a torque tube, were of the differential type and if one were damaged the other remained operational.

The very basic metal pilot bucket seat was removable but was not readily adjustable. It was secured within the cockpit by two spring-loaded pins to prevent the seat from falling out during inverted flight. The seat was hinged, and the pins disengaged to provide access to the radio equipment located aft of the pilot's cockpit. The pilot's seat was provided with a seat and shoulder belt.

Among the items carried in the fuselage were: life jacket, oxygen equipment (cylinder, regulator, and associated tubing), first aid kit, fire extinguisher, life raft, and very pistol and holster with twelve cartridges in their holder.

Radios and Radio Homing Sets

The F9C-2s were equipped with Aircraft Radio Corporation (ARC) GF series radios, which were completely shielded from engine interference, but were nonetheless frequently undependable due to the plug coil and antenna design. The first 1.5-watt GF, introduced in 1932, transmitted only 6,600–7,400kcs and included a single plug-in coil (later GF

F9C-2 radio antennas. (*USN*)

models would contain multiple coils.) The improved 3-watt GF-1, introduced in early 1934, also transmitted only 6,600–7,400kcs and included a plug-in coil. The matching RU-3 receiver also had a single plug-in coil for receiving 5,400–8,100kcs. Because pilots often flew long distances from their airship, their frequently undependable GF-1/RU-3 transmitter/receiver radios would cause them to have to resort to the Morse code key to communicate. More reliable voice communication was needed.

Early F9C-2s were equipped with radio homing gear that was expected to be able to home on a radio signal from the airship. However, this was not reliable until January 1934, when a new radio navigation system with a visual indicator using an arrow indicating the direction to the source of the radio signal was installed on the airship and the aircraft. With this system, pilots could fly away from the airship as far as possible without using the restrictive 60-60 system (described later). During testing of the radio equipment, the aircraft took off from a land-based airfield and, using the new radio system, easily found an airship from 63–81 miles away. Trailing wire antennas to provide better radio communications were tested but they complicated hook-on operations and the storage of the aircraft in the airship hangar bay. The wing-mounted radio mast was eliminated on production models.

Wright R-975E-3 Whirlwind Engine

The XF9C-1's Wright R-975-C was replaced by the R-975-E on the XF9C-2 and then by the R-975E-3 on the production F9C-2s. The Wright R-975 Whirlwind engine was gradually developed and built by the Wright Aeronautical division of Curtiss-Wright. The R-975s were the largest and most powerful of the Wright Whirlwind engine series to be manufactured commercially and were also the most numerous. The R-975 was a series of nine-cylinder, air-cooled, supercharged, radial aircraft engines with a displacement of about 975 cu in, power ratings of 300–450hp, gear ratio of 10.15 to 1 and a compression ratio of 6 to 1. Air-cooled Whirlwinds were lighter and more reliable than liquid-cooled engines of similar power since a liquid cooling system added weight and required extra maintenance.

The magnetos were double-type Scintilla VAG-9DF of a 12-volt ignition system and the carburettor was a Stromberg model NAR-9. An Eclipse Series VII hand electric engine starter was installed. The Sparrowhawk's R-975E-3, introduced during 1931, had greater supercharging capability and a higher rpm limits. There was an adjustable shutter device installed in the engine nose cowling, which the pilot controlled for manual operation for cooling the engine crankcase. The engine starting system consisted of an access hole on the aircraft's port side for winding the inertial starter hand crank, which was mounted to an integral booster magneto and an engine fuel primer. With oil heaters in the tanks, the engine could be started at any time. A fuel shut-off cock was provided in the fuel primer line near the fuel primer pump. The starter trip was controlled by the pilot. However, aboard the airships, with no area for the hand-cranking crewman to stand, a 110v external electric starter was utilised via a cord handed down from the trapeze and plugged into a jack on the pilot's instrument panel. There was a pressurised engine fire extinguisher that was manually controlled by the pilot.

Introduced by the Wright Aeronautical division of Curtiss-Wright during 1931, the Sparrowhawk's R-975E-3 Whirlwind was a 300–450hp, nine-cylinder, air-cooled, radial engine with a displacement of about 975 cu in. (*USN*)

Propellers

The Wright engine swung a Hamilton-Standard (design 4651) 8.5ft diameter, wooden (later aluminium alloy) two-bladed, variable-pitch, hydromatic propeller. It was painted ivory on the

The Wright R-975E-3 swung a Hamilton-Standard 8.5ft diameter, wooden (later aluminium alloy), two-bladed, variable-pitch, hydromatic propeller with three narrow (from tip) red, yellow and blue bands. (*USN*)

outside surface, flat black on three quarters of its inside surface and ivory on its lower one quarter. It was marked with three narrow red (from prop tip), yellow and blue bands, and the Hamilton-Standard decal. The propeller diameter had been increased to 8.5ft on both the F9C-2 and XF9C-2 from the 8ft XF9C-1 propeller. At the time Hamilton was a new company formed in 1929 and its hydromatic propeller introduced in the 1930s was a significant advance over the counterweight, controllable pitch propeller. This propeller would make Hamilton Standard the largest manufacturer of aircraft propellers in the world, with its three licensees producing 530,135 hydromatic propeller assemblies during the war.

Fuel System

The fuel system consisted of a main 60-gallon welded sheet aluminium fuel tank located directly in front of the pilot and behind the firewall, hydrostatic fuel quantity gauges, copper tubing fuel supply lines with Titeflex connections at the engine end of the lines, and the applicable fittings. Later, an auxiliary 30-gallon external fuel tank replaced the landing gear.

Lubrication System

The lubrication system consisted of an engine oil tank, oil supply lines, and a quantity gauge. The welded aluminium oil tank had a capacity of 5 gallons, plus 1.5 gallons of

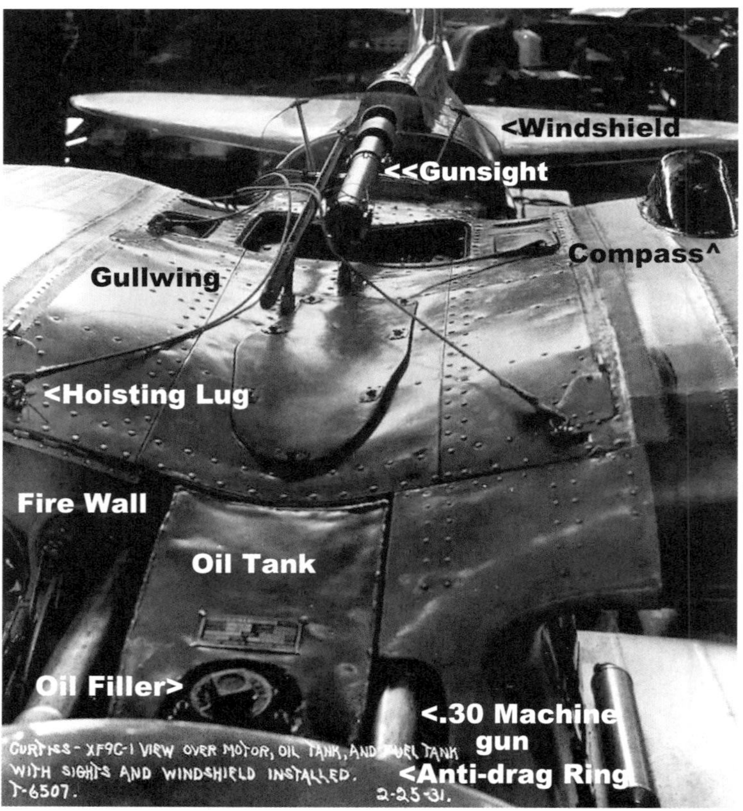

View looking rearward over the oil tank and firewall towards the windshield and cockpit. (*USN*)

expansion space, and was located forward of the firewall of the fuselage. All oil supply lines were constructed of copper tubing except a short section of Titeflex[4] rubber tubing at the engine end of each supply line. An oil temperature regulator and an oil pressure gauge and temperature indicators for the inlet and outlet oil supply were provided. Service oil and oil returning from the engine was strained.

Engine Cooling

The engine nose cowling had a manually adjustable shutter by which the pilot manually/mechanically controlled the cowl flap extension by a handle in the cockpit for increased cooling of the air-cooled radial engine crankcase. It would not be until later that cowl flaps would be opened and closed by electric motors or by hydraulic actuators.

Cowl flaps are small doors located in the bottom of the engine cowling that open to permit greater cylinder cooling during take-off and climb and are closed during cruise, descent, and landing. Baffles help to direct cooling air over the cylinder cooling fins, creating an airflow that travels from top to bottom and eventually returns out of the aircraft through more openings in the cowl.

Cowling, cylinder exhausts, cowl flaps. (*USN*)

Electrical and Lighting

Standard navigation lights and indirect cockpit instrument lights were installed: a red light on the port wingtip, a green one on the starboard tip and a white light on the top, forward of the vertical stabiliser. All electrical wiring was carried in light-gauge aluminium, electrical conduit. A small storage battery was also carried that was charged by an engine-driven generator. There was a plug-in device for starting the engine.

Armament

Two fixed 0.30in (7.62mm) Browning machine guns with 300 rounds of ammunition per gun were mounted in the upper fuselage deck nose, firing between engine cylinders, and synchronised to fire through the propeller arc. Expended cartridges were expelled through individual ejection chutes. A telescopic optical C-3 gunsight passed through the windshield and could be bore sighted by visual methods.

The major machine gun firing and ammunition storage and feed problems were determined and rectified during XF9C-2 testing. During early firing tests a large amount

4. The Titeflex company was formed in 1916 in Newark, New Jersey, and is viable today as the Flex-Tek Group, which supplies the aerospace industry.

of smoke from the guns' firing flooded the cockpit, which was remedied by resealing the engine firewall. Problems in gun maintenance, loading, and achieving correct bore sighting were caused by the inaccessibility and the limited space of the machine gun installation. The original ammunition boxes were fabricated from thin metal to save weight and could be easily damaged, and their incorrect size caused feeding problems, especially during combat manoeuvres, so these were reinforced in production models. The cartridge ejection chutes required redesign. These initial problems were resolved in the six production aircraft and although they probably would not have met Navy combat standards at the time their development was not pursued because of the F9C-2's experimental nature.

Safety Equipment

Aircraft Flotation Gear

Understandably, when scouting well ahead of the Fleet with only the airship able to rescue them, pilots were concerned with ditching in the open ocean. On 16 April 1929, Curtiss engineer Charles Hathorn applied for a patent for 'emergency flotation gear for aeroplanes of the landplane type'. Hathorn's patent provided for two normally deflated rubber gas bags carried packed in elongated envelope-like containers on each side of the fuselage. The containers had a manually controlled release cord, 'in convenient proximity to the pilot's seat' (right-hand side) and, in an emergency, the pilot could activate the internal carbon dioxide bottle to simultaneously open the containers and inflate the cylindrical gas bags in forty seconds. The patent, 1,833,646, was granted on 24 November 1931. Ditching inside a colourful Sparrowhawk equipped with flotation bags gave the downed pilot reasonable hope of rescue, particularly more so than a man bobbing in open water in only his life vest.

Like many Navy aircraft of the era, the F9C-2 was equipped with two emergency rectangular containers that housed rubberised spherical 'ballonet' flotation bags located outboard of the wing struts inside the lower surface of each of its upper wings. An aluminium alloy panel secured these bags in place and an attached manually actuated release mechanism jettisoned this panel. The bags were then inflated by CO_2 contained in a pressurised steel bottle stowed in the lower fuselage. In the event of a water ditching,

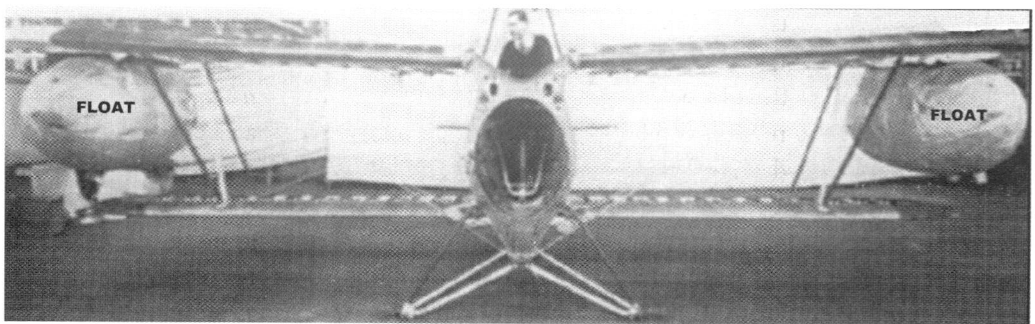

Like many Navy aircraft of the era, the F9C-2 was equipped with two emergency rectangular containers that housed flotation bags located outboard of the wing struts inside the lower surface of each of its upper wings. The rubberised spherical 'ballonet' flotation bags were inflated by a CO_2 cylinder located in the lower fuselage. (*USN*)

the pilot could discharge the internal CO_2 bottle to inflate the floats and wait for the airship or ships of the Fleet for rescue in very large ocean that was, however, made smaller by having to find a large floating aircraft rather than a life raft.

Airship-Deployed Pilot Rescue Life Raft

From the onset, HTA pilots were concerned about being rescued by the airship if their aircraft were ditched. For the next two years the pilots would complain about the need for a rescue method, and one was tested in 1934 for use aboard the *Macon*. A circular 10ft inflatable rubber life raft was converted with a web on the bottom and a safety belt. The airship lowered the raft on a 4,000ft, .025 reeled cable which could also be used to suspend the spy basket and send it to the pilot in the water below, who would climb aboard, fasten the safety belt, and be hoisted up into the airship. The airship, 2,000ft above, could also tow the raft and rescued pilot on the water to a nearby buoy. Fortunately, this technique was never needed as it was probably as terrifying as the ditching.

Airship-deployed pilot rescue life raft. (*USN*)

Paint Schemes

Six Sparrowhawks were considered the heavier-than-air 'squadron' aircraft, and received distinctive, non-regulation paint schemes, reminiscent of Rickenbacker's First World War 'Flying Circus'. Lt Ward Harrigan, the senior HTA officer, implemented the selection of an insignia for the HTA Unit. During the *Akron*'s trapeze trials, the label 'Belly Bumpers' become popular at Lakehurst, and the motto *Ventram Semper Impengentes*, 'Those always bumping the belly', was conceived. However, Harrigan considered this as lacking the blend of humour and dignity that he wanted. A clever proposal was the name 'Little Oaks', which was a play on the old saying into 'Little Oaks From Great *Akron*s Grow'. Other suggestions were a kangaroo and baby Joey in its pouch or a shark and remora pilot fish motif. Pilot Harold 'Min' Miller suggested a stern view of a horse with half a dozen flies buzzing around it, but the *Akron*'s officers found this neither appropriate nor amusing. Harrigan subsequently visited a Philadelphia art school, where a student devised a colourful and imaginative insignia that would become included as a classic Navy squadron insignia of the 1930s (some sources state that this insignia was designed by *Akron* commander, Lt Cdr Hubert Wiley, which seems unlikely). The insignia displayed a brawny and grinning acrobat in red tights and yellow shirt hanging by his knees from a trapeze, reaching out to catch a small, skinny fellow performer who is flying through the air with a worried look on his face. From then on, the pilots of the airships' HTA were known as 'The Men on the Flying Trapeze'. This emblem appeared on the *Akron*'s N2Ys and Sparrowhawks and initial *Macon* Sparrowhawks, on both sides of the fuselage just below and a bit forward of the cockpit. Once the BuAer's Plans Division discovered that the HTA Unit had their planes all 'dolled up in gaudy colours', on 22 September 1933 BuAer directed that the unauthorised 'Man on the Flying Trapeze' insignia be removed from the Sparrowhawks.

The distinctive unauthorised 'Man on the Flying Trapeze' insignia appeared on the *Akron*'s N2Ys and its Sparrowhawks and those F9C-2s of the *Macon*. (*USN*)

Each aircraft had its own colour code on its cowls and wheel-covering spats: 9056: Royal Red, 9057: White, 9058: True Blue, 9059: Black, 9060: Willow Green, and 9061: Lemon Yellow. Harrigan asserted that these distinctive paint schemes were necessary for recognition and identification purposes, but the F9C-2 pilots felt an esprit de corps; so much so that they often flew their formations in a red, white, and blue formation order. There was a 21in coloured fuselage band just behind the cockpit with either white USS *Akron* or USS *Macon* lettering across it. A section leader's chevron appeared on the

Akron Sparrowhawk markings. (*USN*)

US National Insignia at the time (1919–42) was a blue circle encompassing a white star with a red circle inside the star, on the ends of the upper wing (shown on *Macon* Sparrowhawks). (*USN*)

upper wing and on the engine cowl. The wheel spats also bore the aircraft's identification code colour. The top of the upper wings and horizontal stabilisers were painted yellow. A coloured stripe ran from the mid-leading edge of the upper wing ending diagonally to a point above the cockpit.

The US National Insignia at the time (1919–42) was a blue circle encompassing a white star with a red circle inside the star, on the ends of the upper wing, added to the colourful motif. There was no insignia on the rear fuselage sides, where the words USS Akron or USS Macon were placed across the vertical band behind the cockpit where the National Insignia would be placed on later US aircraft.

After the *Macon* joined the Fleet, the three-colour blue-white-red (forward to aft) vertical stripes on the vertical fin and the coloured horizontal stabiliser were removed and the tail repainted in solid blue-black tail to meet unit standards. The vertical band on the fuselage just behind the cockpit was retained, as were the appropriate colour markings on the wing, cowl, and landing gear, but the colour code was removed from the engine cowl and wheel spats.

Macon Sparrowhawk markings. (*USN*)

After the *Macon* joined the Fleet, the three-colour blue-white-red (forward to aft) vertical stripes on the vertical fin and the coloured horizontal stabilizer were repainted as a solid blue-black tail to meet unit aircraft standards. (*USN*)

Launch and Hook-On Mechanisms and Operations

Airship Hangars

The internal aircraft hangar was located inside the massive *Akron*'s and *Macon*'s fuselage, approximately one third of the way aft, in the second bay, aft of the control car. The hangar measured approximately 75ft long, 60ft wide, and 16ft high. The configuration of the airship's three keels made the use of an airship hangar possible. The hangar consisted of two transverse girders that closed in the area between the crew's quarters on opposite sides of the airship forward of a longitudinal girder away from the forward engine rooms. These girders supported a fore and aft structural configuration containing rails in an 'X' configuration. These rails held the rollers and fittings that moved the aircraft to and from the trapeze. Four aircraft could be suspended in the hangar and a fifth could be carried on the trapeze, which was never undertaken as if there was an inoperable aircraft stranded on the trapeze, the other four would also become inoperable. The skin covering of the airship was a type of doped fabric

After the successful *Los Angeles* hook-on trials, the next step was to transport and store dedicated hooked-on aircraft through a T-shaped door into a hangar inside the massive new *Akron* and *Macon* airships to be carried until needed for defence or reconnaissance. (*USN*)

USS Macon Trapeze/Hangar Operations

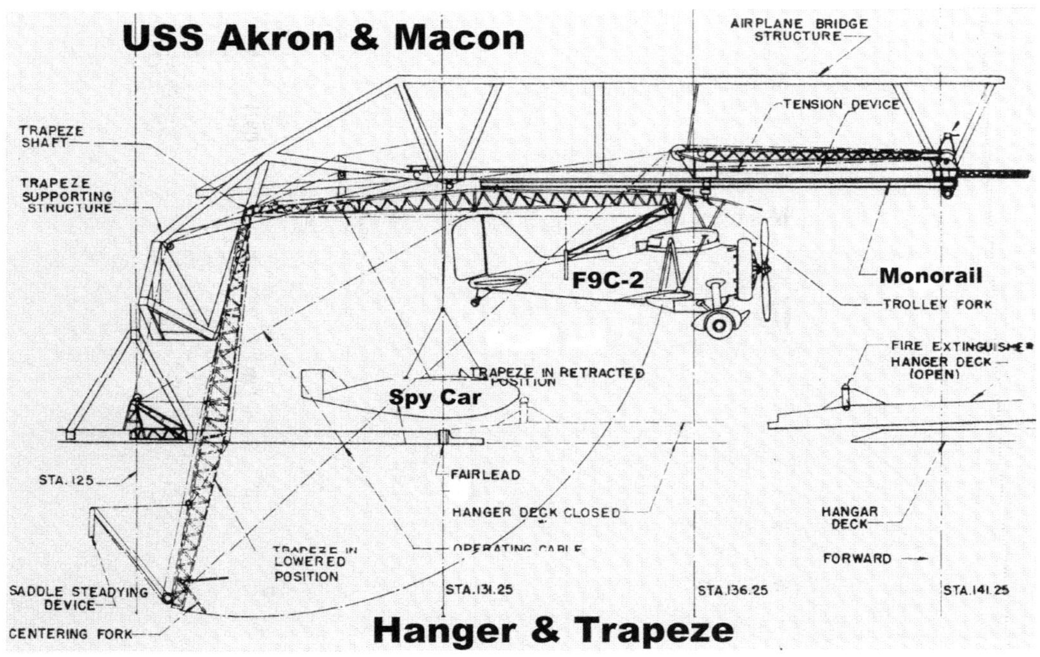
USS Akron & Macon
AIRPLANE BRIDGE STRUCTURE
TENSION DEVICE
TRAPEZE SHAFT
TRAPEZE SUPPORTING STRUCTURE
F9C-2
Monorail
TROLLEY FORK
FIRE EXTINGUISHER
HANGER DECK (OPEN)
TRAPEZE IN RETRACTED POSITION
Spy Car
STA. 125
FAIRLEAD
HANGER DECK CLOSED
HANGAR DECK
TRAPEZE IN LOWERED POSITION
OPERATING CABLE
FORWARD
SADDLE STEADYING DEVICE
STA.131.25
STA.136.25
STA.141.25
CENTERING FORK
Hanger & Trapeze

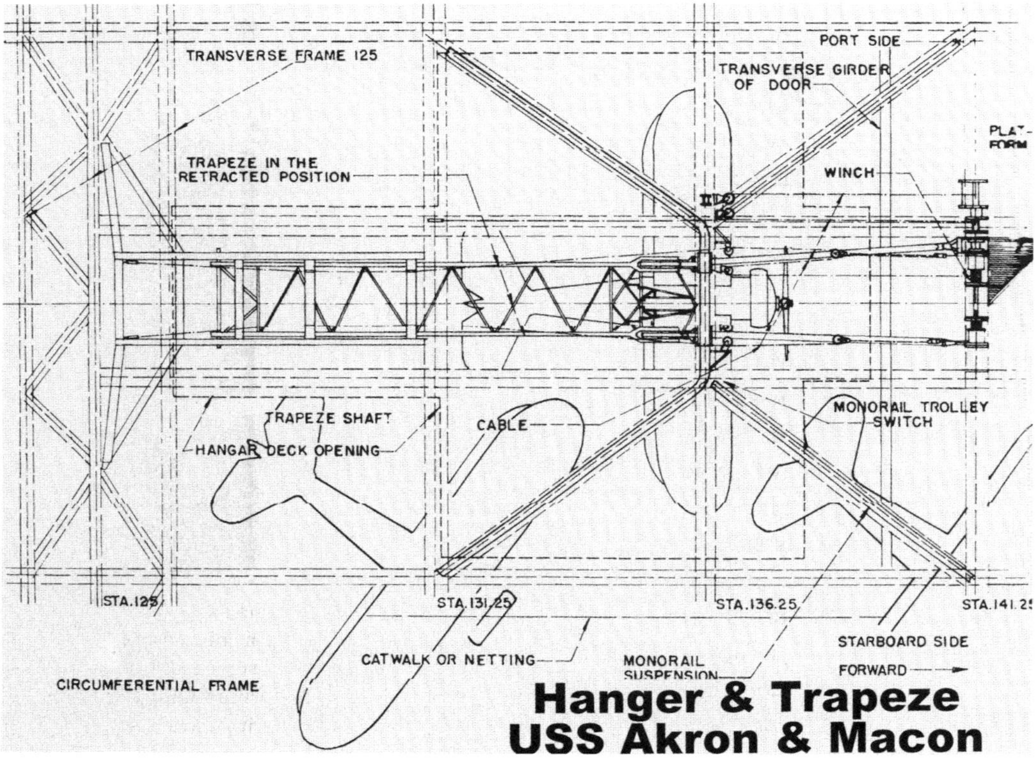

PORT SIDE
TRANSVERSE FRAME 125
TRANSVERSE GIRDER OF DOOR
PLATFORM
TRAPEZE IN THE RETRACTED POSITION
WINCH
TRAPEZE SHAFT
CABLE
MONORAIL TROLLEY SWITCH
HANGAR DECK OPENING
STA.125
STA.131.25
STA.136.25
STA.141.25
STARBOARD SIDE
CATWALK OR NETTING
MONORAIL SUSPENSION
FORWARD
CIRCUMFERENTIAL FRAME
Hanger & Trapeze
USS Akron & Macon

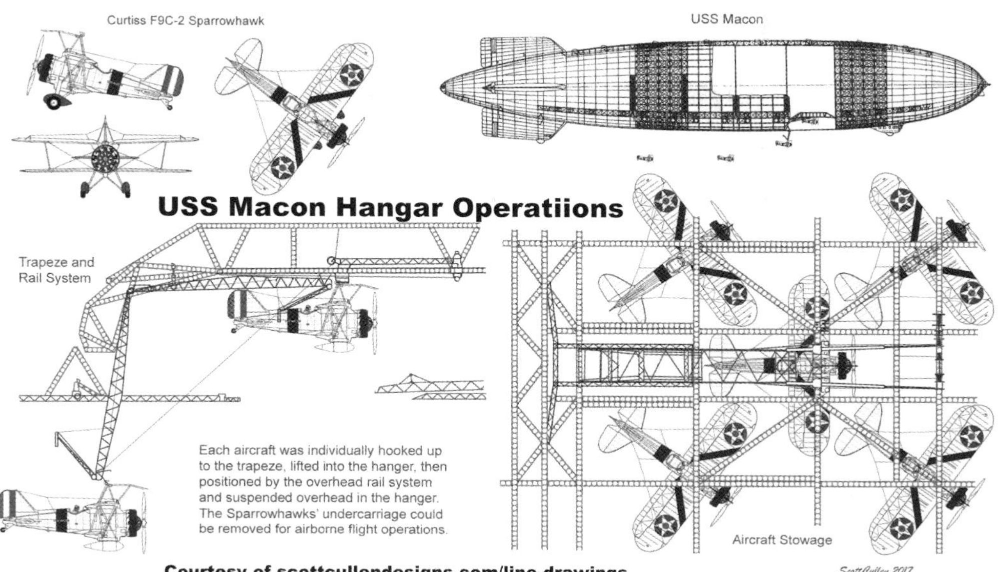

that had to be carefully manoeuvred around while in the hangar. During the hundreds of day and night trapeze and hangar operations it is remarkable that no serious accident or injury occurred there. This was despite the lack of a safety railing around the hangar opening for the handling crewmen and that night hook ons were made with the assistance of a single light that was located on the trapeze. A work platform was provided to perform routine maintenance on aircraft stowed in airship hangars. There were no tie-down rings inside the hangar that could have been used to secure the aircraft as the airship was jostled in turbulent air. Later, to enable the heavy landing gear to be replaced with a belly fuel tank, a support cable was added to fit around the engine crankshaft to stabilise the aircraft.

The performance of routine maintenance on the stowed aircraft was resolved by the design and construction of a work platform with an overhead support cable lifting a framework that fit around the forward fuselage to permit the landing gear to be replaced with a fuel tank. (*USN*)

Trapeze

The *Los Angeles* trapeze removal was a 'temporary' measure; but as America was descending deeper into the Great Depression, on 30 June 1932, the *Los Angeles* was decommissioned, also as a temporary economic measure. However, the airship would never again carry any aircraft on an operational flight. The final streamlined single-point attachment trapeze/hook-on system for the *Akron* and *Macon* was developed from a three-point cable attachment used on the *Los Angeles*. This innovative mechanism was constructed to swing forward and upward at a 45-degree angle, while the main trapeze structure was sprung to absorb the high impact loads. The initial impact was lessened by the airship cruising at 80mph while landing the fighters. Later, the *Macon*'s trapeze had an additional arm pointing at 90 degrees aft that was lowered to hold an aircraft steady while it was being hoisted into the hangar.

Trapeze and Storage Problems

Akron Trapeze and Storage Problems

On 22 August 1932, *Akron* suffered another ground-handling accident, causing another repair hiatus during which the its aircraft-handling capability was greatly improved. During this interlude, Lt Frederick Trapnell made modifications to the trapeze mechanism that would accelerate launch and retrieval times and this also lightened the trapeze by about 300lb. The mechanism of the *Akron*'s trapeze was very similar to that of the *Los Angeles*. After a parasite aircraft had hooked on to the yoke, and before it was moved into the hangar, the yoke and aircraft needed to be reeled up to the end of the trapeze and locked into the mechanism of the 'third pole'. During this procedure a pair of steadying arms swung downward from the trapeze, behind the aircraft, and moved it into a pair of open jaws on the aircraft's upper wings. This provided a three-point attachment to the aircraft while it was being swung rather inelegantly into the hangar. The aircraft often oscillated on its skyhook, delaying the lining up of the steadying arms with the jaws on the aircraft's wings by as much as fifteen minutes. During combat situations, when four aircraft with almost empty fuel tanks were returning to refuel, this certainly would be unacceptable. Trapnell removed the trapeze's third pole, its system of steadying arms, and the need for steadying points on the aircraft wings and replaced them with the 'fork and saddle' assembly. The fork was a padded yoke that was lowered over the aircraft's rear fuselage to check the oscillation and swaying; while the yoke was a pair of prongs at the end of the trapeze that were lowered after an aircraft landed, centring its skyhook on the yoke.

The main problems the *Akron*'s aircraft handlers encountered was the shortage of equipment for securing the aircraft in their stowage positions inside the hangar compartment; the lack of catwalks for use of the servicing personnel; and insufficient storage area for spare parts, ammunition, and auxiliary gear. Hypothetically, five aircraft could be stowed in the hangar, one in each corner on the overhead monorail system, and a fifth on the trapeze in the hangar's centre. In the *Akron*'s hangar two girders obstructed the use of the two after-corner positions and because of these obstructions, the airship never carried more than three aircraft. BuAer authorised a hinge for these struts so they

Evolution of the Trapeze

Los Angeles trapeze three-point cable attachment. (*USN*)

The first hook-on system for the *Akron* was developed from the *Los Angeles*' three-point cable attachment, which was simplified to a single-point attachment and was used on both the *Akron* and *Macon*. (*USN*)

The final and major change to the *Macon* trapeze was the addition of an extra arm structure at 90 degrees directed aft. This arm was lowered to hold the arriving aircraft steady while it was being lifted into the hangar. (*USN*)

F9C-2 9059 inside the *Akron* hangar testing the revised trapeze with the saddle device clamping the rear fuselage steadying the aircraft. (*USN*)

Final *Akron* trapeze. The initial three-point cable attachment was simplified to a single-point set up on the both the *Akron* and *Macon*. (*USN*)

could be swung out of the way while handling aircraft, but the *Akron* was lost before this work could be completed. This shortcoming was rectified in the *Macon* while she was under construction and although it could also accommodate five aircraft, the fifth was infrequently carried because it would have to be carried on the trapeze, and, again, if it had engine problems, the other four would be trapped in the corners of the hangar until the one on the trapeze could be started, repaired or jettisoned.

Launch Procedure

For the ten-minute launching procedure, the Sparrowhawk was attached to an overhead trolley running diagonally on an overhead monorail system to be moved from its hangar corner to the trapeze. Using handholds on the lower wings and boat hooks, the crewmen steadied the aircraft as it was transported to the hangar bay door. The crew worked close to the edge of the railingless hangar door opening without wearing parachutes. With the pilot on board, the trapeze was attached to the F9C's crossbar by the skyhook attached above its top wing and lowered through the T-shaped opening that accommodated aircraft with a 30ft wingspan, 24ft overall length and a tailplane span of 10ft. With the aircraft now hanging in the furious slipstream, the airship crew lowered a power cable to the pilot that he plugged in to energize the electric starter. Once the engine was started, the pilot unplugged the power cable and was ready to launch his aircraft by pulling a handle in the cockpit that unlocked the spring-loaded hook. He then eased back somewhat on the control stick, causing lift to his wings, which took the aircraft's weight off the trapeze. The aircraft would then fall free in a short dive and the pilot quickly gained control. Occasionally, the aircraft's weight pulling down on the hook combined with the insufficient speed of the airship made unlocking difficult.

The Skyhook

The hook-on apparatus was subject to considerable experimentation before a satisfactory configuration was obtained. It is remarkable that although hundreds of hook-on and hook-off operations were performed, no mishap occurred where a pilot suffered injury, or an aircraft sustained major damage or disaster. During early hook-on attempts, one of the most troubling challenges that the pilots had to face was keeping the hook on the trapeze yoke during the initial instant of contact. The Vought OU-1's skyhook was shaped like a shepherd's crook with its forward end curving upward, giving it a shallow depth that did not allow sufficient hooking surface for the aircraft bouncing backward in the first second of contact. The hook's internal plane was designed for level approaches to the trapeze and was parallel to the aircraft's axis, making hook ons from a stalling attitude difficult. The hook's upturned end, which was intended to lead the hook over the trapeze yoke, actually hindered hook ons by providing a surface on which the aircraft too often bounced off the trapeze. Shortly after Lt Jake Gorton's July 1929 hook-on trials, the hook was modified, which made the procedure somewhat easier; but it was not until Calvin Bolster's redesign that the 'perfect' hook was realised. This hook was large and rugged; it offered about 200 degrees of opening between its jaws and achieved its hooking action by its forward end

Sparrowhawk hook-on apparatus. (*USN*)

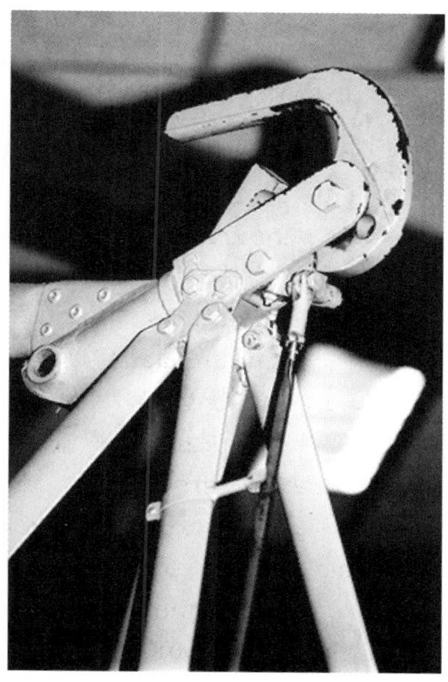
Calvin Bolster's redesign of the final 'perfect' hook. (*USN*)

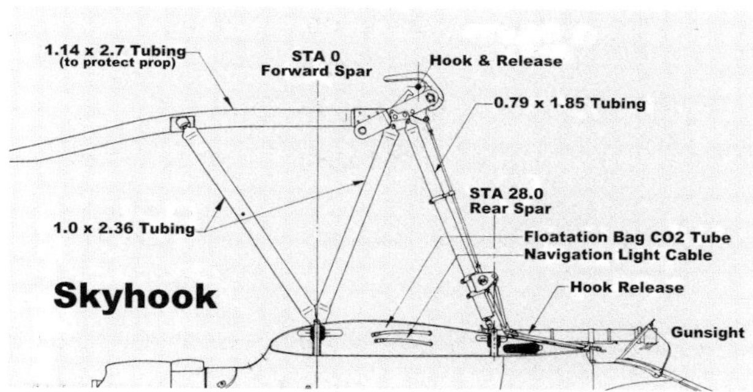

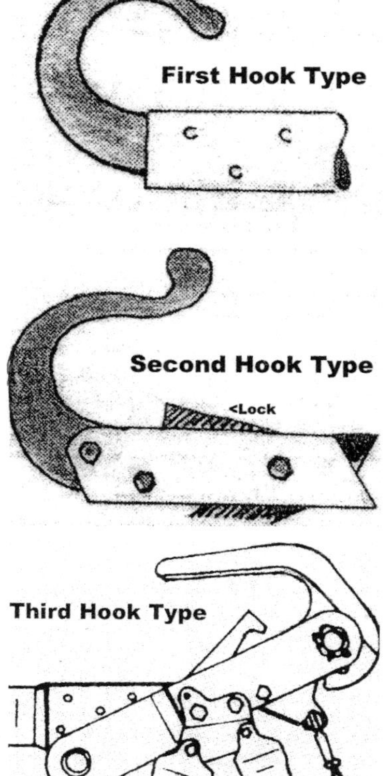

being canted down toward the aircraft's axis. However, most important, when the aircraft was approaching the trapeze in a nose-up attitude, the internal plane of the hook was parallel to the axis of the airship, which allowed the pilot to literally slide his hook on to the trapeze yoke.

It is noteworthy that during the Air Force's post-war October 1947 hook-on experiments involving the XP-85 Goblin jet parasite fighter and the B-29 the *Akron* and *Macon* trapeze design was resurrected. Because the Superfortress was not large enough to carry the XP-85 completely within its bomb bay, the Goblin needed to be carried on a trapeze with its lower fuselage suspended below the bomb bay and its folding wings remaining down and locked. Utilising the *Akron-Macon* airship trapeze layout, the Goblin's McDonnell's engineers designed their trapeze with the hook-on bar horizontal and with a horse collar stabilising gear to seize the XF-85's nose, holding it tightly during retraction and extension.

Hook-On and Hangar Storage Procedure

When the airship had reached the area where its scouting mission was to begin, its aircraft were flown off without the airship's buoyancy being affected. The procedure used in recovering its aircraft was to have the airship be at cruising altitude and speed, so that its dynamic lift would compensate for the additional weight of the aircraft when being taken aboard. The minimum altitude for hook-on operations was considered to be 800ft. During an airship hook-on operation, the airship cruised at maximum speed, with the parasite fighter approaching it at an airspeed just above stalling speed for the engaging operation. All hook-on operations were directed from a platform inside the bottom of the hangar. As the Sparrowhawks returned, the trapeze apparatus, located considerably aft of the airship's control car, about parallel to the airship's No. 1 engine, was suspended. On his hook-on approach the F9C-2 pilot closed alongside the airship control car and watched for the lowering of a green flag to signal him to come aboard. The airship's speed was crucial for successful hook ons. The airship was to increase its speed to a maximum of 85mph if all engines were at full throttle. Even at that speed the Sparrowhawks had to substantially reduce their airspeed to hook on, being careful not to fall below their 70mph stall speed. On closing towards the trapeze bar, the pilot had to adjust his throttle and climb, closing to about 25ft below the airship and just outboard of No. 1 engine, and then skid in under the airship, about 25ft behind and below the trapeze. The pilot aimed the skyhook toward the vee notch on the trapeze hook-on bar that centred the aircraft when it was hoisted aboard, which was essential because of the aircraft's small wing clearance into the hangar. If the pilot landed off centre, he had to kick the rudder and let his aircraft slide down into the centre vee notch. There was a pilot-operated cable release gear for use during a hook-on emergency. A bar was placed over the F9C's prop to prevent it from hitting the trapeze during hook on. There were tension springs on the trapeze bar to absorb the shock of an aircraft landing. Another flag from the airship cabin signalled to the pilot that his aircraft was properly hooked on and that a cable was ready to hoist the trapeze with the attached aircraft. Because there was so little clearance for the aircraft as it went through the hangar door, a device called a 'saddle' was lowered down on its fuselage, holding it steady fore and aft. As the trapeze and Sparrowhawk were raised toward the hangar, the pilot kept his engine idling and cut it as he passed through the door. Once inside, the aircraft was transferred from the trapeze to an overhead monorail trolley running diagonally into one of the four corners of the hangar to be refuelled and rearmed for immediate release or storage. After the aircraft were retrieved, hoisted, and secured within the hangar, its T-shaped opening was closed by a single sliding panel and two trap-type doors.

Hook-on problems could occur if the airship went into an unexpected turn or was not flying at the correct hook-on speed just as the pilot put his aircraft into the critical near

Sparrowhawk Recovery and Stowage

Two Sparrowhawks approach the *Macon* for retrieval. (*USN*)

Frame from a movie still showing the pilot's view of the approach to the trapeze. (*USN*)

On closing towards the trapeze bar, the F9C-2 pilot had to adjust his throttle and climb, closing to about 25ft below the airship and just outboard of the airship No. 1 engine, and then skid in under the airship, about 25ft behind and below the trapeze. (*USN*)

On his hook-on approach the F9C-2 pilot closed alongside the airship control car and watched for the lowering of a green flag to signal him to come aboard. (*USN*)

Another flag from the airship cabin signalled to the pilot that his aircraft was properly hooked on and that a cable was ready to hoist the trapeze with the attached aircraft. (*USN*)

After riding the monorail to its corner of the hangar, the Sparrowhawk hangs stowed to the hangar ceiling. (*USN*)

stall as it approached the trapeze. The pilot's only option, being unable to see the horizon, was to increase to full throttle to 'stagger' up to the trapeze bar while almost stalling, trying to move his hook up to place it on the centre of the trapeze bar. In rough weather the airship would often lunge downward, and the pilot would need to throttle down, to have the hook and bar make the necessary contact. Occasionally the aircraft stalled out and the pilot would have to dive and then go around for another trapeze approach. The pilot needed to keep his prop turning until he was certain he was locked aboard the trapeze as occasionally an unlocked aircraft would fall off it. If the pilot had shut down his engine, he could not restart it as his only external starter power source was on the airship. Also, it must be remembered that any trapeze malfunction would leave any airborne aircraft with nowhere to land, which was especially critical when the airship was patrolling miles offshore and the returning aircraft was low on fuel.

Harrigan-Bolster Scheme For Outside Aircraft Storage

During the summer of 1931, the *Akron* was rapidly approaching completion and while Ward Harrigan was stationed at Lakehurst, he familiarised himself with the airship's blueprints, the full-scale wooden mock-up of the *Akron*'s internal aircraft storage compartment and its aircraft-handling provisions. He concluded that the *Akron*'s internal stowage of the hook-on aircraft would impose significant limitations on their military efficacy.

Airships in immediate need of fighter protection against multiple enemy attackers would have to rely on the release of one fighter already hanging on the trapeze and then would have to wait a very long ten minutes to launch another fighter, moving it from the hangar on to the trapeze.

For adequate protection from enemy interceptors, the airship's aircraft scouting force needed to be as continuous as possible, using a maximum number of aircraft. Because the *Akron* could carry only three aircraft, and at least one needed to be held in reserve, the requirement for rapid servicing was particularly important. While the *Akron*'s internal hangar was suitable for extensive servicing, repairs and for in-flight stowage, under combat conditions its use would be problematic.

To avoid the chokepoint created by the *Akron*'s hangar door, Harrigan met with Calvin Bolster of the Naval Aircraft Factory to obtain an engineer's perspective and they developed a method in which, during a General Quarters situation, the hook-on aircraft could be hung outside the *Akron*'s hull where they could be kept on standby and, in an emergency, all could be released at once, instead of having to be lowered, one by one, outside the hangar on the trapeze. This plan would have supplemented, not replaced, the airship's internal hangar and would have served as an external 'flight deck' from which three or four aircraft could take off immediately instead of one at a time.

The Harrigan-Bolster scheme for outside stowage of the *Akron*'s hook-on aircraft proposed a 100ft-long monorail running along the airship's outer hull underside, immediately aft of the hangar, door with trolleys to accommodate three or four aircraft. The monorail would operate as the airship's 'flight deck', and would be utilised for all extensive flight operations.

The aircraft was to land on a trapeze at the far end of the external monorail track. This trapeze would swing the aircraft towards the track, where it would be transferred to a trolley on which it would be slid forward to make room for the next aircraft. Refuelling connections were to be placed along the monorail, together with ladders to facilitate the exchange of pilots. If an aircraft required extensive servicing, it would be taxied on its trolley to the forward end of the monorail, where the hangar trapeze would swing it up into the airship's hangar. All extensive flight operations would be carried on from this external track, while the internal hangar would only be used for independent flights, and for repairs and in-flight stowage.

The external monorail 'flight deck' would also allow larger ground-based aircraft arriving from ashore or those from aircraft carriers whose wing spans were too large to pass through the hangar door to be equipped with temporary skyhooks that would permit them to operate to and from the *Akron*'s trapeze, supplementing by almost doubling the airship's usual aircraft scouting force.

The Harrigan-Bolster external monorail scheme was received with interest by BuAer and Cdr Garland Fulton, Chief of the Lighter-Than-Air Design Section, who recommended that an experimental installation of the outside track be made aboard the *Los Angeles*. In the autumn of 1931, fabrication of this system was begun for the *Los Angeles*, but the project was temporarily abandoned due to Lakehurst's small engineering staff being overwhelmed by the delivery of the *Akron* and its multitude of teething problems. The scheme was finally waylaid when the *Los Angeles* was decommissioned during the summer of 1932.

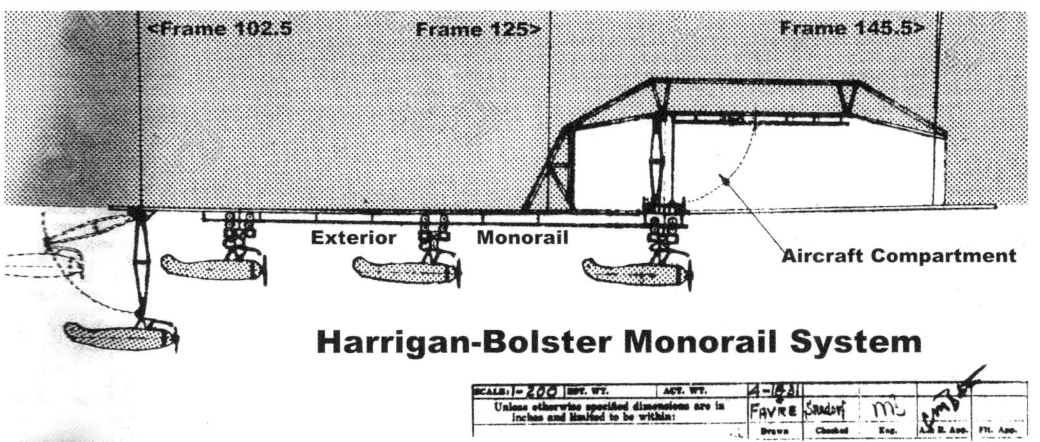

Perch

Although the elaborate Harrigan-Bolster exterior monorail track system was never installed, a compromise solution was to have additional F9Cs immediately ready for release by stationing them at exterior positions on the airship hull other than on the hangar trapeze. Dubbed 'perches', these small, simple, U-shaped bars on the exterior of the airship hull were essentially fixed auxiliary trapezes. One or even several perches could accommodate aircraft with their pilots seated and ready for immediate release to defend the airship, only

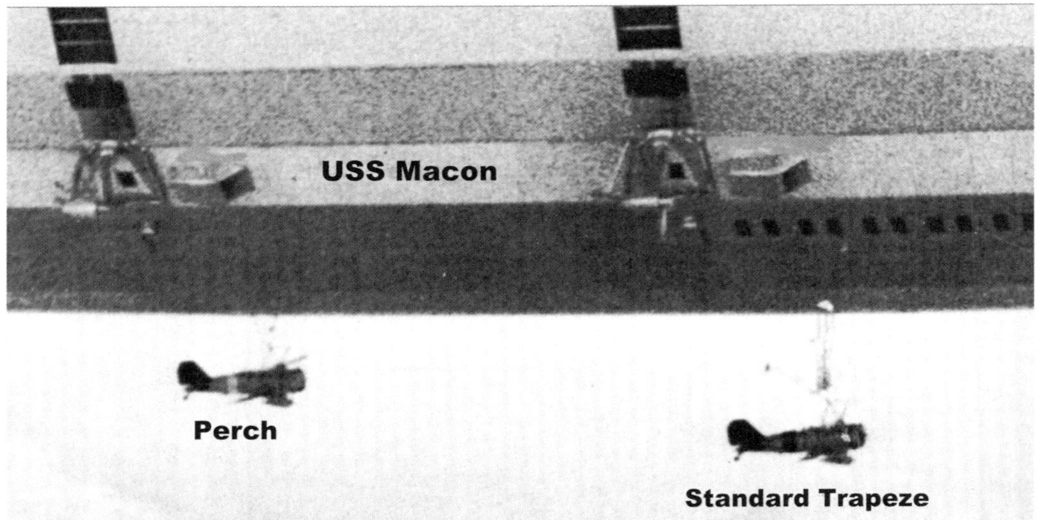

Perches were small, simple, U-shaped bars on the exterior of the airship hull essentially fixed auxiliary trapezes. Here *Macon* Sparrowhawks are attached to a perch (right, pilot Lt (JG) Fred Kivette) and trapeze (left, pilot Lt Harold 'Min' Miller) near Moffett Field on 12 October 1934. (*Frame from USN movie film*)

needing to start their engines and release the perch hooking mechanism. These perches also provided a returning fuel-starved aircraft a place to park while awaiting its turn on the trapeze for refuelling or stowage, or offered an emergency landing place if the main trapeze became inoperable. By 1933 a single, fixed perch trapeze was permanently rigged further aft along the bottom of the *Akron* at station 102.5, only about 5ft from the hull. Pilots found that it was much easier to hook on to the aft perch, closer to the airship, than it was on to the main trapeze, because the main trapeze received turbulence from the forward control car engines. Three more perches were planned (at stations 57.5, 80 and 147.5) but these were never installed and neither the *Akron* nor *Macon* ever had more than one.

The F9C-2 as Flying Ballast

One interesting use of the Sparrowhawks was to act as 'flying ballast' as the airship was unable to lift off with the aircraft on board and also because of additional ballast or fuel aboard. Once the airship was cruising, the aircraft would be flown aboard, the additional weight being supported by dynamic lift until the airship lightened. The airship's static condition was radically affected by its aircraft operations. When two F9Cs were launched, she immediately became 5,540lb lighter; with four, 11,080lb lighter. In this condition the airship had to fly dynamically, nose down, to prevent rising over pressure height. It required hours to compensate for the weight of the patrolling F9Cs and by that time they would usually be back on board.

Later *Macon* Airship Utility Aircraft

Although the Curtiss Sparrowhawk had established itself as the Navy's standard hook-on aircraft, the need arose for small utility aircraft to service the *Macon*.

Akron and *Macon* N2Y-1s

Delivered in mid-1930, these aircraft were originally intended to serve as the scouts for *Akron* and *Macon* airships until a suitable operational hook-on aircraft (the Sparrowhawk)

N2Y-1 (8604) *Akron* The N2Y-1s were initially tested on *Los Angeles* in 1931 and six (8600–8606) later served as training/familiarisation/liaison aircraft with *Akron*. (*USN*)

N2Y-1 *Macon* After *Akron*'s loss, three N2Y-1s (8604–8606) remained on board the *Macon* while 8600, 8601 and 8602 were detached and sent to the Naval Aircraft Factory for storage. (*USN*)

was procured. The N2Y-1s were tested on *Los Angeles* in 1931 and later served with the *Akron* and *Macon* as training and familiarisation trapeze hook-on aircraft (mostly with the *Akron*), liaison and taxi aircraft, and as targets for the *Akron*'s gun crews to practise their training camera gun skills. Three N2Y-1s, Nos. 8604–8606, remained with the *Macon*, while Nos. 8600, 8601 and 8602 were detached and sent to NAF for storage.

When the *Macon* flew west to its new base at Moffett Field in October 1933, one N2Y-1 (8604) joined the airship there. On 17 July 1934, it was destroyed during a training crash while simulating an emergency landing.

Waco UBF/XJW-1

During 1933, once the new *Macon* became operational, the Navy required a small utility aircraft to augment to the dirigible's HTA Unit. Although the N2Y-1 had served competently as a hook-on trainer and as 'running boats' to and from the *Los Angeles* and *Akron*, it had limited load capacity, speed and range. The Bureau of Aeronautics examined the civilian aircraft market for a replacement with increased range and payload and yet would be small enough to fit into the airship's hangar (following some minor wingtip trimming).

During early January 1934, the Navy issued a contract to the Waco Aircraft Company, Troy, Ohio, one of the leading American manufacturers of open-cockpit training and sports biplanes since 1926, for two modified XJW versions of its UBF biplane. The two XJW-1s (BuNos. 9521 and 9522), procured on contract No. 34222 of 9 January 1934, were modifications of the Waco UBF, a three-place sport plane (two passengers side by side in the front cockpit, ahead of the pilot). They were purchased 'off the shelf' from the civil aircraft market because there was nothing of similar performance in the Navy inventory that would fit through the *Macon*'s hangar door.

Several months later, on 16 March 1934, the Navy received BuNos. 9521 and 9522 at Moffett, after both had been equipped with skyhooks at the Naval Aircraft Factory over their upper wing for engaging the *Macon*'s trapeze. Like the N2Y-1 configuration, their top fuselage sheet metal covering could be removed to accommodate a patient's evacuation litter. Trials were satisfactory and the Waco became *Macon*'s utility aircraft. Neither was on board the *Macon* when she crashed off the California coast on 12 February 1935.

Waco UBF/XJW-1 Specifications and Performance

Specifications
Crew: 1 plus 1 trainee or passenger
Length: 23ft 1in (7.04m)
Height: 8ft 5in (2.57m)
Wingspan: 30ft (9.14m)
Wing Area: 244 sq ft (22.67 sq m)
Empty Weight: 1,870lb (848.22kg)
Gross Weight: 2,650lb (1,202.02kg)
Powerplant: 1 × 220hp Continental W-670-6A seven-cylinder radial engine

Performance
Maximum Speed: 128mph (207kmph)
Cruise Speed: 114mph (185kmph)
Range: 400 miles (644km)
Service Ceiling: 14,800ft (4,511m)

Waco XJW. The Navy purchased two civilian Waco sport biplanes and modified them with skyhooks at the Naval Aircraft Factory as XJWs, 9521 (shown) and 9522, where they served the *Macon* as utility aircraft at Moffett Field. (*USN*)

Martin T4M-1

The previous study for a service and utility aircraft for refuelling the airship aloft was revived by Lt Cdr Charles Rosendahl, who had recently returned from sea duty to take command of the Lakehurst Airship Station. Adm. King approved of the project and provided a Martin T4M-1 (BuNo. 7640), then in storage at the Naval Aircraft Factory, which was to be modified for its new use. The T4M-1 was a large, single-engined, three-seat, obsolete biplane that had been the standard USN torpedo bomber of the mid-1920s, flying off the carriers *Saratoga* and *Lexington*. The aircraft was modified into a cargo-tanker weighing 5,900lb including a cargo of 1,000lb but could only carry 166 gallons of fuel, which was to be pumped aboard the *Macon* while hanging on its trapeze. In a study of the Martin's fuel tanker viability, Garland Fulton calculated that during the time required to transfer 166 gallons, nearly half would be expended by the *Macon* during the process and that a minimum of 500 gallons needed to be transferred to make the project viable. Fulton also determined that the aircraft's 5,900lb weight would exceed the safety limit of 4,500lb gross weight of the trapeze and airship frame 125 it hung on. The expense to strengthen this frame was prohibitive and the Navy had no aircraft of 4,500lb gross weight that included a 1,000lb payload. It investigated five commercial aircraft prospects but none could carry more than 160 gallons of cargo fuel. Adm. King recommended that the project be discontinued and while the T4M-1 joined the *Macon* aircraft complement in California, it was only used as a no hook-on, ground-back-to-ground transport, meeting the *Macon* between moorings.

Martin T4M-1 (7640) was a large, single-engined, three-seat, obsolete biplane that had been the standard USN torpedo bomber of the mid-1920s and was taken out of storage for use with the *Macon*. It was initially modified for use as a utility aircraft for refuelling the airship aloft but was only used as a no hook-on, ground-back-to-ground transport meeting to supply the *Macon* between moorings. (*USN*)

The 'Spy Basket'

Although not a powered aircraft, the 'spy basket' deserves mention here as it was manned and did 'hook on' to the *Akron*. The spy basket was variously known as a 'spy car', 'angel basket', or more officially as the 'sub-cloud observation post'. The concept was originally developed by the Zeppelin company as the Spähgondel or Spähkorb and was used as an observation means during the First World War by the German Army and Navy. The German version looked like a small, rotund bomb with its enclosed prone pilot being lowered on a 2,460 to 3,300ft-long winch cable. The US Army's version was the 'cloud car' deployed from a blimp.

The Navy version was a small wingless aircraft fuselage with an open cockpit, a seat, tail fin, and rudder pedals that only gave the pilot marginal control to steer the basket left and right. It was lowered through the airship's trapeze door on 1,000ft of 0.25in cable with a microphone connection for telephone communication to the spy in the basket below while the dirigible stayed hidden in the clouds. The spy basket was difficult to control, open to the elements, and even its toughest occupant was assured of acute airsickness. On its first

The spy basket, also known as the 'spy car', was lowered from the airship's trapeze door on a 4,000ft cable with a microphone connection for telephone communication to spy on the enemy below while the dirigible stayed hidden in the clouds. (*Frame from USN movie still*)

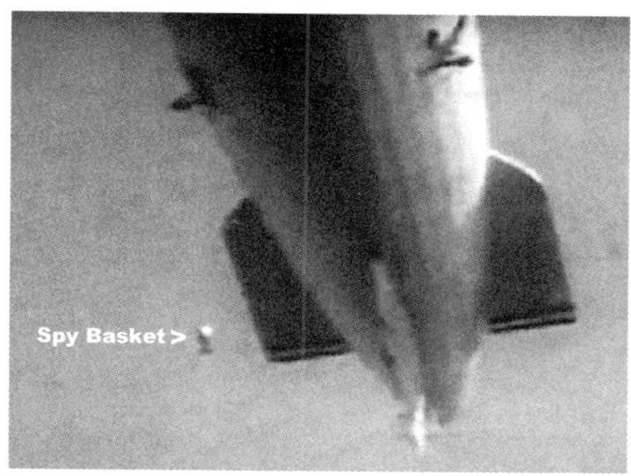

The spy basket was open to the elements, and even its toughest occupant was assured of acute airsickness. Worst of all, it was difficult to control and is shown in this movie still swinging alongside the airship's lower hull. (*Frame from USN movie still*)

use the basket was tested with a dummy, weighted with sandbags and lowered 1,000ft. Soon it was flying alongside the *Akron* and quickly zoomed up to the airship's midline, stalled and dropped quickly, only to zoom up the airship's opposite side. Rosendahl slowed the *Akron*, and the spy basket was reeled into the *Akron* for the last time to be shipped off to an outside facility for study. The spy basket would be resurrected during 1934 aboard the *Macon*.

Chapter Seven

The *Akron* Flying Aircraft Carrier Operations 1931 to 1933 Crash

Introduction: The *Akron* Described

Goodyear-Zeppelin's design for the USS *Akron* stipulated a huge airship measuring 785ft long with a maximum diameter of 132ft 11in and weighing 242,356lb. It had an operational gas volume of 6,850,000 million cu ft of helium in eleven gas cells that gave it a total lift of 403,000lb. She was powered by eight 560hp Maybach 12-cylinder V-type water-cooled engines, mounted inside the hull and driving their propellers via extension shafts. Airships and balloons are aerostats because they obtain their lift aerostatically rather than aerodynamically. Briefly, static entails no motion while dynamic does. Aerostatic lift is obtained without the use of motion from propellers or other thrust, while aerodynamic lift does require propellers or some other means of thrust. The benefit of aerostatic flight is that much less energy is required since the lifting gas, rather than propellers, generates most of the lift. The Maybach engines gave it a maximum designed speed of 87mph (140kmph), an a maximum range of 6,836 miles at 63.3mph speed. *Akron* had a flight crew of ten officers and fifty enlisted men, plus a HTA group of four officers and fifteen aircraft mechanics. Its aircraft complement was as many as four Curtiss F9C-2 Sparrowhawk fighters, launched and recovered via a mechanical trapeze extended below the airship's hangar compartment. Building upon the mistakes of the USS *Shenandoah* and the successes of the USS *Los Angeles*, the *Akron* incorporated many new and innovative design features. The *Akron*'s total cost of $4.5 million ($100 million in 2025) made it the most expensive aircraft ever built up to that time.

Construction of the *Akron* (ZRS-4) began on 31 October 1929 at the Goodyear Airdock in Springfield Township, Ohio, by the Goodyear-Zeppelin Corporation under the direction of a team of experienced German airship engineers, led by Chief Designer Karl Arnstein, who had supervised the design of both the *Akron* and *Macon* and would later construct the *Macon*. Secretary of the Navy Charles Francis Adams chose the name *Akron* for the city near where it was built. The airship was christened by the First Lady, Lou Henry Hoover, on 5 August 1931 in ceremonies held inside the Goodyear-Zeppelin hangar. The ceremony was presided over by R. Adm. William Moffett, Chief of BuAer; and David Ingalls, Assistant Secretary of the Navy for Aviation.

By 1930, while the construction of the *Akron* was ongoing, the Curtiss XF9C-2 Sparrowhawk had been chosen as suitable for airship launching and recovery, and an operational trapeze system had been designed, constructed, and tested on the *Los Angeles*. The first phase in flying aircraft to and from the airships was the organisation and training

After nearly two years of construction, the *Akron* left the Goodyear Airdock for its first flight on 23 September 1931 piloted by veteran airship commander Lt Cdr Charles Rosendahl, who would then fly her to her new home at NAS Lakehurst (shown). (*USN*)

of their HTA units. The Bureau of Navigation (then responsible for Navy personnel) called for volunteers for aircraft flight duty aboard airships and their ranks were immediately filled by exceptionally talented pilots, to augment veterans Ward Harrigan and Howard Young, who had flown hook-on operations with the *Los Angeles*.

A Question of Airship Vulnerability and Defences

After her commissioning in October 1931, there were great expectations for the *Akron* despite her being effectively in the shakedown, experimental phase without the internal aircraft hangar completed or trapeze installed. But in a 17 October 1931 letter to Capt. H. E. Schoemaker, Commander, NAS Lakehurst, Admiral Moffett began to increase pressure on the lighter-than-air branch:

> We are now at the threshold of a great opportunity, and I feel that all lighter-than-air personnel must realise this or be made to realise it and see that these ships operate to the fullest possible amount. If they cannot operate as I have indicated, then they are of little value, and we might as well abandon them. It may be advisable to take one of these ships out and keep her out, even looking for bad weather, to see what she can do; if necessary, protecting the personnel by making everyone on board wear a parachute, so we can actually find out what these ships can really do, and whether or not they are of any value.

In the upper Navy echelons, there existed a general bias against the *Akron* due to its supposed vulnerability as a huge target for enemy dive bombers and fighters. The lasting impressions of old-line US Naval officers was the spectacular images of First World War hydrogen-filled German Zeppelins falling in flames after being attacked by British fighters.

While Lt Cdr Rosendahl assumed that the *Akron* would be able to repel its attackers with its own armament and hook-on aircraft, an airship's vulnerability to machine gun fire was also found to be less than expected. The helium that supported the *Akron* was not flammable and would suffocate a fire. Many bullet hits striking the gas cells' upper areas would be required to cause depressurisation or structural damage but they would not cause a devastating fire or explosion. The gas in the cells was not pressurised and the pressure was so small that it was measured not in pounds per square inch but in inches of water. Excluding large tears in the tops of the cells, gas loss would be relatively small and at a slow rate, while even a very large hole in a cell bottom would inflict a negligible loss of helium, which exerted upward pressure and did not leak downward. Fighters of the early 1930s were armed with small twin .30-calibre machine guns, which only in a massive, concerted attack would be capable of destroying an airship.

A bomb hit would most likely pass straight through the airship without exploding unless it hit and exploded on a main frame, a keel, or an engine room, in which case it would probably be fatal to the airship. Later, hook-on pilots flying simulated attacks on the airship indicated that conventional dive-bombing attacks by 150–250mph aircraft against the 75–85mph *Akron*, which took evasive action, were mostly unproductive.

Akron Flying Aircraft Carrier Operations 1931–33

First Flights

Akron made its first flight on 23 September 1931, commanded by Lt Cdr Charles Rosendahl, with Secretary of the Navy Charles Frances Adams and R. Adm. William Moffett on board. The *Akron* then made ten trial flights before being commissioned on Navy Day 27 October 1931 as a Navy 'vessel'. On 2 November 1931, BuAer and the Navy Department sent the *Akron* on its official maiden voyage, flying south down the eastern seaboard to Washington, DC. The next day the *Akron* set the world's aircraft record by taking 207 passengers aboard. Over the subsequent weeks she logged more than 300 hours aloft from its Lakehurst base, including a 48-hour endurance/publicity flight over the Midwest. Ambitious plans scheduled but not culminated were a proposed 7,000-mile 'rim flight' around the continental United States and a flight to Hawaii to join Fleet Problem XIII during February 1932.

1932 Operations

From 9 to12 January 1932, the *Akron* participated in exercises with the Scouting Fleet off the US east coast on a search mission and was considered to have 'achieved a qualified success' but its 'performance could have been better with radio detection finding equipment, and scout planes'. During these exercises its aircraft handling provisions were incomplete and she did not operate the scout planes.

On 22 February 1932, while exiting the Lakehurst hangar an unexpectedly strong wind drove the airship's ventral tail fin into the ground, causing damage that required six weeks to repair. (*USN*)

The NAF was officially contracted for *Akron*'s trapeze in late December 1931 with completion and installation due for February 1932. Accordingly, when the *Akron* participated in January 1932 scouting exercises with the Fleet, Lt Cdr Rosendahl was unable to employ aircraft for reconnaissance. These exercises concluded with mixed results, as while the *Akron* located the enemy forces using direct scouting methods, the enemy also located the *Akron*.

Although the installation of the *Akron*'s trapeze continued 'as in progress', she was scheduled to participate in Fleet Problem XIII, the one-month Army/Navy Grand Joint Exercise 4 Blue, based in Hawaii, during March. During February 1932, Adm. Moffett invited members of the House Naval Affairs Committee to fly in the *Akron* to 'dispel their concerns about the rigid airship's military worthlessness'. While exiting the Lakehurst hangar, an unexpectedly strong wind severed her aft mooring line, causing the airship's ventral tail fin to strike the ground and causing damage that required six weeks of repairs.

Throughout March and most of April, the *Akron* was hangar-bound undergoing repairs to its damaged fin. This two-month hiatus gave the Naval Aircraft Factory the opportunity to cannibalise *Los Angeles*' trapeze for parts to complete the *Akron*. *Akron* was not certified as airworthy again until later in that spring, at which time its trapeze was

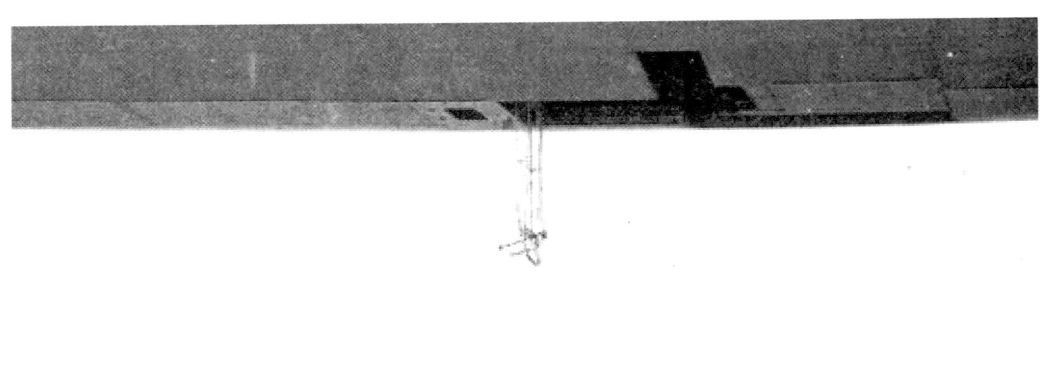

On 3 May 1932, *Akron* cruised over the New Jersey coast to test the trapeze installation for the first time. Lieutenants Ward Harrigan and Howard Young alternated in their Consolidated N2Y-1 trainers, hooking on and dropping off, while being filmed by a cameraman in another aircraft. (*USN*)

As a finale, Harrigan flew the new, larger, heavier, and more powerful XF9C-1 to successfully demonstrate its hook-on capabilities. A view from the *Akron*'s hangar door shows Lt Ward Harrigan approaching the trapeze to accomplish the first Sparrowhawk hook on. (*USN*)

completed, installed, and ready for hook-on retrieval and launch trials. On 28 April the *Akron* was ready to fly again and took Adm. Moffett and Secretary of the Navy Charles Adams aboard.

On 3 May 1932, *Akron* cruised over the New Jersey coast to test the trapeze installation for the first time for in-flight handling of aircraft. R. Adm. George Day, the President of the Board of Inspection and Survey, and members of that BIS were on board to assess the trapeze. Lieutenants Harrigan and Young alternated in their Consolidated N2Y-1 trainers, hooking on and dropping off, while being filmed by a cameraman in another aircraft. As a finale, Harrigan flew the new, larger, heavier, and more powerful XF9C-1 to successfully demonstrate its hook-on capabilities. The following day, *Akron* performed another demonstration flight, this time with members of the House Committee on Naval Affairs on board and Harrigan and Young gave the Congressmen a demonstration of *Akron*'s ability to handle and store parasite aircraft.

Following the conclusion of those successful flight trials, on 8 May 1932 *Akron* departed Lakehurst for Sunnyvale, California, for exercises with the Pacific Fleet. After *Akron* took off, Harrigan followed in the XF9C-1 and Young and passenger Lt Scott Peck in the N2Y-1. They hooked on and were stowed in the airship's hangar to continue to the west coast. The reason for this procedure was so that the aircraft's weight was not part of the airship's static lift during its take-off. Once the *Akron* was airborne, it generated enough dynamic lift to easily transport the additional weight of the aircraft down the Eastern Seaboard, across the Gulf Coast towards Texas and the challenging New Mexico desert and mountain passes.

The *Akron* arrived for its final stop at Camp Kearny (MCAS Miramar), San Diego, on 10 May to moor, refuel, then launch to join the Scouting Fleet in the Pacific during the next morning. Harrigan in the XF9C-1 and Young and Peck in the N2Y-1 launched from the *Akron*. The reason for Peck flying as a passenger in the N2Y was that not only was he the *Akron*'s cross-country navigator but also was the airship's mooring officer on the ground. Mooring was problematic at Camp Kearny, where the Navy had recently installed a mast. Young transported Peck to the ground to aid in the mooring by poorly trained ground handlers, who did not have all the specialised mechanical equipment available. During the flight *Akron*'s helium gas had been warmed by sunlight, increasing lift, and the

Prior to mooring, Lt Scott Peck, the *Akron*'s mooring officer, was flown as a passenger in the N2Y to Camp Kearny to aid in the mooring by poorly trained ground handlers, which led to the death of two mooring men. Peck was one of the few airship and aeroplane-qualified pilots and would later become a lieutenant commander and full commander during the Second World War. (*USN*)

The *Akron* moored outdoors at NAS Sunnyvale, California, with its uncompleted hangar in the background. (*USN*)

During its west coast sojourn, the *Akron* spent much of its time cruising California's central valleys and coast (shown over San Francisco) and then made a good showing in the Fleet scouting exercises. (*USN*)

airship became uncontrollably light. The attached mooring cable had to be cut to prevent a catastrophic nose stand, and the *Akron* then floated upward. Most of the inexperienced mooring crew released their lines, although four did not and hung on; two plunging to their deaths.

After her arrival at Sunnyvale, over the following weeks the *Akron* 'showed the flag' over the west coast, ranging as far north as the Canadian border. *Akron* participated in her second, and final, exercise with the Scouting Fleet, serving as part of the Green Force attempting to locate the White Force. The *Akron* failed to employ her aircraft due to Lt Cdr Rosendahl's preference for direct observation scouting methods. Subsequently, the *Akron* came under attack by enemy aircraft multiple times, confirming senior officers' opinions concerning the 'vulnerability' of the rigid airship during Fleet operations.

In need of maintenance and repairs, *Akron* departed Sunnyvale on 11 June 1932 bound for Lakehurst, proceeding on a laboured cross-country flight. After servicing, at Lakehurst the *Akron* engaged in local flights for the remainder of July and into August, collecting data on fuel consumption, water recovery rates; and speeds at different flight modes that would later prove useful in determining improvements to be incorporated into the new airship *Macon* (ZRS-5), then under construction.

Dresel Replaces Rosendahl in Command of the *Akron*

After eight months in command of the new *Akron*, on 22 June 1932, Lt Cdr Rosendahl was relieved by Cdr Alger Dresel. During this time USN senior officers and Rosendahl repeated First World War German Zeppelin tactics by regarding the rigid airship as primarily a reconnaissance platform to directly observe and track enemy ground units. Rosendahl's predilection for these outdated German airship tactics was probably due to his collaborations with Zeppelin commanders Ernst Lehmann and Hugo Eckener. By the 1930s, owing to the advances in aircraft performance and the widespread implementation of Fleet-based aviation, German First World War direct observation techniques were considered dangerous. Because of Rosendahl's assessments of rigid airship predominance, he regarded the *Akron*'s on-board aircraft as supplementary and defensive, and they were seldom employed during exercises. In the *Akron*'s final Fleet exercise, Rosendahl had his aircraft remain at Lakehurst and then only brought them on board

Cdr Alger Dresel relieved Rosendahl of his command of the *Akron* on 22 June 1932. (*USN*)

at the time to land the airship, using their weight as ballast. During Fleet exercises, the Navy brass' assessments of rigid airship vulnerability and obsolescence were bolstered when the *Akron* was encountered and 'destroyed' by enemy aircraft several times while directly observing enemy surface units.

New Pilot Arrivals

During June 1932, vital for the *Akron*'s future as a flying aircraft carrier was that Harrigan and Young were joined by lieutenants (junior grade) Harold 'Min' Miller, Robert 'Swede' Larson, and Frederick 'Nappy' Kivette, who reported for duty with the HTA Unit. A sixth pilot, Lt (JG) Frederick Trapnell arrived in July. Also, during June the first F9C-2, the production model XF9C-1 fighter, was received at Lakehurst for trials. These new pilots and their new aircraft would require hundreds of hours of training for the HTV unit to become a proficient scouting element, which would not be entirely accomplished while serving with the *Akron*.

Robert 'Swede' Larson. (*USN*)

After his 1924 graduation from the USNA, Ensign Robert 'Swede' Larson served aboard the USS *Rochester* from July 1924 to October 1927, after which Lieutenant (Junior Grade) Larson was assigned for flight instruction at NAS Pensacola, Florida. After receiving his wings during July 1928, Larson was assigned to Scouting Plane Squadron (VS) 3B, aboard the USS *Lexington*, where he served until October 1930. He then returned NAS Pensacola, where he was stationed until his assignment to the Rigid Airship Training & Experimental Squadron, USS *Akron*.

Following graduation from the Naval Academy in 1924, Harold 'Min' Miller, spent two years on the battleship USS *California* (BB-44) before going to flight training. As an aviator, he was initially on the battleship USS *West Virginia* (BB-48) and then the carrier USS *Langley* (CV-1) before joining the *Akron*. During his HTA tenure Miller wrote the first of his popular 'Bob Wakefield' aviation stories for boys.

Harold 'Min' Miller. (*USN*)

Frederick 'Nappy' Kivette graduated from the Naval Academy in 1925 and continued to flight school. He received his Naval Aviator rating at Pensacola in 1928 as a fighter pilot. He was stationed at San Diego from 1929 into 1932, where he was assigned to the aerobatic team named the *Nine High Hats* of the VF-1, the High Hat Squadron, which performed in Clark Gable's 1931 movie *Hell Divers* flying Boeing F2Bs.

Ensign Fred Trapnell graduated from the Naval Academy in 1923 and after serving for two years at sea on the battleship USS *California* and the cruiser USS *Marblehead*, he was assigned to NAS Pensacola in 1926 for flight training. During 1927 he was assigned to Torpedo Squadron 1-S attached to the Fleet Air Base, Norfolk, Virginia, and later operated with aircraft squadrons, battle Fleet. In March 1928 he joined Fighting Squadron 5. He transferred to San Diego aboard the aircraft carrier USS *Lexington*. In 1930, he was transferred to the Flight Test Section at NAS Anacostia. In June of that year, along with two other pilots, he was assigned to a new unit, the Three Flying

Frederick 'Nappy' Kivette (centre) posing earlier with the Nine High Hats aerobatic team. (*USN*)

Frederick Trapnell (centre) as part of the Three Flying Fish, the Navy's first official aerial demonstration team. (*USN*)

Akron HTA Unit 1932. (*USN*)

Fish, the Navy's first official aerial demonstration team. Flying specially modified Curtiss F6C-4 biplanes, they toured across America performing intricate, aerobatic exhibitions. After the team was disbanded in April 1931, Trapnell was soon assigned to the small plane unit attached to the USS *Akron*.

Once they arrived at Lakehurst, the new pilots were familiarised with the trapeze by Harrigan and Young, who enlightened them through lectures and films on the art of hooking on. On 14 July, all pilots were flying their N2Ys for their initial trapeze hook-on

British airship pioneer RAF Squadron Leader Ralph Booth. (*RNAS*)

attempts. After watching Harrigan and Young make a few successful attempts, the rookie pilots followed and at the end of the practice they had made fifty-four successful hook ons. During one of these hook ons a N2Y's hook seized, and *Akron* officer Lt Roland Mayer, clambered down the trapeze from the airship, slipped into the N2Y's front cockpit, and hammered the hook's cam loose.

During July the British airship pioneer RAF Squadron Leader Ralph Booth came on board the *Akron* as an observer. Booth had been the captain of the privately built British airship R100 on its successful crossing and return across the Atlantic during July–August 1930 but following the crash of R101 in October 1930 the Imperial Airship Scheme was terminated and R100 was scrapped. Booth witnessed all six of the *Akron*'s N2Y pilots practise on the trapeze and was duly impressed by the Navy's progress in LTA aeronautics.

Akron Repaired and Continues Operations

Repairs to the *Akron*'s lower fin, damaged during a ground-handling accident on 22 February 1932, were not completed until 21 September. During this time Harrigan and his pilots had ferried all six F9C-2s from the Buffalo Curtiss factory to Lakehurst and by the end of the year, the *Akron* HTA Unit would comprise all the F9C-2s, one XF9C-1, one F6C-3 and three N2Y-1s. One additional XF9C-2 (BuNo. 9264) would be delivered to Lakehurst in January 1933. The BuAer informed the *Akron* that these aircraft would be its last and four of them would have to be transferred to the *Macon* when she was commissioned.

After the *Akron*'s fin repairs were completed, she made eight extended flights over the Atlantic until the end of 1932 during operations involving intensive work with the trapeze and the F9C-2s, as well as the drilling of lookouts and gun crews, with the Sparrowhawks simulating attacks. Among the tasks undertaken were two aircraft patrolling and scouting the *Akron*'s flanks.

During the first week of November, Garland Fulton visited Lakehurst and boarded the *Akron* during a twenty-three-hour flight. Also on board was Capt. Ernest King of the Naval War College, who had previously shown little interest in the rigid airship but now did so as it was the only potential means of very long-range reconnaissance available. On this flight King observed the first tests of the Trapnell-modified trapeze and became impressed by the possibilities demonstrated by the scouting aircraft-carrying ability of the *Akron*.

'60-60' Scouting System

During late 1932, the Sparrowhawk pilots began to use the scouting tactic called '60-60', which allowed them to fly further away from the airship with the assurance of a safe return, thus extending the airship's vision well beyond the horizon. Lt Donald Mackey, a Lakehurst station officer, had developed this pre-navigation system while at the Naval Postgraduate School studying the application of vector analysis to relative motion problems. The secret of the 60-60 system was uncomplicated as two F9Cs flew in different directions at angles of 60 degrees relative to the longitudinal line of the airship and maintained a speed exactly twice the speed of the airship. After any period, the pilots could turn 120 degrees and meet with the airship. The first flight using MacKey's 60-60 system was conducted on 18

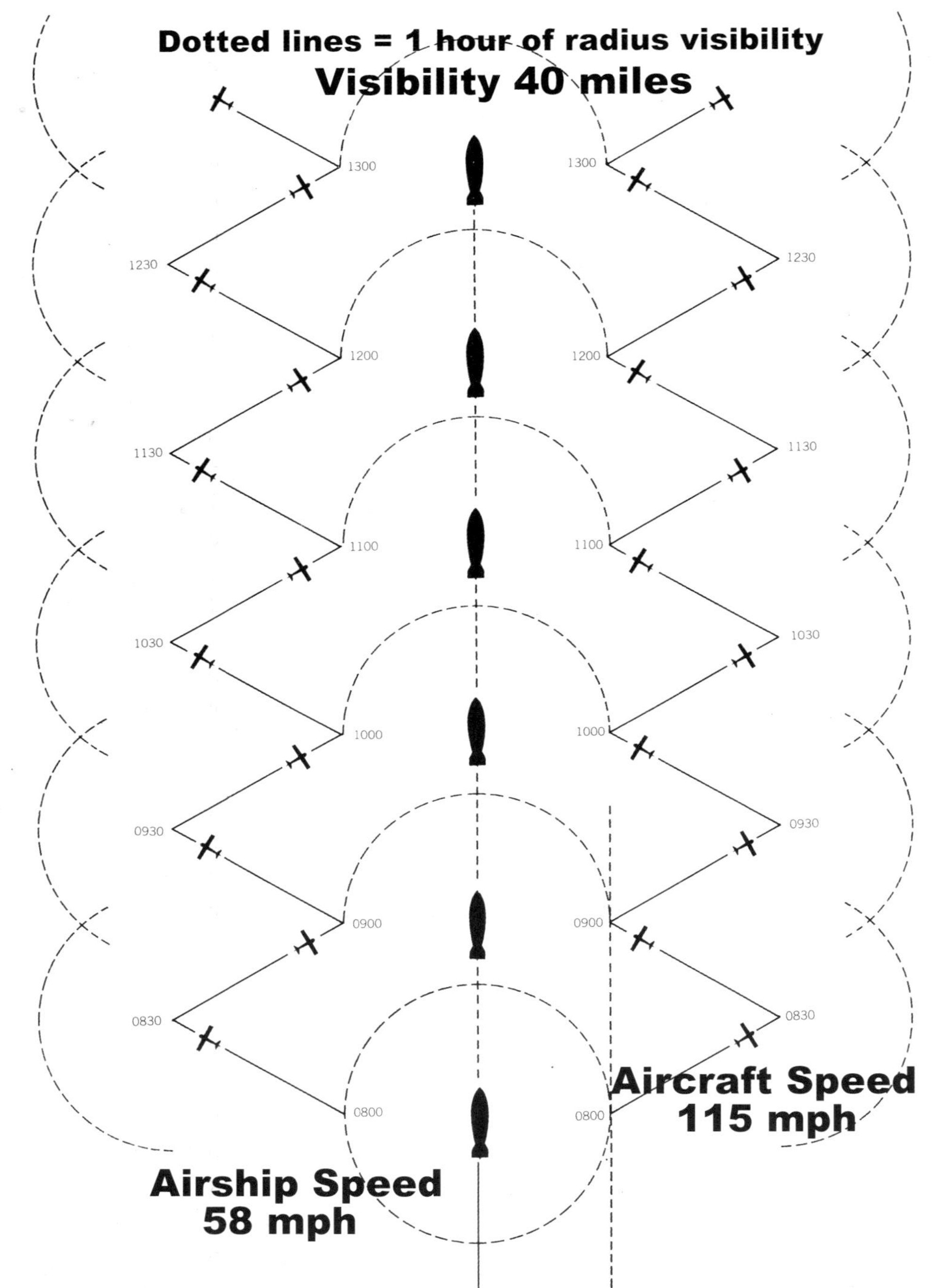

60-60 Search System

November 1932, with the *Akron* sweeping the Atlantic coast south of New York City. The flight was flown along the coast so that if any of the aircraft encountered difficulties, they would be able to divert to a landing field ashore. The Sparrowhawks were to fly relatively close, 20–30 miles, to the airship because of their inadequate and unreliable homing and radio equipment that was intended to home on the airship's radio signal. The F9C's radio communication transmitting/receiving sets had only a range of about 25 miles, so it was risky to be out of visual contact with the airship when operating at sea. During the test the *Akron* and its three aircraft maintained their scouting line on a path 100 miles wide for seven hours. During that afternoon, 'Swede' Larson approached the trapeze to refuel but due to a mechanical glitch in the trapeze he had to search for a landing field in Maryland. Although the trapeze was repaired in twenty minutes, its failure underlined the need for the 'perch' auxiliary trapeze.

The 60-60 scouting tests were considered productive, and with upgraded radios and navigation equipment, it was determined that an airship with two scouting aircraft deployed could sweep an area 200 miles wide, at 70mph over twelve hours of daylight covering an impressive 165,000 square miles of ocean. While these exploratory trials were a limited success, navigation and communications would be two important issues that would hinder a more rapid development. The small aerobatic F9C-2 demanded its pilot's complete attention and had only elementary navigation devices, and its cramped cockpit allowed its pilot no room to unfold and study navigation charts and maps. The F9C's radio homing equipment and its radio communication sets would remain unreliable until replaced in 1934.

However, there was the increasing demand by airship proponents for the Sparrowhawk's employment as a scout and to appoint a flight control officer (Mackey), a position that was opposed by senior BuAer officers, who continued to insist that the Sparrowhawk was a fighter, not a scout. They maintained that the aircraft would only operate as the airship's defensive screen and were not to be deployed very far from the vulnerable and costly weapon.

Harrigan Report

In mid-December 1932, Cdr Alger Dresel received a forty-two-page report composed by HTA leader Lt Ward Harrigan that was thought to be one of the most significant documents of the Navy's LTA/hook-on era. Considering that at the time the HTA Unit had had only four months of periodic and tenuous hook-on experience with the *Akron*, the Harrigan Report was thoughtful and comprehensive and would delineate the military future for the rigid airship during the 1930s.

The Harrigan Report began by recapping the history of hook-on development and described the technical aspects of the *Akron*'s aircraft-handling facilities; pilot training doctrine; and hook-on technique and hazards. However, the most important subjects broached 'scouting', 'communications' and 'future projects'.

Harrigan's narrative on 'Scouting' disclosed nothing fundamentally different, but it restated and detailed viewpoints he expressed in a 1931 thesis that characterised the

Akron, 'not as an airship' but as a 'carrier'. Harrigan began this segment of the report by opening with a restatement that the mission of aircraft operating from a LTA carrier was to broaden the scouting operations of the airship carrier, and that providing the airship with fighter protection was a 'collateral' duty. Harrigan considered the prospect of the airship establishing contact with the enemy to be 'decidedly dangerous'. He maintained that the airship's principal method of protection was to have its aircraft act as 'pickets', stationed far out on its flanks and ahead of her, where they would make the first contact with the approaching enemy and warn the airship so she could turn away and remain unobserved.

Harrigan stressed the lack of adequate radio equipment used for communication and navigation. The F9Cs could communicate with the airship by telegraphic key over 200–250 miles, but only under the very advantageous atmospheric conditions could their radio-telephone sets be depended on for more than 35 to 50 miles. The F9Cs' radio sets were not shielded from the aircraft's ignition system interference and until this was realised, airship/aircraft scouting would have to continue within visibility of the airship. Accurate navigation was the crux of accurate scouting and Harrigan again recommended establishing a 'flight control officer' who would be posted in the airship's navigation compartment. This officer would maintain a plot on the launched aircraft's positions and direct their navigation and courses by radio communication. Besides simplifying flying for its HTA pilots, the airship would have control over its aircraft and independence in its own movements. The airship could correlate the navigation of its aircraft with its own movements, and, if a major course change was necessary, it would be able to do so immediately and direct its launched aircraft to a new rendezvous rather than having to wait for them at the original rendezvous point. However, the flight control officer would not become a reality until 1934, again delayed by the development of dependable radio communication out to 200 to 250 miles.

As part of the 'future projects', the report recommended more perches, improvement of the *Akron*'s hangar aircraft servicing facilities, and the development of a reliable radio homing apparatus. Harrigan suggested the experimental installation of wing slots or flaps on one of the F9Cs to reduce its landing speed, which would allow the airship to reduce its own speed during aircraft recovery operations and so cut the *Akron*'s fuel consumption. The removal of the F9C's landing gear was anticipated as a wheel landing gear was unnecessary during trapeze operations and during over-water flying; its removal would reduce drag and increase the F9C's performance.

Lt Daniel Ward Harrigan, Senior Aviator, HTA Unit, composed the Harrigan Report, which was thought to be one of the most significant documents of the Navy's LTA/ hook-on era. (*USN*)

The report's significance was that it defined the reasons for a rigid airship's military future and two years later its substance became the *Macon*'s aircraft operating doctrine. However, of more significance was that in the meantime it was practically disregarded. Among Cdr Dresel's last actions before leaving as the *Akron*'s commander was to forward Harrigan's report to the BuAer head, Cdr Garland Fulton, who remarked enthusiastically that 'great credit is due this H/A unit for their zeal, and to them should go most credit for progress'. But when Fulton distributed the report to other BuAer divisions it met, at most, indifference.

The Harrigan Report suggested equipping the Bellanca Airbus with a skyhook and using it as a cargo and tanker aircraft. (*USN*)

During 1929 V. Adm. Rosendahl had originally expressed interest in the Bellanca Airbus as a supply aircraft, and Harrigan revived the idea in his report, suggesting equipping an airbus with a skyhook and using it as a cargo and tanker aircraft. The Bellanca was a high-wing, single-engine aircraft built by Bellanca Aircraft Corporation of New Castle, Delaware, as a 'workhorse' intended for use as a passenger or cargo aircraft. The aircraft was powered by either a 750hp Wright Cyclone or 675hp Pratt and Whitney Hornet engine. This tanker could shuttle between the ground and the airship to keep it supplied with fuel if landing was impractical. Because of its size and weight, this aircraft could not be accommodated inside the hangar and would have to hang on the trapeze and pump fuel to the airship. This and other aircraft of this type could also be used to ferry dry stores and personnel, permitting the airship to be provisioned and its personnel exchanged in areas where the airship had no landing provisions. The trapeze would have to be modified to include a hoist for handling stores, hoses for transferring fuel, and a ladder accessing an internal walkway for personnel. Using this method, the airship could be serviced from any field that could accept the utility planes, or from aircraft carriers at sea. The Bellanca idea never came to fruition, but the idea of a service and utility aircraft would be revived in 1934.

1933 Operations

During an afternoon ceremony on 3 January 1933, Cdr Frank McCord relieved Commander Alger Dresel as the *Akron*'s commanding officer, the latter becoming the first commanding officer of *Akron*'s sister ship *Macon*, whose construction was nearly complete. A 1910 USNA graduate, McCord had commanded a torpedo boat during the First World War and later served as executive officer of the Lakehurst Naval Air Station. On 30 June 1932 he was assigned to serve on board the USS *Akron*, assuming command until his death in the airship's crash.

On 3 January 1933, Cdr Frank McCord relieved Cdr Alger Dresel as the *Akron*'s commanding officer. (*USN*)

Within hours of the change-of-command ceremony, *Akron* headed south down the eastern seaboard toward Florida with Harrigan, Young, and Trapnell following in the two F9C-2s and the N2Y-1, which were then retrieved and stowed in the hangar compartment. During the flight the N2Y-1 tested the newly installed perch, which was judged to be satisfactory.

After McCord took command, the BuAer permitted the *Akron* and her crew a January to March 1933 training period to develop and refine internal organisational and operational practices that required 425 hours through 'all kinds of weather'.

The *Akron* was the 'star' of the fifth annual All-American Air Races at Miami on 5–7 January 1933. This air race was never as important as the National Air Races, particularly that year as it had been compromised by the Depression. Prize money was reduced, few trophies were donated, and there was no free fuel for competitors. The races themselves were described as 'entertaining but not remarkable'. A spectacular feature of the weekend meet was the visit of the *Akron* and its hook-on aircraft. A local Miami newspaper reported that:

> Visitors discovered that every road from which they could catch even a distant glimpse of the moored ship led also to the airport, that those roads were blocked by Miami policemen selling tickets to the meet. Before departing for Cuba, the *Akron* hovered over the airport, launched its five planes which engaged in a mock fight and then, one by one, returned to be taken back into the belly of the mother ship.

The next day, after refuelling at the nearby Naval Reserve Aviation Base, Opa-Locka, Florida, the *Akron* continued to Guantanamo Bay, Cuba, for an inspection of base sites. Early the next morning, while *Akron* circled Guantanamo Bay, Harrigan provided 'taxi' service with the N2Y-1, ferrying four *Akron* officers individually to the ground for a survey of possible sites for an airship mooring facility. After dropping off each passenger, Harrigan returned to the airship transporting a cargo of local lobsters for the mess!

The *Akron* was the 'star' of the fifth annual All-American Air Races in Miami on 5–7 January 1933, at which the local news report erroneously stated that the *Akron* launched five aircraft. (*USN*)

The *Akron* refuels at the Naval Reserve Aviation Base, Opa-Locka, Florida, near Miami, which would serve as the major stopover for Navy airships during Caribbean Fleet exercises. (*USN*)

The *Akron*'s return from Cuba to Opa-Locka and back to Lakehurst was uneventful and *Akron* continued local operations, which were interrupted by a two-week overhaul and poor weather. On 18 January she resumed a programme of extended local flights out to sea, during which navigation problems were practised and more hook-ons conducted, with the Sparrowhawk testing its aptly named perch.

During the last week of January, the *Akron* with two F9Cs aboard flew out to sea for an overnight navigation problem. However, squally winds related with an approaching storm prevented the scheduled mooring at Lakehurst and the *Akron* spent several days in the air avoiding the storm.

Hoping to escape the Lakehurst winter weather, and to increase his operating time, Cdr McCord proposed another flight to Florida for February. However, during a conference with the Lakehurst CO, Cdr Fred Berry, and Cdr Garland Fulton of the BuAer, McCord requested a March flight to Panama instead. Fulton agreed as he wished to inspect possible Canal Zone mooring sites. Meanwhile, *Akron*'s February Lakehurst operations consisted of only one forty-eight-hour flight, as others were curtailed by a two-week overhaul and stormy weather.

During March, *Akron* conducted intensive training with the F9C-2s, honing their hook-on skills. On 1 March, *Akron* carried three F9Cs out to sea, where they drilled to

During March 1933, *Akron* conducted intensive training with the F9C-2s, honing their hook-on skills and improving their trapeze recovery times. (*USN*)

improve trapeze recovery times. The best time, from the opening to the closing of the airship hangar doors, was fifteen minutes, which was considered too slow for combat operations. The main cause of the delays occurred while transferring the aircraft from the trapeze to the hangar trolleys, and then in getting them clear of the trapeze so it could be swung out for the next aircraft.

On 4 March *Akron* performed an overfly of Washington, DC for Franklin D. Roosevelt's first inauguration as President, which probably would have been more imposing if the Sparrowhawks had escorted the impressive airship.

Akron's Panama trip was scheduled for 8 March, but heavy winds prevented it from leaving its protecting hangar until 11 March, the same day its sister ship *Macon* was christened. At 0249 it was pulled out of the hangar in 18-to-25 knot crosswinds and took off for the Canal Zone at 0405. Immediately after take-off, Harrigan and Robert 'Swede' Larson, flying N2Ys, were taken aboard and eighteen hours later *Akron* arrived to be moored on the Opa-Locka mast. On 14 March the Panama flight continued with Cdr Garland Fulton and two civil engineering officers from the Navy Department on board to inspect possible mooring sites. While the *Akron* wandered over the Canal Zone, Harrigan and Larson transported the inspecting party to the ground in the N2Ys. On their return to the airship, the two pilots carried officers from the Coco Solo Naval Base on a sight-seeing visit to the *Akron*.

On 16 March, on their way back to Lakehurst, the *Akron* stopped at Opa-Locka for six days, where the N2Ys acted as targets for the *Akron*'s gun crews, who practised their training camera-gun skills. After leaving Florida for Lakehurst on 22 March, *Akron* made only one more flight in March, a twenty-three-hour flight at sea conducting navigation problem trials, during which the F9Cs were flown to test their direction-finding equipment.

During mid-March 1932, the *Akron* flew over the Canal Zone with Cdr Garland Fulton aboard to inspect possible bases. (*USN*)

On the morning of 3 April, *Akron* was preparing for an extended flight to New England to support the calibration of Shore Radio Direction Finding (RDF) stations. Cdr McCord directed his Executive Officer, Lt Cdr Hubert Wiley, to have a N2Y flown aboard as a running boat and to have three Sparrowhawks ready for hook on immediately after the *Akron*'s take-off. However, during the day, the visibility deteriorated, and McCord cancelled the Sparrowhawk rendezvous. Weather permitting, McCord still wanted a N2Y, piloted by Lt Fred Trapnell, to be prepared to fly aboard. *Akron* took off at 1728 and climbed into the fog with R. Adm. William Moffett on board accompanied by his aide, Cdr Henry Barton Cecil, Cdr Fred Berry, and Lt Col Alfred Masury (US Army Reserve).

As the fog grew thicker than expected, McCord radioed Lakehurst to order Trapnell not to take off in the N2Y. Disaster struck the belaboured *Akron* just after midnight when she encountered a violent storm front, stalled, and then crashed into the Atlantic. The *Akron* disaster was likely the result of poor command decisions relating to weather, navigation, and poor handling. While it is likely that *Akron*'s tail was driven into the sea by a strong downdraft, it is also probable that Capt. McCord simply flew his ship into the sea as he

The only three survivors of an *Akron* crew of seventy-three: (R to L) Lt Cdr Herbert Wiley; Boatswain's Mate Second Class Richard Deal; and Aviation Metalsmith Second Class Moody Erwin, seen the day after their rescue. None of *Akron*'s aircraft nor their pilots were on board. (*USN*)

was flying too low for the conditions and did not consider the *Akron*'s 785ft length while attempting to climb out of a downdraft. With the nose of the ship raised sharply to climb, the *Akron*'s tail may have turned downward into the water.

Most of the seventy-three deaths, including Adm. Moffett, were caused by drowning and hypothermia, since the crew had not been issued life jackets, and there had not been time to deploy the airship's single life raft. All three men accompanying Moffett perished in the crash. Cdr Henry Barton Cecil (USNA 1910/naval aviator No. 42 qualified in both HTA and LTA craft) was aboard the *Akron* as the Flight Division Head of Bureau of Aeronautics. Cdr Fred Berry (USNA 1908) was the former *Los Angeles* commander. Lt Col Alfred Masury was an ardent proponent of the potential civilian uses of rigid airships and as the Vice-President of Mack Trucks he was famous as the designer of the Mack Truck Bulldog ornament. Six of the enlisted men killed in the crash had survived the crash of *Shenandoah* in 1925. There were only three survivors, including *Akron* XO Wiley, while none of its aircraft nor their pilots were on board. The *Akron* had made seventy-three flights totalling 1,695.8 hours before the loss.

Akron's loss marked the beginning of the end for US Navy rigid airships, especially since one of their leading proponents, R. Adm. William Moffett, was among the dead. President Roosevelt declared, 'The loss of the *Akron* with its crew of gallant officers and men is a national disaster.' *Macon* and other airships would receive life jackets to avert a repetition of the *Akron* tragedy. When *Macon* was damaged in a storm in 1935 and subsequently sank after landing in the sea, only two of the seventy-two crew were lost. Nonetheless, despite the broadcasts and photographs of the great fiery explosion, the *Hindenburg* was not the world's greatest airship disaster with thirty-five fatalities (thirteen passengers and twenty-two crewmen) of the ninety-seven people aboard. While the *Hindenburg* tragedy was the event that turned the public against airship travel, the USS *Akron* is history's worst airship disaster.

After the loss of the *Akron* on 4 April and the recent launching of its sister ship *Macon* on 11 March, questions arose about the continuance of America's airship programme. The *Akron*'s indifferent performance in Fleet exercises and its fatal crash furthered perceptions among the Navy leadership that even the most modern rigid airships were useless. When CNO William Pratt asked Admiral Schofield how he felt *Akron* could have benefited the Fleet, Schofield responded, 'The need of the Fleet is not more *Akrons* but more carriers.' Airship advocate Adm. Moffett was gone and could no longer support the rigid airships or further his objective vision of naval aviation that included rigid airships. After the loss of the *Akron* and Moffett, the future of the rigid airship programme would rely entirely on the performance of the *Macon*, the new 'Queen of the Skies', which was built, paid for, and operating.

In a May 1933 *Aero Digest* article, Cy Caldwell defended the continuance of Navy airships: 'An airborne or sea-going scout both can cover expanses where an enemy's navy might be lurking. Airships in quantity would cost not over $3 million and be manned by a crew of 75 men. A cruiser costs nearly three times as much and requires a crew of 500.'

Chapter Eight

The *Macon* Flying Aircraft Carrier Operations 1933 to 1935 Crash

The *Macon*, the last of the Navy's dirigibles, was built at a cost of $2.5 million ($60 million in 2025) at the Goodyear Airdock as a joint venture between the Goodyear Tire and Rubber Company and the Zeppelin Company of Germany. Because she was by far the largest airship ever to be built in America, a team of experienced German airship engineers was led by Chief Designer Karl Arnstein, who had previously participated in the design and construction of the *Macon*'s sister ship *Akron*.

For the *Macon* christening on 11 March 1933 at the Goodyear Air Dock, BuAer Chief R. Adm. William Moffett spoke of possibly enlarging the ZRS ships and later obtaining larger ships capable of carrying more aircraft. After he spoke, Moffett then stood next to his wife, Jeanette Beverly Moffett, as she christened the new USS *Macon*. President Roosevelt, who never forgave a court loss to Goodyear in 1924, conveyed a very public snub by not sending the First Lady to christen the new airship, as both Herbert Hoover and

After its christening on 11 March 1933 the *Macon* first flew on 21 April, and was commissioned on 23 June 1933, with Cdr Alger Dresel in command. On 24 June 1933, *Macon* left its Ohio Goodyear plant for NAS Lakehurst, where the new airship was to be based for the summer while undergoing a series of training flights (in photo). (*USN*)

Calvin Coolidge had done. Moffett had been aboard the *Akron* during its first flight on 23 September 1932 and would die three weeks after the *Macon*'s christening, on the *Akron*'s last flight on 3 April 1933. In obvious military service nepotism, the airship was named after the city of Macon, Georgia, which was the largest city in the Congressional District of Democrat Carl Vinson, then the Chairman of the US House of Representatives' Committee on Naval Affairs! After its christening, the *Macon* first flew on 21 April, and was commissioned on 23 June 1933, with Cdr Alger Dresel in command. On 24 June 1933, *Macon* left its Ohio Goodyear plant for NAS Lakehurst, where the new airship was to be based for the summer while undergoing a series of training flights.

Cdr Alger Dresel. (*USN*)

After her commissioning, the *Macon* was confronted with an enormous challenge in gaining the Navy's confidence after the *Akron*'s brief and underwhelming performance. Moffett's successor as BuAer Chief, Adm. Ernest King, was determined that the rigid airship demonstrate its value. King needed the *Macon* to be employed as much as possible to determine its future: 'We have only one airship. We must not be reckless, but if airships are to justify themselves, the *Macon* has got to show more than she has shown.' King realised that the time for publicity flights needed to end, and that the rigid airship had to perform to prevent termination of the programme.

The new CNO,[5] Adm. William Standley, was not an airship advocate and had successfully used his aircraft to attack the *Akron* in the June 1932 Scouting Force Exercise. He granted the *Macon* ten months to demonstrate her military effectiveness and ordered her to the west coast in October 1933. Standley informed Adm. David Sellers, the new C-in-CUS,[6] that the *Macon* was 'to be employed to the fullest extent possible in Fleet exercises, so that her military value could be determined'. Sellers was ordered to prepare a report, due in September 1934, on the *Macon*'s performance to advise the future development, or termination, of rigid airships in the Navy.

During its service the *Macon* was to have a much more productive career than the *Akron*. *Macon*'s commanders developed the doctrine and techniques of using her on-board aircraft for scouting while the airship remained safely out of sight of the opposing forces during exercises. *Macon* participated in several Fleet exercises, but the officers of the Fleet who planned and conducted the exercises had little perception of the airship's capabilities and weaknesses and often misused her.

5. Chief of Naval Operations.
6. C-in-CUS, pronounced 'sink us', means commander-in-chief, United States Fleet.

Adm. William Standley (above), the new Chief of Naval Operations (CNO) a vocal airship non-advocate, ordered Adm. David Sellers (below), the new Commander in Chief, United States Fleet (C-in-CUS), to prepare a report on the *Macon*'s performance to advise on the future development, or termination, of rigid airships. (*USN*)

Macon officers and crew: Seated in front, left to right: Lt Anthony Danis; Lt Howard Coulter; Lt Calvin Bolster, Construction Corps; Lt Scott Peck; Lt Cdr Bertram Rodgers (or Lt Cdr Joseph Arnold; Cdr Alger Dresel, Commanding Officer; Lt Cdr Edwin Cochrane; Lt Donald MacKey; Lt Charles Roland; Lt Walter Zimmerman; and Lt Frederick Trapnell. Standing in back, left to right: Chief Boatswain William. Buckley; Lt (JG) George Campbell; Lt (JG) John D. Reppy; Lt (JG) Robert W. Larson; Lt Howard Young; Lt Harold Miller; Lt (JG) Frederick Kivette; and Chief Machinist Emmet Thurman. (*USN*)

1933 Operations

Just over two weeks after the loss of *Akron*, the *Macon* made its first flight on 21 April 1933, remaining aloft over northern Ohio for nearly 13 hours with 105 people aboard. After several test flights, she was commissioned on 23 June 1933, with Cdr Alger Dresel in command. On 24 June 1933, *Macon* left Goodyear for Lakehurst, where the new airship was to be based for the summer while undergoing a series of training flights.

On 7 July *Macon* practised its first hook ons with four Sparrowhawks flown by Lieutenants Harrigan, Trapnell, Larson, and new arrival Frederick Kivette (USNA 1925). Additional hook ons were made several days later over New York City, welcoming Italo Balbo's Italian Air Armada of twenty-four seaplanes that had moored in Jamaica Bay during their round trip from Rome to the Century of Progress in Chicago between 1 July and 12 August 1933. During these July flights, further Sparrowhawk hook ons were made, both to the trapeze and to the newly installed perch.

On 7 July 1933, Macon practised its first hook ons with four HTA Unit Sparrowhawks flown by lieutenants Harrigan, Trapnell, Larson, and Kivette. (*USN*)

NAS Moffett Field

During October 1928, contracts were signed for the construction of two new airships and the Navy found that it now required accommodation for them. In January 1929, Secretary of the Navy Curtis Wilbur requested that Congress appoint a board of officers to inspect possible sites for a new west coast airship station to supplement Lakehurst. Adm. Moffett was appointed to head the 'Moffett Board', which comprised R. Adm. Joseph Reeves, Garland Fulton, Cdr Charles Rosendahl, and Lt Cdr Edward Marshall of the Civil Engineering Corps. The Board met on 15 May 1929 to study ninety-seven west coast sites located between Puget Sound and the Mexican border and reduced the candidates to two in California. One was of 1,700 acres in the Santa Clara Valley near Sunnyvale; and the other, Camp Kearny, was an abandoned 2,032-acre Army base about 11 miles north of the Navy's large Pacific Fleet base at San Diego. The Board (except Adm. Reeves) recommended the Sunnyvale site because of better weather conditions for airship operations and also because it would provide naval aviation with initial large-scale facilities in the San Francisco area. The Board also proposed that if Sunnyvale were selected, Camp Kearny should also be purchased as an aircraft base and a secondary airship facility because of its immediate vicinity to the Fleet in San Diego.

In 1930, the city of Sunnyvale acquired a 1,000-acre parcel of farmland bordering San Francisco Bay for $480,000 ($11.5 million in 2022) and then sold it to the US government for $1 as the home base for the new Navy airship USS *Macon*. The area was ideal for an airport since it was often clear while other parts of the San Francisco Bay area were covered in fog. The Naval Air Station was authorised by an Act of Congress, signed by President Herbert Hoover on 12 February 1931. Construction of the original facilities was begun 8 July 1931. The originally named Airbase Sunnyvale CAL was commissioned on 12 April 1933 and dedicated as NAS Sunnyvale. On 1 September 1933, after the death of R. Adm. William Moffett, who is credited with the creation of the airfield, it was renamed NAS Moffett Field.

On 12 October 1933, the *Macon* left Lakehurst on a transcontinental flight to Sunnyvale, which at maximum speed would require over thirty-seven hours. At Sunnyvale, the *Macon* was to be housed in the impressive Hangar One designed by German airship and structural engineer Dr Karl Arnstein, Vice President and Director of Engineering of the Goodyear Zeppelin Corporation in association with Wilbur Watson Associates Architects and Engineers of Cleveland, Ohio. Hangar One, constructed in 1931, remains one of the world's largest free-standing structures, constructed on a network of steel girders sheathed with galvanised steel that envelops 8 acres and measures 1,133ft long and 308ft wide. Moffett's Hangar One once simultaneously accommodated not only the massive *Macon* but several smaller non-rigid airships. The hangar's interior is so large that fog was said to sometimes form near the roof. The hangar doors were of a distinctive clam shell design, each weighing 200 tons each and powered by a 150hp motor. Standard-gauge railway tracks traversed the length of the hangar and extended into the large area at each end of the hangar to enable the transportation of the airship on the mooring mast into the hangar or back outside to the flight position. This hangar is still standing at the

Aerial view of the Moffett Field airship complex with Hangar One in the centre and the two very evident large mooring areas divided into the North and South Circles. (*USN*)

The impressive Hangar One at NAS Sunnyvale was designed by German airship and structural engineer Dr Karl Arnstein and remains one of the world's largest free-standing structures. (*USN*)

NASA Ames Research Facility in Sunnyvale and is a Naval Historical Monument, Historic American Engineering Landmark, on the National Trust for Historic Preservation List, and a State of California Historic Civil Engineering Landmark.

The Macon Moves West

Only a month after the *Macon* was completed, she travelled across the country to Sunnyvale. Lt Trapnell, flying the N2Y 'running boat', was the only aircraft to accompany the *Macon* to California as the other aircraft of the HTA Unit were flown to the west coast by their pilots. However, leader of the HTA Unit since its establishment, Lt Daniel Ward Harrigan, would be left behind as he had contracted a serious case of pneumonia that threatened his Naval career. Although he recovered, he would not return to fly on the *Macon* and was transferred to the new cruiser *Minneapolis*. For his ground-breaking work on the *Akron*, Harrigan received a Letter of Commendation from Secretary of the Navy Claude Swanson for his leadership of the HTA Unit:

> During this time, the problems in connection with operating a unit aboard dirigibles have been successfully met, and you, by your initiative and study, have greatly contributed toward this success ... The Department congratulates you upon your contributions to the successful operations of HTA aircraft from dirigibles and commends you upon the zeal and energy displayed by you as evidenced by the present high degree of efficiency of such operations.

A N2Y, acting as a 'running boat', was the only aircraft (arrow on photo) to accompany the Macon to California as the other aircraft of the HTA Unit were flown separately to the west coast by their pilots. (*USN*)

About noon on 15 October 1933 a crowd of 20,000 greeted the *Macon* as she approached the newly named Moffett Field. Although the other buildings were still under construction, Hangar One had been hastily completed. To somewhat compensate for the 38 tons of fuel the *Macon* had consumed on its transcontinental journey, during the four-and-a-half-hour mooring procedure, Lt Young took off from the field in a Sparrowhawk to hook on to provide 2,700lb of ballast and, more so, a photo opportunity.

For its first west coast flights, the *Macon* made two initial trips in early November: one a five-hour circuit to familiarise the crew with the nearby west coast and the Channel Islands; the other a short demonstration flight over San Francisco conveying Adm. Daniel Sellers and some of his staff. During this flight, Lts Young and Kivette demonstrated hook-on operations using Sparrowhawks.

Three Sparrowhawks flown by Young, Kivette, and Larson arrive at NAS Sunnyvale just before the *Macon*. (*USN*)

At about noon on 15 October 1933, after a thirty-seven-hour, non-stop, cross-country flight, the Macon arrived at its new home base at NAS Sunnyvale, California, outside San Francisco. (*USN*)

Macon HTA Group: (L to R) Lt (JG) Robert Larson, Lt Harold Miller, Lt Frederick Trapnell, Lt Howard Young, and Lt (JG) Frederick Kivette. (*USN*)

Macon Participates in Fleet Exercises D and E

Macon was assigned to the Fleet and was scheduled to participate in two extensive war games, Exercises D and E, as a scout for the defensive Blue Force. The limited geographic area of the exercise made *Macon*'s role more tactical than its designated strategic mission, and although not a true measure of her potential, the exercises did introduce her to the way she would be integrated into the Fleet machinations. Exercise D began at 0500 on 14 November 1933, with the *Macon*, carrying two Sparrowhawks, on station off Point Arguello and ordered to conduct a search to cover the Blue flank. After cruising through clouds for two hours, the *Macon* dropped out of the clouds and unexpectedly found herself directly over a Brown Force (enemy) cruiser, which opened simulated gunfire, causing the exercise referee to declare the airship shot down. For exercise purposes, *Macon* (ZRS-5) was reconstituted as ZRS-6 and continued its search. At 0917, Lt Kivette's Sparrowhawk was launched to drive away two Brown flying boats. At 1125, the *Macon*'s lookouts spotted an unidentified ship on the western horizon and Lt Trapnell's F9C-2 was launched to reconnoitre. The ship was identified to be a friendly Blue cruiser, but Trapnell continued to fly on to locate a division of Brown cruisers. However, soon after retrieving Trapnell, the *Macon* roamed out of the clouds and was again 'shot down' by a Brown cruiser and destroyer AA fire, but again was allowed to continue in the exercise as ZRS-7. During the remainder of the exercise the *Macon* continued scouting but did not launch its aircraft.

Exercise E began on the morning of 16 November, when the *Macon*'s lookouts spotted unidentified ships and Trapnell and Young, pre-positioned in their Sparrowhawks on the

During December 1933, to maintain their carrier proficiency, *Macon* HTA pilots landed and launched their Sparrowhawks aboard the carrier USS *Lexington* (CV-2). (USN)

trapeze and the perch, were launched and reported sighting Brown enemy ships to the *Macon*, which informed Blue HQ. When the Sparrowhawks returned, the *Macon* broke off contact and hid in the clouds until 1010, when she began scouting but did not contact Brown enemy forces until 1315. She was attacked by Brown fighters and declared to have been shot down. During these exercises, because of their inadequate radio and navigation equipment, the *Macon*'s Sparrowhawks saw limited use and were not authorised to fly more than 25 miles from any Fleet unit. In his report, the Fleet umpire, Lt Donald Mackey, aboard the *Macon* declared that 'tactical scouting was not a function of a rigid airship'. He also identified the *Macon*'s problems as being 'navigation and vulnerability in close contacts with enemy forces … Heretofore, the airships were to be used mostly in point-to-point flying over great distances and flying was to be conducted in a fashion to facilitate the navigator's work.' Regarding the airship's vulnerability, Mackey suggested that the 'only' solution was for the airship to remain out of sight and 'let its planes do the searching'. During 1934, Mackey would become the *Macon*'s tactical officer and would develop the technics that would allow the Sparrowhawks to search beyond constant visual contact with the *Macon*. During the Second World War Mackey would become the commanding officer of Moffett Field.

During December 1933, to maintain their carrier proficiency, the HTA pilots flying Sparrowhawks 9056 and 9058 landed on board the USS *Lexington*. The main landing gear wheel pants on these two aircraft had been reoutfitted with curved fins fixed to their forward midline to prevent the arresting gear wires jumping up and over the pants into the gear struts.

At the end of 1933, the HTA Unit was equipped with six F9C-2s, one XF9C-2, three N2Y-1s, and two new additions: a Vought O2U-1 Corsair interchangeable wheel/float biplane scout and a Loening OL-8 two-seat amphibious biplane. The XF9C-1 had been transferred to the Naval Aircraft Factory, where it was eventually scrapped on 8 January 1935.

Vought O2U-1 Corsair interchangeable wheel/float biplane scout. (*USN*)

Loening OL-8 two-seat amphibious biplane. (*USN*)

1934 Operations

A Crucial Year For Airships

During the first half of 1934, the *Macon* would participate in exercises six times and each time failed to demonstrate the airship's military effectiveness. While the *Akron* had operated in large search areas that were suited to its capabilities, the *Macon* would operate in smaller areas that were congested with 'enemy' carrier aircraft participating in the exercises, which were designed to prove and develop the offensive capabilities of carrier-launched aircraft. This biased scenario was not at all favourable for the *Macon* to demonstrate her military proficiencies.

Adm. Ernest King observed that 1934 was a 'crucial year for airships, with the *Macon* carrying practically all hopes for the future of airships in the Navy'. (*USN*)

In a letter to *Macon* Commander Alger Dresel, Adm. Ernest King observed, 'This is a crucial year (1934) for airships, with the *Macon* carrying practically all hopes for the future of airships in the Navy.'

At the same time Adm. King wrote to R. Adm. John Halligan, Commander Aircraft, Battle Force, providing some modicum of advocacy for the Navy airship's future:

> This is a crucial year for airships ... the *Macon* has got to show more than she has shown. I am trying to keep an open mind on the airship question, but the more I see of airships the more I can visualize a useful field for them in searching operations, especially in conjunction with their aircraft, provided we can get the airships to perform.

January West Coast Exercises

The beginning of 1934 saw the *Macon* engaged in further Fleet exercises off the California coast, which were a continuation of the November 1933 exercises. During the afternoon of 3 January 1934, *Macon* departed Moffett Field as a scout for the Blue (defending) forces during Fleet Exercises D and E. Once she was airborne, Trapnell and Miller joined the airship in their Sparrowhawks. A third F9C-2 was scheduled to be carried but the airship's helium lost lift, and 2.5 tons of ballast had to be dumped for the *Macon* to continue climbing and also carry two aircraft. By that evening, *Macon* was stationed off San Pedro with orders from the Commander of the Blue Force to search an area between San Nicholas Island and Santa Cruz Islands, beginning at 0600 the next day. The *Macon* began the search in excellent visibility, which was to continue throughout the day. At 0649 the *Macon* sighted nine enemy flying boats and although they never closed to within 2 miles, they claimed to have damaged the airship. At 0733 *Macon* lookouts reported shipping to the north-west, and Trapnell and Larson were launched in their Sparrowhawks. An hour later they reported a Brown Force convoy of twelve cruisers, four transports, and many destroyers en route to reinforce its San Nicholas Island base. *Macon* relayed the report to the commander of Blue Force, who launched a carrier air strike that 'almost wiped out' the Brown Force convoy. There is no report of the *Macon* launching its aircraft for the remainder of the day. During that night she drifted off San Clemente Island, and at 0700 on the 5th she was on station just off that island for the next phase, Exercise G. The Sparrowhawks were launched and flew to the western sector of *Macon*'s assigned search area, while the *Macon* covered the eastern sector. Feeling confident in their navigation abilities, the pilots used Mackey's vector analysis system of pre-navigation, which allowed them to search beyond visual contact with the airship. *Macon* made the initial sighting of the enemy Brown Force assets and then ordered its Sparrowhawks to maintain tracking. Voice radio communication between the aircraft and airship was very poor and the pilots were obliged to use the clumsy hand-keyed Morse code from their cramped cockpits. About noontime the *Macon* was attacked by eighteen enemy fighters and was judged to have been shot down. Again, for exercise purposes, *Macon* was reconstituted as ZRS-6 and continued to operate until released to return to base.

After these exercises the *Macon*'s Tactical Officer, Lt Donald Mackey, reported the following critique of the *Macon*'s aircraft to Adm. Daniel Sellers:

> Experience to date seems to indicate that manoeuvrability, strength, and high speed are characteristics not required of an airship's planes. Prime considerations should be long endurance, good reliable communications by voice up to at least 100 miles, and a speed of 126–138mph ... These planes can protect the airship most effectively by giving its ample warning of enemy approach. It is further felt that the airship planes should not engage in combat except as it is forced on them, or in an effort to give the airship a chance to escape when seriously threatened.

The aging but reliable N2Y, flown from Lakehurst, was about to be replaced by two Waco UBFs designated as XJW-1s to be used by the Navy as hook-on trainers and utility aircraft for the airship skyhook/trapeze aircraft programme. (*USN*)

In his report Adm. Daniel Sellers noted the *Macon*'s thirteen useful contacts during Exercise F and 11 during Exercise G but criticised the *Macon*'s loitering over the Fleet's cruisers for AA protection as it was a large visible indicator for enemy aircraft. He thought that the airship was flying too low and too close to the Fleet and should be best deployed as a 'tactical scout by operating at high altitudes'.

Macon was scheduled to take part in Fleet Exercise H on 20 February and although she departed Moffett Field carrying three Sparrowhawks, bad weather prevented their use. *Macon* then did not fly again for four weeks.

On 16 March the Navy received two skyhook-equipped Waco XJW-1s, BuNos. 9521 and 9522, which were replacements for the trusty N2Y-1. Then, on 20 March, *Macon* participated in Sparrowhawk hook-on exercises and also tested the XJW-1s. The N2Y-1 had served adequately as a hook-on trainer and to transport passengers to and from the airship but had limited load capacity, speed and range.

April 1934 West Coast Fleet Exercises

Macon was scheduled to participate in massive west coast Fleet exercises during April and Caribbean exercises during May. Its first assignment was to scout for the Blue Fleet as it deployed from the west coast to Panama. On 9 April she left Moffett Field to rendezvous with the Blue Forces off Guadalupe Island for Exercise J, about 200 miles west off the Mexican Baja California coast. The exercises began at 0500 on 10 April with the *Macon* assigned to search the area west of Guadalupe. Two Sparrowhawks were aloft during each of two search periods and *Macon* confirmed that no enemy forces were found to the west. During its next searches there is no record of *Macon* launching its Sparrowhawks. At 1055, *Macon* was directed to search between Guadalupe and the Mexican coast and during this reconnaissance, soon after 1300, it was attacked by two enemy dive bombers and while trying to evade them, flew over enemy cruisers and was 'fired' upon. An hour later she was attacked again by enemy dive bombers and was judged to have been shot down. She was reconstituted as ZRS-6, but again shot down and reconstituted as ZRS-7. *Macon* escaped another reconstitution and was released from the exercises on the 11th to return to Moffett Field.

Caribbean Fleet Exercises

Macon left Moffett Field on 22 April for Opa-Locka, Florida, its base for the May Caribbean Fleet exercises. Two of its Sparrowhawks and one XJW-1 were flown across the country beforehand. While crossing the Texas mountains, the *Macon* encountered turbulent air and a large altitude increase that induced a helium cell to rupture, causing the airship to lose valuable lift near Van Horn, Texas. While the crew was dumping large amounts of fuel and ballast to regain the needed lift, part of its internal structure failed and was severely damaged. After she landed, repairs were only partially completed, but the *Macon* needed to remain operational for her continued existence and she returned to California in February 1935 for nine days of intensive repair by Goodyear and Navy personnel.

The repaired *Macon* returned to Florida and took off from Opa-Locka for Exercise M in the Caribbean on 5 May to join the friendly Blue Force, which was to retake Puerto Rico and the Virgin Islands from the enemy Grey Force. After *Macon*'s take-off, Trapnell and Miller flew up in their Sparrowhawks for them to be stowed. On the morning of the 6th, *Macon*'s lookouts spotted several ships and launched Trapnell's Sparrowhawk to reconnoitre and identified ships as Grey destroyers before returning to *Macon*'s hangar. Later, another F9C-2 was launched to investigate another flotilla, which was identified as Grey cruisers. Between 0845 and 1005, two Sparrowhawks searched ahead of *Macon*'s search track and returned to the airship without results. As the F9Cs were being stowed in the hangar, the airship's radio warned that enemy planes were directly above the *Macon* at 12,000ft and were about to attack. The F9Cs were ordered to launch immediately. Trapnell cleared the trapeze, but Kivette was just being swung out of the hangar when a horde of Grey fighters arrived, and the exercise umpire pronounced that *Macon* was destroyed. Just before its 'destruction', the *Macon*'s spotters had sighted the Grey carrier *Lexington* about 20 miles distant. Between the time *Macon* sighted the *Lexington* and the airship was judged destroyed, *Macon* had reported the carrier's position, but not its course and speed. The commander of the Blue Force demanded that information even though *Macon* no longer 'existed'. The umpire permitted the information to be circulated, as he ruled that Trapnell in his F9C supposedly survived the attack and detected and

To participate in the Caribbean exercises the Sparrowhawks and Waco flew to Opa-Locka ahead of the *Macon*. The airship was damaged on the way there, causing the pilots to wait at the primitive base until it was repaired back in California and then returned to Florida. (*USN*)

reported the *Lexington* through a hole in the clouds. *Macon* remained out of the exercise until 1048, when the umpires allowed it to resume operations as the ZRS-6 and it was ordered to find *Lexington*. At 1158. *Macon*'s commander, Alger Dresel, believed that the *Macon* was about 30 miles astern of the carrier and launched his planes. However, the Sparrowhawks were unable to find it until just over an hour later as the carrier had made a number of course changes. The F9Cs shadowed the carrier until 1442 without being discovered but their radio reports were frequently distorted by static and had to be often repeated, before they could be relayed by the *Macon* to the Blue fleet. This information permitted the Commander of the Blue Air Forces on the *Saratoga* to launch a successful attack against *Lexington*. After its successful radio report, *Macon* was ordered to return to its originally assigned search area. About half an hour later its aircraft identified and reported a large group of Grey cruisers and destroyers. *Macon* continued an unsuccessful search for the remainder of the afternoon and at 1847 she was released from the exercise to return to Opa-Locka.

Macon left Opa-Locka on 11 May for the final Exercise N of the Caribbean Fleet problem with two Sparrowhawks hooking on after take-off. The exercise began off Puerto Rico at 0955 on 12 May and an hour later *Macon*'s lookout spotted many ships of the enemy's advance force. *Macon* dispatched Sparrowhawks flown by Larson and Young to fly 40 miles south-east an attempt to locate the enemy main body, but their chronic radio problems prevented them from receiving updated intelligence from Fleet HQ on the enemy's position and the search was unsuccessful. At 1310, Miller and Young were launched on

Lt Harold 'Min' Miller became the HTA's Senior Naval Aviator (SNA), and would follow the inimitable Ward Harrigan as an effective CO. (*USN*)

Lts (JGs) Harry Richardson and Leroy Simpler replaced pilots Trapnell, Young, and Larson, who were transferred to cruiser duty. Simpler is shown during his 1942 Guadalcanal duty as CO of VF-5 aboard the USS *Saratoga*. (*USN*)

another search but during this flight they were updated with intelligence by Mackey sent from the nearby airship's radio. By having the *Macon* fly at a constant speed, Mackey was able to maintain an accurate plot of their flight on the airship's manoeuvring board and the Sparrowhawks contacted the enemy carrier division at 1400. The two pilots throttled back their F9Cs and were able to shadow the enemy Grey carriers for over an hour. *Macon* was then discharged from the exercise and moored at Opa-Locka during the morning of 13 May. During these exercises the *Macon* and its aircraft were used as tactical scouts, for which they were unsuited but nonetheless much was learned about the future employment of the aircraft by airships, especially the need to resolve the aircraft's continuing navigation and communication problems. Mackey again reported to Adm. Sellers:

> I believe that the concept of a rigid airship, of itself, being a scout is false. It is more on the order of an aircraft carrier ... the attached aircraft must accomplish the scouting, the airship's sole function ... is to impart mobility and endurance to its planes.

On 16 May, *Macon* left Opa-Locka for Moffett, arriving on the 18th with its aircraft again individually flying transcontinental. Once the *Macon* returned to Moffett, three pilots, Trapnell, Young, and Larson, were transferred to cruiser duty with Lts (JGs) Harry Richardson and Leroy Simpler transferring in as replacements on 2 June. Lt Min Miller became the HTA's senior naval aviator, and would follow the inimitable Ward Harrigan as an effective CO.

After graduating from the Naval Academy in June 1929, Simpler had sea duty for a year, assigned first to the USS *Idaho* and later the USS *Colorado*. On 23 May 1930, he reported to the Naval Air Station, Pensacola, Florida, where he completed flight instruction and was designated Naval Aviator on 7 April 1931. On 2 June 1934 he was attached to the *Macon*.

During May 1934 the *Macon* took part in the Warner Brothers' movie *Here Comes the Navy*, starring James Cagney, Pat O'Brien, and Gloria Stuart. (*Warner Brothers*)

The *Macon* Goes Hollywood

During May 1934 the *Macon* and its Sparrowhawks briefly participated in the Warner Brothers' movie *Here Comes the Navy*, a 'fast-moving comedy enriched by an authentic naval setting', starring James Cagney, Pat O'Brien, and Gloria Stuart. During the next year, the *Macon* and its Sparrowhawks would make a cameo appearance in the *Devil Dogs of the Air*, which was reviewed as a 'flag-waving piece of propaganda for the Marines'. It again starred Cagney and O'Brien in their pursuit of Margaret

Lindsay. In a very brief scene, an admiral directs the *Macon* to drop its observation aircraft and report on a major Fleet exercise.

Sellers' Report

The most significant airship event of June 1934 was a damaging ten-page report prepared by Adm. Daniel Sellers for CNO Adm. William Standley, which opened the airship's future to serious doubt. The Sellers' Report asserted that the *Macon* was 22,000lb 'overweight', which reduced her range and endurance, that it was impossible for the airship to operate at high altitudes; that its maximum speed was only 85mph, and that she was 'vulnerable' to weather, aircraft attacks, and to anti-aircraft fire. She had been unable to operate in Fleet exercises for more than an average of twelve hours without being determined as 'shot down', and was 'definitely unable to remain in the area of operations for more than 36 hours'. Sellers concluded that 'the USS *Macon* has failed to demonstrate its usefulness as a unit of the Fleet'; and Sellers was 'decidedly of the opinion that the further expenditure of public funds for this type of vessel for the Navy is not justified'. To construct another airship of its type would cost $4 million ($94 million in 2025), and in Sellers' opinion these funds would be better spent on thirty or forty flying boats, which had an operating radius of 3,000 miles. Sellers conceded that the *Macon* had demonstrated steady performance improvement, which was 'remarkable and commendable'. He also acknowledged that the airship's use in 'congested tactical exercises' placed it at a disadvantage; but he emphatically declined to consider how else she could have been or could be used. He concluded that 'the USS *Macon* has failed to demonstrate its usefulness as a unit of the Fleet'; and he was 'decidedly of the opinion that the further expenditure of public funds for this type of vessel for the Navy is not justified'.

Adm. Daniel Sellers prepared a damaging ten-page report for CNO Adm. William Standley, which opened the airship's future to serious doubt. Sellers (L) is shown with Lt Cdr Alger Dresel, who was the captain of the *Macon* at the time. (*USN*)

After reading the Sellers' Report, Adm. Ernest King's opinion was that it was 'very confused' and that in view of Sellers' 'recognition of the *Macon*'s remarkable progress', his 'final judgement seemed contradictory'. King called attention to the fact that the rigid airship was the only aircraft then available capable of undertaking over-water operations more than 500 miles from base. Regarding the flying boats with a 3,000-mile operating radius that Sellers anticipated, King countered that these flying boats were unavailable in 1934, and that using an airship carrying aircraft was faster and less expensive than by any other means available for acquiring information per square mile of ocean. He addressed the *Macon*'s tactical employment and contended that this was 'not the airship's practical function, and it was not advocated by anyone acquainted with the airship's obvious shortcomings and unique capabilities'. King insisted that while the *Shenandoah* and *Akron* appeared to confirm an 'unqualified notion of the airship's "vulnerability", this was a relative matter, especially under combat conditions, and was equally applicable to aircraft and surface vessels'.

Despite King's status and the supposed validity of his claims, since the *Shenandoah* and *Akron* losses, the Navy was unconvinced of the airship's place in combat, considering its continuing experimental status and that there was only one of the expensive airships available to the Fleet at any one time. There were those upper-tier naval officers who thought the millions of dollars spent building expensive airships could be better used to build one destroyer, half a cruiser, and many patrol aircraft. If the *Akron* had not been lost, and two airships and two HTA units had been available for the Fleet exercises during the first half of 1934, perhaps the rigid airship would have played a more significant role, gained more information and experience, and impressed Adm. Sellers more. However, during the second half of 1934, it became imperative that the *Macon* develop an operational agenda, and then test it in future Fleet exercises.

Lt Cdr Hubert Wiley Named *Macon* Commander

On 11 July 1934, Lt Cdr Hubert Wiley was named Commander of the airship, relieving Cdr Dresel. Wiley had served aboard the *Shenandoah* and then the *Los Angeles*, which he commanded from May 1929 to April 1930. He served as executive officer aboard the *Akron* until its loss on 4 April 1933 and was the only surviving officer.

On 11 July 1934, Lt Cdr Herbert Wiley (R) was named commander of the airship, relieving Cdr Dresel. (*USN*)

Subsequently, Dresel became commanding officer at NAS Moffett Field, where he served for five years, then was executive officer of the USS *Raleigh* for a year, commanded a destroyer squadron in the Pacific, and entered the United States Naval War College in Newport, Rhode Island, where he graduated in the class of 1937. From 1938 until he was forced to retire from the Navy due to physical disability in the early 1940s, Dresel served on the staff of the Naval War College.

After he relieved Dresel, Wiley drove the *Macon* and her crew vigorously and achieved significant results in increasing her operational effectiveness and that of her HTA contingent. He and the BuAer considered any time in the hangar was time not spent in the air proving themselves. The *Macon*'s HTA pilots were initially concerned about Wiley assuming command as they thought him to be too conservative and would maintain the established LTA doctrine, relegating the HTA Unit to a secondary scouting role. Wiley had more experience with HTA units than any other airship captain as he had been the *Los Angeles*' XO when Lt Gorton hooked on for the first time and during his time on the *Akron* Wiley had operated closely with that airship's HTA Unit.

Lt (JG) Gerald Huff (shown in his 1929 USNA photo) was finally assigned as the fourth *Macon* HTA pilot in October 1934 after not having one for four months. (*USN*)

On 12 July, the day after assuming command, the new *Macon* commander allayed the HTA pilots' concerns when he launched Miller and Kivette's Sparrowhawks for hook-on exercises over the Los Angeles area. They also practised Mackey's 60-60 manoeuvring board search pattern, during which their Sparrowhawks disappeared out at 90 degrees from the airship directed by Mackey on the radio, who charted their courses on a plotting board. During this trial Wiley also had the pilots test the Fisher-Coulter experimental radio compass and Fisher-Miller voice communication equipment, which was designed to extend scouting range. The trial was a success as the aircraft reappeared about an hour later holding at the same 90 degree bearing from the *Macon*. Meanwhile, pilots Richardson and Simpler made their first trapeze flights using the Waco XJW-1s.

On 17 July, Richardson fractured both ankles in a training crash while simulating an emergency landing, which marked the demise of N2Y-1 (8604). It left the *Macon*'s HTA Unit with three pilots, and a replacement fourth was not received until 19 October when Lieutenant (JG) Gerald Huff was finally assigned. Huff had graduated from the Naval Academy in 1929 and served on the battleship *Colorado*, becoming a Naval Aviator at Pensacola in 1930. After serving with Utility Squadron One and Patrol Squadron 9 (USS *Wright*) he was assigned to the *Macon*.

Wiley Leads the *Macon* on a Historic Sea Search

During mid-July, Wiley seemingly requested a 'protracted flight' as an open sea search operation, but he also saw it as a prospective public relations ploy, demonstrating to its sceptics what the *Macon* could accomplish as an aircraft carrier. Wiley intended to intercept the heavy cruisers USS *New Orleans* (CA-32) and *Houston* (CA-30), which were en route through the Panama Canal on a 12,000-mile trip to Hawaii, with President Roosevelt and First Lady Eleanor as passengers on the *Houston* on their way to a Hawaiian vacation. FDR's stop at Cartagena, Colombia, made him the first President to visit South America and he was the first to visit Hawaii. The *Macon* departed Moffett Field on 18 July and

The cruiser USS *Houston* (CV-30) was en route after passing through the Panama Canal to Hawaii with President (X on photo) and Mrs Roosevelt (X) aboard when Wiley adeptly directed the *Macon* 1,500 miles in poor weather to find the ship despite every measure to keep its location a secret. (*USN*)

Wiley's navigation team determined the *Houston*'s position to be about 1,500 miles east after leaving the Panama Canal several days earlier.

As the *Macon* approached the two cruisers' predicted position, at about 1030 Miller and Kivette donned their winter flight gear and were launched to scout ahead of the airship with their landing gear replaced by 30-gallon fuel tanks. They conducted their search patterns in the cold drenching rain squalls, with Kivette spotting the cruisers at about 1145 and Miller quickly joining him. The *Houston*'s lookouts were surprised to see two unidentified aircraft with possible 'bombs' hanging below their fuselages appear out of nowhere so far out to sea, especially when all the Navy's aircraft carriers were in the Atlantic. Soon, the F9Cs were recognised by their skyhooks and their 'bombs' as their auxiliary fuel tanks, and the cruisers waited for the appearance of the *Macon*. Roosevelt wired his congratulations to Wiley: 'The President compliments you and your planes on your fine performance and excellent navigation.' While avoiding rain squalls, *Macon* recovered its planes and then asked the *Houston* for permission to drop two gift packages for the president. Wiley relaunched the two Sparrowhawks, each 'armed with gift bags' containing a *San Francisco Chronicle* from the day the *Macon* left, the latest issues of *Time* and *Newsweek*, and some mail. Some mail included specially stamped and addressed commemorative letters from the *Macon* to President Roosevelt, taking into consideration FDR's interest in philately. Both Miller's and Kivette's Sparrowhawks trailed a line with waterproof bags attached and both released them close enough into the sea that the cruisers could slow to launch their landing boats to make a recovery. Shortly afterwards the *Macon* manoeuvred its way between a pair of rain squalls to join its planes loitering over the cruisers, while the president and his party watched. The appreciative president wired Wiley: 'Well done. Thank you for the papers.'

Afterward, Miller's F9C-2 was recovered easily in heavy rain, but Kivette's approached in worsening weather with gusty winds. A gust caused his plane to hit the trapeze yoke so forcefully that two struts of its tripod were broken off, leaving only one strut hook to hook on to the airship. Kivette either had to hook on or to ditch at sea. Kivette skilfully made the 'trap', leaving his F9C-2 hanging on one strut to the trapeze. Miller and the hangar crew went down on to the trapeze with a cable and shackle and placed a loop of cable around the propeller shaft with the other end shackled to the yoke of the trapeze so that the plane could be hoisted aboard.

Wiley's direction of the *Macon* was commendable as, with minimal information ,the airship had flown 1,500 miles in poor weather and found the president despite every measure to keep his location a secret. While this accomplishment should have made Wiley a hero; it was not appreciated by many surface Navy officers as Wiley had had demonstrated the *Macon* to be a valuable long-range scout. That the president and a gaggle of reporters was aboard the *Houston* to witness the feat made matters worse.

When Wiley and the *Macon* arrived back at Moffett on 21 July, with its F9Cs flying practising search tactics en route, the *Macon* had not only completed its longest flight to date, but Wiley had accomplished what previous Navy airship captains had not: he'd shown the *Macon* could be a more effective scout than a surface cruiser in finding the enemy.

While the mail delivery to the president generated beneficial publicity, top Navy brass considered it a 'stunt', particularly Commander of the Fleet and airship detractor Adm. Joseph Reeves, who had relieved Adm. Daniel Sellers as c-in-c. Reeves was incensed, considering Wiley's description of the *Macon*'s flight as 'a long-range scouting operation for a ship at sea' without divulging the intended target (*Houston*). Sellers considered this as 'insubordination', as revealed in a cable from Reeves to Adm. King the next day:

> *Macon* requested and received from Commander Battle Force authority to make protracted flight to sea commencing Wednesday, 18 July. There was no reference made in request from *Macon* to making contact with *Houston*. Commander Battle Force had no information regarding any papers carried by *Macon* on this trip. *Macon* directed to submit full report.

Adm. Joseph Reeves, Commander of the Fleet, lambasted Wiley's brilliant discovery of the *Houston* with the President aboard as ill-timed, ill-advised, and conceived with disregard for proper Naval procedure. (*USN*)

Reeves continued his tirade in another memo: 'The Commander-in-Chief [Reeves] considers the flight, ill-timed, ill-advised, and conceived with disregard for proper Naval procedure.' Adm. William Standley, Chief of Naval Operations, stated that he considered it as a 'publicity stunt … he [Wiley] had no business doing'. With rumours of a court martial stirring, Wiley's Naval career could be in jeopardy, but he was saved only by the intervention of airship advocate Ernest King, the Chief of the Bureau of Aeronautics.

July–November 1934: The *Macon* Conducts Extensive Training, Tactical Experimentation and Equipment Development Operations

During July until November, the majority of the Navy's Fleet was in the Atlantic and the *Macon* was unrestricted and could conduct extensive individual training, tactical experimentation, and equipment development conducted during 14 flights totalling 404 hours. During this time, the *Macon* assisted in the calibration of the West Coast Navy Radio Direction Finder (RDF) installations, and performed experiments with the observation spy basket, pilot rescue equipment, and with a prototype device to pick up water ballast from the sea.

The *Macon* became involved in especially important radio direction finding and voice communications trials, which were vital for airship–aircraft operations. During January 1934, German-born electronics engineer Dr Gerhard Fisher contacted *Macon* communications officer Lt Howard Coulter to demonstrate a simple low-frequency, radio direction-finding design he was developing. Coulter recognised that Fisher's device could allow safe Sparrowhawk operation out to the maximum aircraft range. Conventional RDF sets broadcast an auditory signal that needed to be translated into a bearing while Fisher's new set delivered an easily read visual indicator. While bearings could be taken with it; when its loop antenna was locked in its neutral position it also functioned as a homing set, allowing the Sparrowhawk pilot to be able to home on any radio signal just by flying a course that maintained the set's visual indicator on zero. Thus, the pilot could

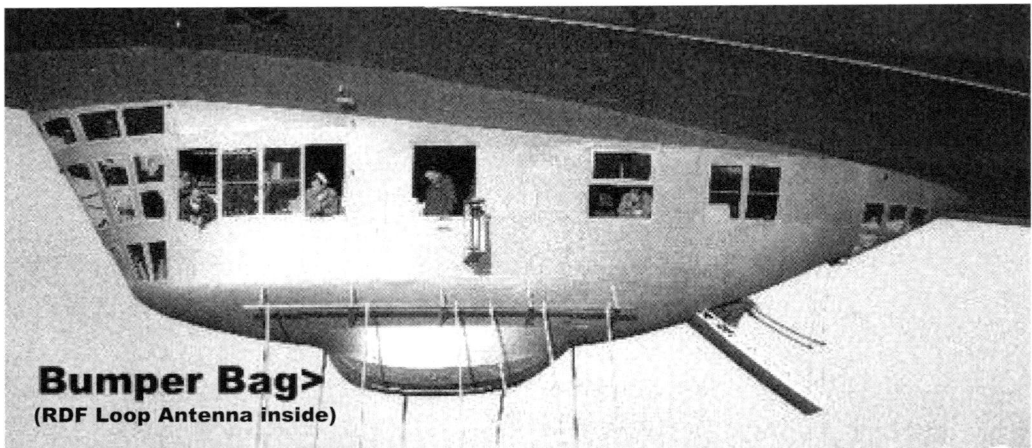

The new RDF Fisher-Coulter radio set, which gave much-improved communications and bearings taking, was installed aboard the *Macon* with its loop antenna inside the bumper bag under the control car. (*USN*)

not follow the signal in the wrong direction as he could with aural RDF equipment. The Fisher-Coulter set was installed aboard the *Macon* with its loop antenna in the bumper bag under the control car, ready for communications and to take bearings. At its inception its range was only 500 miles; by the end of the year, it was improved so that the *Macon* could obtain accurate triangulations from stations 3,000 miles away. Also, at that time, Dr Fisher collaborated with Lt Harold Miller to combine a 500kc homing set with a 4,000kc radio receiver, which was installed in F9C Nos. 9056 and 9058, with the antenna carried in a huge loop around the upper and lower wings. The Fisher-Miller set would solve most of the F9C's communications and navigation problems, needing only minimal modifications to increase range. However, initially a pilot, now flying his Sparrowhawk with its landing gear replaced by a range-increasing 30-gallon fuel tank needed confidence in the set to fly miles out of sight of the airship, so, on their first flights from the *Macon*, pilots trained and practised in its use flying 50–75 miles just out of sight of and then back to their mothership.

The Spy Basket Gets a Second Chance

After its turbulently failed 1932 tests strung out under the *Akron*, the spy basket had been disregarded by the BuAer but after the Army Air Corps had successes using a spy basket with its new TC-13 blimp, a refurbished Navy spy basket was shipped to Lakehurst during the spring of 1934. The basket was tested hanging from overhead cranes at Lakehurst's hangar, and later from under a K-1 blimp. Although the spy basket had a sound design, the arrangement of its suspension bridles caused excessive yawing (rotation). On 8 August 1934, after modifications, the spy basket was lowered from the *Macon* for the first time, but its performance continued to be 'unpredictable'. It was then shipped to Stanford's Guggenheim Aeronautical Laboratory, where additional testing determined that the addition of an auxiliary vertical stabiliser beneath its tail was required. Upon its return to Lakehurst, the unmanned contraption was weighted with 200lb of sandbags and was successfully tested under the *Macon*. On 27 September it received its first passenger, Lt Cdr Jesse Kenworthy, for a fifteen-minute ride. As the basket was lowered, the quarter-inch cable formed into a wide U-shape (catenary) and the basket trailed the airship down astern to 1,500ft, trailing 200ft behind and 500ft above the ocean below. After Kenworthy was reeled in, HTA pilots Min Miller and Scott Peck enjoyed their turns at riding it. Several subsequent experiments were

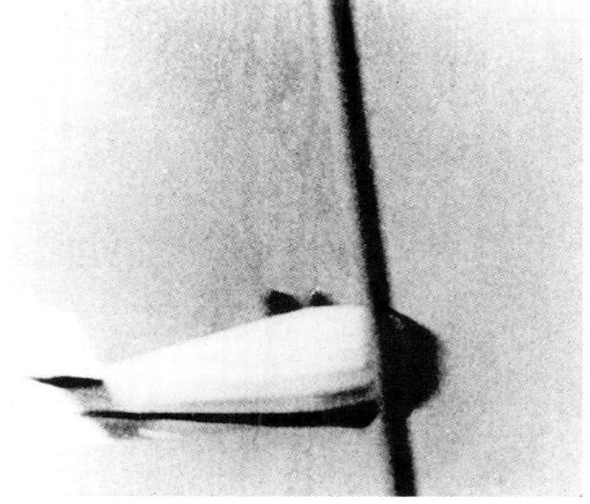

After its turbulently failed 1932 tests under the *Akron*, the spy basket had been forgotten by the BuAer but was resurrected during August 1934. It was used several times with better results by the *Macon* when the Sparrowhawks were hangar-bound due to poor weather. (*USN*)

conducted with the spy basket, but no matter how exciting it was for its riders; the airship's aircraft certainly superseded it, and the *Macon* only used it a few times when the Sparrowhawks were hangar-bound due to poor weather.

October 1934 Sparrowhawk Search Exercises

On 8 October, *Macon* departed Moffett Field at 1755 for an open-ocean search. Miller, Kivette, and Simpler followed in their Sparrowhawks and were taken aboard. During the morning of 9 October, the *Macon* flew out about 450 miles on the first phase of the search to begin a hunt for a Japanese freighter inbound to the west coast. Low ceilings prevented the use of the Sparrowhawks, but the spy basket was used most of the day without any sightings. Commander Wiley then decided to change the search focus to the Matson Lines SS *Lurline*, known to be en route from Honolulu to San Francisco. *Macon* located *Lurline* on the morning of the 10th and for the next two hours she purposely opened the range and then launched two Sparrowhawks to relocate *Lurline* using 60-60 search patterns and their radio homing sets. The F9Cs, without their undercarriages and using auxiliary fuel tanks, found and tracked the *Lurline*, then broke contact, returned to the *Macon* and then conducted a new search, which was successful. While returning to Moffett, *Macon* launched its Sparrowhawks, which practised preplanned search patterns and the use of the radio homing equipment en route.

During the morning of 11 October, *Macon* launched Simpler's and Miller's Sparrowhawks at 900 but recalled them after about an hour due to rapidly deteriorating weather. Wiley dropped the *Macon* down to 800ft to provide better visibility for the returning Sparrowhawks. As Simpler was approaching the trapeze, *Macon* was not yet up to recovery speed of about 70mph and Wiley started the Nos. 5 and 6 engines. But Simpler received a premature landing signal from the airship and a wind gust caused him to collide with the trapeze during his short climb up to it. Simpler was unable to hook on and the trapeze's yoke broke the guard tube of his skyhook a few inches forward of the hook. The guard tube was the only fore and aft member of the hook mechanism. Simpler's hook was locked with the yoke and there was only a gap of a few inches in the damaged guard tube through which Simpler could get free. While Simpler made a very cautious disengagement, a gust caused his hook to bend 30 degrees, which left little left of the hook to re-hook. On his hook-on approach, fog shrouded the *Macon*'s hull and only the trapeze could be seen. With his fuel almost expended, Simpler had only one chance to hook on. Wiley increased the airship's speed to its maximum of 85mph to make the landing easier and Simpler approached the trapeze at a power-stalled attitude and incredibly hooked on with a resounding thud. But the F9C-2 only hung on to the trapeze by one bolt. It was not possible to move the trapeze because if the remaining bolt sheared the Sparrowhawk would fall tail first with its engine shut off. A looped rope was quickly dropped to Simpler, who was carefully drawn up into the hangar. Meanwhile, the aircraft could not be transported into the hangar until Lt John Reppy climbed down on to the trapeze and reinforced the hook with wire straps. After the aircraft was inside the hangar, its landing gear was reattached and Kivette flew it to Moffett in place of the very shaken Simpler. This incident was the only near-accident in almost five years of hundreds of airship hook-on retrievals and launches, and considering the experimental character of the techniques, this record was extraordinary and an acknowledgement of the proficiency of the HTA pilots and the maintenance crews. After delivering Simpler's damaged F9C-2 to Moffett, Kivette returned to the *Macon* in an XJW-1 and then ferried Simpler and Miller back to Moffett in the front cockpit. They then flew two spare Sparrowhawks to the *Macon*, adding 5,600 more pounds of ballast to the three F9Cs already aboard the *Macon* to help with mooring.

Macon flew again on 12 October to participate in *Fox Movietone News* film displaying the operations of two Sparrowhawks without landing gear performing airship launches and retrievals on both the trapeze and the perch. The newsreel, released in commemoration of Navy Day, 27 October 1934, received nationwide attention.

November 1934 Exercise Z

On 7 November, while based at Camp Kearny, *Macon* participated in Fleet Exercise Z as part of Orange Forces defending the west coast against the Fleet sailing north from Panama along the Mexican coast. Early the next morning, Adm. Alfred Johnson, Orange Commander, sent the *Macon* an urgent message disclosing that his flying boats were grounded in San Diego due to dense fog and the airship was also to search their area. At 0555, two *Macon* F9Cs, piloted by Miller and Kivette, were launched and at 0708 spotted the main body of the 'enemy' fleet. However, at 0913 *Macon* was also detected by the enemy carrier but could not leave the area as she had to retrieve the two F9Cs. Meanwhile, *Saratoga* launched six Vought SU-1 dive bombers to attack the airship. Although the dive bombers made an attack, Wiley's expert and unexpected defensive manoeuvring thwarted them from receiving credit for a kill. The two Sparrowhawks returned during the attack and Miller, low on fuel, headed directly to the trapeze while Kivette chased after the attackers. After Kivette was retrieved, both aircraft were refuelled, launched, and continued covert tracking of *Saratoga* at 16,000ft (4,877m) until the end of the exercise at 1600. After the exercise, Adm. Henry Butler, Commander Air Battle Forces, commended *Macon*'s 'excellent scouting and the character of the radio reports by its planes'.

Macon flew from Moffett to San Diego during 20–22 November and en route Wiley had the F9Cs simulate dive bombing attacks on her, so the airship could practice evasive manoeuvres, and to drill its gun crews. She returned to Camp Kearny during the first week of December for a formal inspection by Adm. Henry Butler.

6–7 December 1934: *Macon* Participates in Fleet Exercises

Macon participated in Fleet exercises on 6–7 December, covering the Fleet during its move from San Pedro to San Francisco. For the first time during an exercise, *Macon* carried four Sparrowhawks. On the 6th at 0600 *Macon* began its participation from about 50 miles west of the coast and began a southerly search. About an hour later, Miller and Huff, the latter on his first operational flight from *Macon*, were launched to initiate their search to the west. Forty minutes after the first flight, Kivette and Simpler were sent out on a search to the east, where they found part of the enemy's scouting line and were recalled to the airship. In the meantime, at about 0900, *Macon*'s lookouts spotted an enemy battleship to

During the December 1934 Fleet exercises, six *Lexington* Vought SU-2 bombers approached the *Macon* from out of the sun for a successful attack, causing the exercise umpires to rule that the airship was destroyed. It was then reincarnated as the ZRS-6 to continue. (*USN*)

the west, and Wiley swung the airship around to circle the enemy. While circumnavigating the enemy, the *Macon* received reports from Kivette and Simpler that the battleship was trailed by a heavy escort. At that time the first Miller and Huff flight was returning. By 1100 *Macon* was back on its original course, receiving reports from the second flight, which was tracking the enemy carrier *Lexington* and its escorts. *Macon* tried the same manoeuvres that she used with such success against *Saratoga* in November, but without the same success. At 1230 six *Lexington* Vought SU-2 dive bombers approached out of the sun for a successful attack on the airship, and the exercise umpires ruled that *Macon* was destroyed. *Macon* continued in the exercise, 'reconstituted' as ZRS6, but only for a brief time as within an hour of its first destruction she was 'shot down' again.

Macon was more successful on 7 December. Throughout that morning, she and her aircraft located and tracked various enemy units, but did not find the important enemy carriers. At 1325, the exercise was suspended when two floatplanes off the cruiser *Cincinnati* had become lost after running out of fuel and forced to land at sea. The entire fleet was ordered to search for the lost planes and at 1348 Kivette and Simpler were launched from *Macon* for a search to the south, and at 1507 Miller and Huff were sent out to the north. Some thirty-five minutes later, Miller and Huff located the floating planes and dropped smoke flares to mark the area. About ten minutes later, *Macon* joined its Sparrowhawks and loitered above the downed floatplanes for thirty minutes until the cruiser *Portland* arrived and retrieved the floatplanes and their crews. After the exercise, Adm. Henry Butler again commended the *Macon* and its aircraft for their 'valuable service in a highly efficient manner' in locating the *Cincinnati*'s lost float planes. However, Adm. Joseph Reeves again criticised the *Macon* as 'again failing to demonstrate fitness for service under conditions where assailment by enemy planes is a probability'.

1935 Operations
Airship Future Improves

Despite Reeves' gloomy assessments of the *Macon*'s performance, the future of Navy airships appeared to be improved as she was scheduled to begin operations between California and Hawaii. Compared to the congested exercises of 1934 that placed the airship at a great handicap, these operations would be held over many miles of open ocean where no aircraft of the time could fly. Fleet Problem XVI, scheduled for spring 1935, deployed the Fleet west of Hawaii. where the *Macon* and its aircraft would have ample area in which to authenticate their true scouting capabilities.

During January the Federal Aviation Commission showed renewed interest in the airship, endorsing the Navy to expand its airship operations. The FAC General Board granted $17 million ($377.7 million in 2025) for a training airship to be built immediately to replace the *Los Angeles* and for a programme to be approved to initiate commercial airship operations. The General Board evaluated the Navy's airship policy and recommended immediate construction of a 2.5 million cu ft rigid training airship that would carry two or three aircraft. The commercial programme was to include two large Zeppelin-type airliners, a moderate-sized, metal-clad airship transport, and an airship passenger terminal on the east coast. Although CNO Adm. Standley clearly disagreed with this recommendation, he grudgingly approved the construction of the training airship.

January 1935 Operations

On 2 January 1935, *Macon* departed Moffett Field to rendezvous with *Lexington* off San Pedro for daytime airship visibility tests that concluded her 'conspicuousness could be of a lesser problem if she were careful'. No hook-on flights were recorded for this test.

During 11–12 January the *Macon*'s aircraft were on eleven scheduled two-hour standby patrols during Amelia Earhart's flight from Honolulu to the west coast if she were forced down at sea.

On 15–16 January *Macon* participated with the Fleet off the California Channel Islands to test Fleet detectability under darkened ship conditions. *Macon* carried four aircraft but there is no record that they were operated.

On 31 January, *Macon* left Moffett Field for a two-day open sea flight to participate in a series of drills. The F9C-2 pilots flew simulated attacks on the *Macon* to give its lookouts and gun crews additional detection and gunnery defence experience. The Sparrowhawks flew a series of successful direction-finding and communications tests and were able to take accurate radio bearings on the airship from 185 miles away; clear Morse code communication was established from out to 140 miles, and intelligible voice transmission was obtained out to 95 miles. The F9Cs then practised night hook ons, during which they demonstrated that they had no difficulty in operating from *Macon*'s trapeze in the dark. The next day they participated in further long-range radio homing tests. Wiley had his pilots practise these drills to prepare for a tactic they intended to employ during the next large-scale Fleet Exercise XVI to be held from 29 April until 10 June, between Alaska, Hawaii, and the US west coast. They planned for the *Macon* to track the *Lexington* until

To control nocturnal F9C-2 trapeze practice, for the first time complete control of the *Macon* was successfully transferred from the control car bridge to the auxiliary control station in the rear fin, where visibility was much better. (*USN*)

nightfall, and then launch its four F9Cs in a simulated dive-bombing attack on the carrier, after which the aircraft would return to the airship with the aid of their homing sets, rearm and refuel and then be launched to conduct second and possibly third attacks. It was correctly supposed that the *Lexington* would be very vulnerable to the *Macon*'s dive bombers as night operations by carrier aircraft were virtually unknown. On 1 February, the aircraft continued their nocturnal trapeze drills, as well as exercises for the lookouts and gun crews. To control nocturnal F9C-2 trapeze practice, for the first time complete control of the *Macon* was successfully transferred from the control car bridge to the auxiliary control station.

11–12 February 1935: The *Macon* Disaster

During September 1934, the BuAer determined that the *Macon*'s tail section required additional structural reinforcements and sent the necessary parts to Moffett Field with caveats:

> While the Bureau hesitates to prescribe the additions which are perhaps unnecessary, since the present structure is considered to be amply strong for any operations over the sea, it does seem wise to provide additional strength in order that the *Macon* may be prepared to carry out any mission without risk of local damage to the ship's vertical and horizontal fins. Because the work is not urgent, it is considered that it can be accomplished from time to time, as opportunity offers, at the discretion of the Commanding Officer, and, therefore, will not interfere with operating schedules.

BuAer Chief Adm. Ernest King and CNO Adm. William Standley needed the *Macon* to be employed as often as possible to determine her value and thus her future. Wiley's need to establish the *Macon*'s worth coerced him to prioritise operations over maintenance as hours in the air, necessary for training and testing, were obtained by delaying the hours on the ground required for installing the tail reinforcements.

With the *Macon* moored at Sunnyvale during the morning of 2 February, Wiley and his crew were confident that she was ready to demonstrate outstanding scouting proficiency during the next Fleet operation scheduled for 11–12 February 1935. During these exercises, the Fleet was to move north from San Diego and Long Beach to San Francisco, conducting minor tactical exercises en route. Adm. Henry Butler, Commander Air Battle Force, specifically ordered the *Macon* not to directly participate in the Fleet exercises, but to use the Fleet's movements for training in strategic airship scouting. The *Macon* was specifically directed to search and identify all Fleet units and to maintain a plot of their movements and dispositions. *Macon* and its Sparrowhawks were to remain undetected and maintain radio silence until 1800 on 12 February.

At 0710 during the morning of 11 February 1935, *Macon* departed Moffett Field and headed out to sea. Thirty minutes later, Miller and Huff flew aboard. As soon as their Sparrowhawks were stowed in the hangar, Chief Aviation Machinists Mate William Cody had his mechanics remove the Sparrowhawk's landing gear and install and top off their long-range auxiliary tanks for the scouting flights. At approximately 0800 the *Macon* crossed the Pacific coast and headed south and about 1015, near Point Arguello Light House, off Santa Barbara, Miller and Huff were launched. They were to make a sweep down the Santa Barbara Channel to investigate the Fleet anchorages at Long Beach and San Diego. Five minutes after Miller and Huff left, Kivette and Simpler arrived from

Moffett and were taken aboard to also have their landing gear removed and reconfigured with the auxiliary fuel tanks.

Macon began loitering around Point Arguello, delegating active scouting to its aircraft. At 1235, Kivette and Simpler were launched to overlap the first flight and at 1410 Miller and Huff returned. During their four-hour flight they had flown 200 miles south to arrive at the Fleet anchorage at San Diego, which was almost at the limit of the F9C-2's extended range. At about 1500 Kivette and Simpler returned from the south after having checked possible Fleet rendezvous areas off the Channel Islands extending along the southern California coast near Santa Barbara to north of Los Angeles. The Sparrowhawks had determined the positions, dispositions, and general movement of the Fleet units and Wiley used this information to circle the *Macon* over the advancing surface forces. At 1705 Miller and Huff were launched and the two aircraft sortied to the north and returned with information confirming the composition of the Fleet and its northward movement during the night.

During the night, the *Macon* circled north of Catalina Island and at dawn on 12 February, Kivette and Simpler were launched near Anacapa Island. Since the 'enemy' was moving north, the pilots were directed to conduct their search up the Santa Barbara Channel as far north as Point Arguello, then to return to the *Macon* west of the Channel Islands. The *Macon* recovered Kivette and Simpler at about 0950. Soon after 1000 *Macon* turned north and at 1230 Wiley ordered Miller and Huff to be launched on another search to the north, where he anticipated the Fleet to be assembling. At 1310 *Macon* received orders releasing it from the operation and at 1550, off Point Piedras Blancas, Miller and Huff were recovered, and the *Macon* continued north for Point Sur and headed back to Sunnyvale with all four Sparrowhawks aboard.

At 0504, near the Point Sur Lighthouse, Wiley turned the *Macon* further seaward, at which time the airship's upper fin suddenly broke free and the *Macon* ascended rapidly. Wiley worked hectically to bring the wounded airship under control using its one available rudder but instead it began to descend from 4,000ft at 300ft per minute. After jettisoning all ballast, Wiley attempted to release the Sparrowhawks from their hangar but the *Macon*'s steep descent jammed them on their rail mechanism. The descent continued until the *Macon*'s stern hit the water. Wiley quickly ordered everyone to leave the control car before it submerged, and lifeboats were released as the *Macon* sank slowly stern first at about 1820. Several signal rockets were fired, which attracted the cruisers in the vicinity. Unlike the loss of the *Akron* when Wiley was only one of three of the seventy-six crew to survive, thanks to his emergency pilotage only two crewmen were lost and eighty-three were rescued. The *Macon* had flown 54 flights in 1,798.2 hours before its loss. Four Sparrowhawks were lost and had flown their last ever sorties from an airship.

After the crash Adm. Standley expressed his viewpoint to the media: 'This should be a solemn warning to this country with respect to the use of LTA aircraft. I have never approved of the use of LTA aircraft for other than commercial purposes, and I am more than ever convinced of their unsuitability for military and naval purposes.' Anti-rigid airship bias had already become entrenched among senior Navy decision-makers.

Macon officers rescued by the USS *Richmond* (L to R): Lt (JG) George Campbell; Lt (JG) Gerald Huff*; Lt Anthony Davis; Lt Harold Miller*; Lt Cdr George Mills; Lt Cdr Calvin Bolster; Lt (JG) Earl Van Swearingen; Lt Howard Coulter; Chief Boatswain William Buckley; Lt (JG) Leroy Simpler* (USN). (* = HTA pilot).

Wiley and the Development of the Macon's HTA Component

On 9 May 1929, Lt Cdr Charles Rosendahl passed the command of the *Los Angeles* to Lt Cdr Hubert Wiley, an airshipman with no previous experience with aircraft. After the trapeze equipment was approved for operations on the *Los Angeles* on 24 June 1929, under Wiley's command aircraft hook-on procedure made great strides. On 20 August, Jake Gorton, piloting the Vought UO-1, made the first successful hook-on attempt on the *Los Angeles*. On 28 August 1929, the *Los Angeles* made a much-anticipated first public demonstration of its hook-on development at an appearance at the National Air Races held over Cleveland, Ohio. Hook-on tests continued and were perfected during the autumn and winter of 1929 using the Vought UO-1. On 31 January 1930 Navy glider specialist Lt Ralph Barnaby flew the Navy's Prufling glider from the *Los Angeles*. On 31 March 1930 Wiley was replaced as *Los Angeles* commander by Lt Cdr Vincent Clarke. Using his *Los Angeles* experience, in the years directly ahead Wiley showed an appreciation of the role that hook-on aircraft needed to play for the next two huge rigid Navy airships to be a military success.

HTA pilot leaders, like Lts Ward Harrigan and Harold Miller had previously recognised and recommended that the airship's aircraft should assume reconnaissance duty while the airship should function as a command, control, communications, and logistics centre. It was not until 1933–34 that airship officers receptive to this point of view assumed command. The *Macon*'s last commanding officer, Lt Cdr Herbert Wiley, correctly understood that the rigid airship carrying aircraft was a completely new concept requiring adjustments in tactics and doctrine.

Wiley became the first commander of a ZRS airship who actively implemented the concept of the LTA as an aircraft carrier and made extensive progress in developing the tactical and doctrinal integration of aircraft with the rigid airship. Wiley explained his rationale in a 1934 US Naval Institute Proceedings article, 'The Value of Airships':

> The airship carrier has certain advantages over the surface carrier. It does not have to head into the wind to launch or to recover its planes as both craft are floating in the same medium and, relative to each other, there is no wind. Planes can be operated from it at night with a facility equal to that of daylight operation and without bright lights on the airship. The use of planes to enlarge the scouting area gives enormous advantage to the airship. With five planes, the outfit at present (and more could be provided on present or future ships), one plane can be stationed continuously on each side of the airship. If the visibility is 40 miles and the planes are 80 miles abeam of the airship, this allows the sweep of an area 240 miles wide at a cruising speed of

Although during his seven months of command Wiley's collaboration with his hook-on pilots resulted in innovations and the implementation of some very inventive scouting tactics, these would not be enough to save the Navy's rigid airship programme after the *Macon*'s loss. (USN)

> 60 knots. Covering 172,000 square miles in a day's work is quite a feat for a vessel costing less in men and money than a destroyer!

During his seven months of command, Wiley collaborated with HTA hook-on pilots in the innovation and implementation of several very inventive scouting tactics. Under Wiley, the *Macon*'s aircraft were continually capable of flying beyond line-of-sight reconnaissance by incorporating radio direction-finding equipment, adding external fuel tanks, and undergoing rigorous training in scouting methods that would establish him as the most successful of the Navy's airship captains.

However, what Wiley and his crew accomplished during his seven months of command, the combining of *Macon* and its F9Cs into a viable means of very-long-range reconnaissance, would not be sufficient to continue the programme after the *Macon* crashed into the Pacific Ocean in February 1935. The crashes of three airships and earlier application of antiquated methods of the airship and its aircraft utilisation by Rosendahl and other airship commanders had already delegitimised the rigid airship in the Navy's view.

The *Macon*: Appraisal as an Aircraft Carrier

Ultimately, the *Macon* participated in seven exercises from 1933 to 1934 that were designed to emphasise the offensive and scouting capabilities of airship aircraft carrier aviation during a tactical Fleet action. Because the exercise areas were constrained, this, consequently, nullified the strategic reconnaissance capabilities of the rigid airship and its aircraft. Despite doctrinal innovations implemented by the *Macon*'s two commanders and crew, the *Macon* suffered heavily in the exercises when forced into direct contact with orthodox carrier aviation directed by exercise control measures. In seven exercises, exercise umpires ruled the *Macon* destroyed nine times, causing Adm. Sellers to conclude that the *Macon* could not survive longer than twelve hours in naval operations against any enemy force. Sellers reported to CNO Standley that 'the USS *Macon* has failed to demonstrate its usefulness as a unit of the Fleet' and that 'the further expenditure of public funds for this type of vessel for the Navy is not justified'. Admiral King defended the *Macon* and insisted that the artificial constraints of the exercises did not allow the *Macon* to operate in its intended role as a strategic reconnaissance platform. Eventually, King managed to convince the General Board that the rigid airship and its aircraft were best suited for strategic reconnaissance over the open ocean and should be re-evaluated in this role rather than in confined tactical scenarios. Adm. Standley disagreed, but eventually consented to test the concept in Fleet Problem XVI scheduled to take place west of the Hawaiian Islands during April 1935. However, factions within the Navy Department continued to view the expensive rigid airship as a competitor for resources. When the General Board supported a request from King to build a new training airship to replace the *Los Angeles*, Adm. Standley denied the request, stating that the funds would be better spent on 'items of greater-known value'. The deceased *Macon* would not participate in Fleet Problem XVI and the Navy Department never built another rigid airship.

Lessons Learned

After the crash of the *Macon*, R. Adm. Ernest King, Chief of BuAer and future C-in-C Fleet, issued a letter instructing *Macon* and Sunnyvale officers to investigate and report on lessons learned from rigid airship operations, especially from the *Akron* and *Macon* acting as flying aircraft carriers. Their report commended *Macon*'s trapeze and aircraft parasite handling, and it was observed that three aircraft could be recovered and stowed within ten minutes. Without the utilisation of external aircraft storage, the report stated that any interior aircraft hangar should be located nearer to amidships to facilitate airship trim when launching and recovering aircraft. Since the aircraft's engines were not to be started in the hangar bay, their warm-up time once started in the slipstream slowed launching operations. Therefore, it was recommended that the next generation of airship aircraft should have heavy duty oil heaters to shorten the warm-up times before launch. Report consensus concluded the correct use of the airship fighter aircraft was not to circle in a defensive ring, but to disperse ahead and abeam to detect and report would-be enemy interceptors to the mothership, which then could take evasive action. Since recoveries and relaunches could not always be staggered, a second trapeze and fuel-equipped perch stations were considered as essential.

Before the *Macon*'s loss, a rehearsal was planned by its officers for its aircraft to evaluate the airship's role for more than only scouting:

> Suppose the airship scout should discover an enemy carrier several days before the enemy expects to make contact with our forces. The surprise element and the probable damage which could be done to the planes on deck by a dive-bombing attack delivered by the airship's planes would be of tremendous value. Such a use of the airship-based planes must not be overlooked in the design of new aircraft.

Nonetheless, the Navy's golden age of flying airship aircraft carriers had finally ended, being replaced by thousands of long-ranging flying boats and 154 anti-submarine blimps that served during the Second World War.

The XP3Y-1, the PBY Catalina prototype, made its maiden flight on 21 March 1935. It was a significant improvement over any previous patrol flying boats and would further doom any thought of building any new large Navy airships for patrol duty. The subsequent 3,300 Consolidated PBY Catalinas would become a most versatile and durable patrol aircraft that served in various roles during the Second World War. (*USN*)

Bibliography

Books

Allen, Hugh, *House of Goodyear*, Goodyear, OH, 1949

Althoff, William, *Sky Ships*, Orion, NY, 1990

Althoff, William, *USS* Los Angeles*: The Navy's Venerable Airship*, Brassey's, Washington, DC, 2004

Bowers, Peter, *Curtiss Aircraft 1907–1947*, NIP, MD, 1947

Burgess, Charles P., *Airship Design*, Ronald Press Company, NY, 1927

Grossnick, Roy, *Kite Balloons to Airships: The Navy's LTA Experience*, GPO, Washington, DC, n.d.

Hoffman, Richard, *Curtiss F9C Sparrowhawk*, Ginter, CA, 2008

Hook, Thom, *Flying Hookers*, Airship Publications, MD, 2001

Hook, Thom, *Shenandoah Saga*, Air Show Publishers, MD, 1973

Hook, Thom, *Sky Ships: The* Akron *Era*, Air Show Publishers, MD, 1976

Larkins, William, *Alameda Naval Air Station*, Acadia, SC, 2006

Mitchell, William, *Winged Defense*, Putman & Sons, NY, 1925

Pace, Kate, Montgomery, R. and Zitarosa, R., *Naval Air Station Lakehurst*, Acadia, SC, 2006

Robinson, Douglas, *Giants in the Sky*, University of Washington, Washington, 1973

Robinson, Douglas and Keller, Charles, Up Ship! *US Navy Rigid Airships: 1919–1935*, NIP, MD, 1982

Rosendahl, Charles, *Snafu, the Strange Story of the American Airship*, Atlantis, NY, 2004

Rosendahl, Charles, *What About the Airship? The Challenge to the United States*, Charles Scribner's Sons, NY, 1938

Shock, James, *American Airship Bases and Facilities*, Atlantis Productions, FL, 1996

Shock, James, US Army Airships, 1908–1942, Atlantis Productions, FL, 1996

Smith, Richard, *The Airships* Akron *and* Macon*: Flying Aircraft Carriers of the US Navy*, NIP, MD, 1965

Swanborough, *Gordon and Bowers, Peter, United States Navy Aircraft Since 1911*, Naval Institute Press, Maryland, 1976

Toland, John, *The Great Dirigibles: Their Triumphs and Disasters*, Dover, NY, 1957

Topping, Dale, *When Giants Roamed the Sky*, University of Akron, Ohio, 2001

Vaeth, J. Gordon, They Sailed the Sky: US Navy Balloon and Airship Program, NIP, MD, 2005

Articles

Aero Digest, 'Gyroplane XOZ-1', *Aero Digest*, 26, April 1936

Air Service News, 'Hooking an Aircraft to an Airship', *Air Service News*, 3 March 1925

Andrews, Hal, 'Sparrowhawk: Airship Fighter', *Naval Aviation News*, April/May 1980

Aviation Week, 'Leaving and Hooking on to Airships in Flight Show Future', *Aviation Week*, 28 March 1927

Aviation Week, 'Plane Hooks and Unhooks Airship', *Aviation Week*, 29 December 1924

Buckley, R.L. and F.D., 'Carrier Crisis', Proceedings, March 1943

Carroll, George, 'Airship', Naval Aviation News, September 1975

Clift, A. Denis, 'Gliding from the *Los Angeles*', US Naval Institute Proceedings, July 2022

Dean, Francis and Hagedorn, Dan, *Curtiss Fighter Aircraft, A Photographic History 1917–1948*, Schiffer, PA, 2007

Dean, Jack, 'Hawks Galore', Airpower, July 2000

Elliott, John, 'Sparrowhawk Remarked', *AAHS Journal*, Summer 1972

Geoghagan, John, 'Watery Grave of the Sparrowhawks', *Flight Journal*, October 2008

Haig, Rollo de Haga, 'Large Airships as Aircraft Carriers: British Experiments with Aircraft Leaving and Hooking on to Airships in Flight', *Aviation Week*, 28 March 1927

Koch, August, 'Free Human Flying, as the Preliminary Condition of Dynamic Aeronautics', Aeroplane (Part XIV) August 1893

Miller, Harold, 'Navy Skyhooks', US Naval Institute Proceedings, February 1935

Mitchell, John; 'Chronological History of the F9C-2 and its Use on the *Akron* and *Macon*', *AAHS Journal*, April–June 1958

Mizakami, Kyle, 'Bring Back the Airship Aircraft Carrier', US Naval Institute Proceedings, September 2019

Naval Gazing, 'Naval Airships Part 6', 12 May 2021

Norfleet, Lieutenant Commander Joseph, 'Have Airships a Military Value?', US Naval Institute Proceedings, August 1930

Nye, Willis, 'Genealogy of the Curtiss "Sparrowhawk" Dirigible Fighters', *AAHS Journal*, April–June 1958

Polmar, Norman, 'Ships That Were Lighter Than Air', *Naval History* magazine, May 2011

Popular Mechanics, 'Flying Carrier of Warplanes', *Popular Mechanics*, May 1942

Popular Science, 'The Airwing: Huge troop and Cargo Aircraft Carrier', February 1943

Ray, Thomas, 'Army Air Service: Lighter-Than-Air Branch, 1919–1926', *AAHS Journal*, Winter 1980

Rosendahl, Charles, 'USS *Los Angeles*', US Naval Institute Proceedings, June 1931

Smith, Richard, 'The Airship as an Aircraft Carrier', *AAHS Journal*, Autumn 1960

Smith, Richard, 'The *Akron-Macon* Heavier-Than-Air Unit', US Naval Institute Proceedings, February 1966

Smith, Richard, 'The Navy's First Skyhook', *AAHS Journal*, Summer 1961

Smith, Richard, 'The ZRCV', Aerospace Historian, October 1965

Wiley, H.V., 'Value of Airships', US Naval Institute Proceedings, May 1934

Wilmoth, Gregory, 'False-Fail Innovation', JPQ, Autumn–Winter 1999–2000

Wonders of Aviation (Editors), 'How Airships are Flown', *Wonders of Aviation*, 5 July 1938

Wonders of Aviation (Editors), 'The Mooring of Airships', *Wonders of Aviation*, 17 July 1938

Index